Praise for *Bloody Sunday...*

'Murray, while still keeping the victims and families in focus, has produced a riveting account of the Saville Inquiry for which it will serve both as summary and commentary.' Maurice Hayes, *Irish Independent*

'A book distinguished as much by unflinching honesty as well as empathy.' *Standpoint*

'[Murray's] compelling account of key moments from the enormous amount of evidence gathered by the Saville Inquiry is no revision of Saville's conclusion that there was no excuse for Bloody Sunday. His accounts of the evidence of the anonymous paratroopers who took the witness stand are forensically dismissive of their lies.' *New Statesman*

'Murray's achievement is to turn what happened four decades ago into something like a real-life whodunit.' Melanie McDonagh, *The Spectator*

'To distil the essence of the Saville Inquiry, its twelve years of deliberations and final report of ten volumes, into such a lucid and illuminating account, and at the same time to make it read like a thriller, is a very impressive achievement.' *Salisbury Review*

'Murray has made himself the chronicler par excellence of the public hearings. Nobody has handled the dramatis personae with the same sensitivity and insight ... for those interested in the actual facts – as well as the political reworkings of the story of Bloody Sunday – this is an indispensable guide.' *Literary Review*

'[A] superb analysis of the Saville Inquiry.' Kevin Myers, *Irish Independent*

'Murray has sifted all the evidence, heard a great deal of it being delivered, and has made the whole thing comprehensible. It's even a page turner. What emerges is that the tale was a great deal more murky and complicated than anyone is prepared to concede or believe.' Simon Hoggart, *The Guardian*

Praise for Douglas Murray...

'[Murray writes with] a nice combination of reason and irony... a very cool but devastating analysis. This is a period when tough-mindedness and clarity are at a discount, and it is highly encouraging to find someone youthful, defiant and principled who can both write and think at the same time.' Christopher Hitchens

'Whether one agrees with him or not Murray has made a valuable contribution to the global battle of ideas.' Amir Taheri, *Asharq al-Awsat*

'Douglas Murray writes so well that when he is wrong he is dangerous.' Matthew Parris, *The Spectator*

DOUGLAS MURRAY

BLOODY SUNDAY

TRUTHS, LIES AND THE SAVILLE INQUIRY

ISBN: 9798510291810

Cover design by: Brett Houston-Lock – Nabu Media Ltd.

For Ruth

In admiration

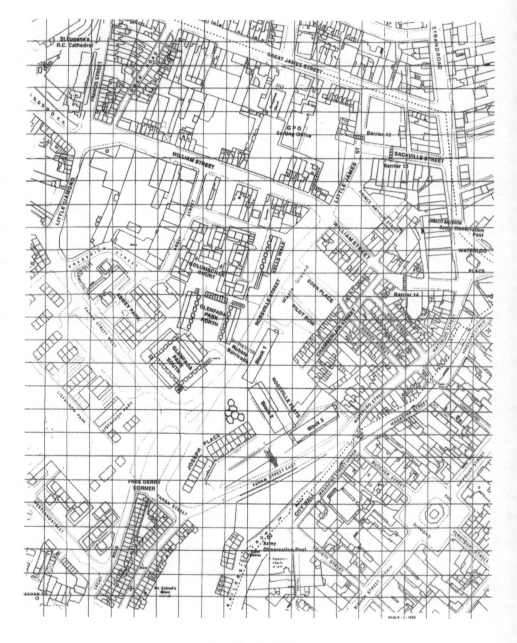

The Bogside, 1972

QUESTIONING OF SOLDIER O,
DAY 336

LORD SAVILLE: A VERY SUBSTANTIAL NUMBER OF SHOTS WERE FIRED WITHIN A VERY SHORT DISTANCE OF YOU AND A NUMBER OF PEOPLE WERE KILLED AND A NUMBER OF PEOPLE WERE WOUNDED, AGAIN WITHIN A VERY SHORT DISTANCE OF YOU; DO YOU HAVE NO RECOLLECTION AT ALL?

SOLDIER O: NO, SIR, IT HAS ALL FADED AND GONE.

QUESTIONING OF SOLDIER L,
DAY 381

q: AND THE NIGHTMARES THAT YOU HAVE, ARE THOSE RECURRENT NIGHTMARES?

a: YES, YES.

q: DO THEY DISTORT REALITY FOR YOU?

a: I DO NOT THINK THEY DISTORT IT, THEY BRING IT OUT MORE VISIBLY, DETAILS I MISSED BEFORE, YOU KNOW, SOMETIMES SEEM MORE VIVID.

CONTENTS

ACKNOWLEDGEMENTS

The author would like to thank a number of people for their help during the research and writing of this book.

First to the staff of the Bloody Sunday Inquiry, both in London and Derry, whose assistance throughout was exemplary and invaluable.

Second to my first employers, at Open Democracy, who allowed me to start attending hearings and forgave me when the subjects of this book took me over.

Third to my family, friends, and particularly Marco, for putting up with me through the months and years that this subject and book stole all my attention.

Also to Ruth and Crispian, who read it first, gave invaluable advice, and corrected mistakes. Any errors that remain are my own. Also to Rafe and Kevin for reviewing drafts and assisting with a mountain of research materials during writing.

INTRODUCTION

This book is about a set of individuals whose stories echo further than Britain or Northern Ireland. Among them are people who cannot believe that anything bad can be done by their own side as well as people who believe no good can be done by their enemies. There are people who are ready to forgive and people who refuse to forget. There are people from all sides who are sorry for their actions and those from all sides who will never admit guilt or express an apology. This book is about something else as well: what happens when ordinary people are thrown into the middle of horrific events. And what forgiveness can ever mean when all the killers are loose.

On the afternoon of 30 January 1972 a civil rights march set off from the Creggan area of the city of Derry[1] in Northern Ireland. The crowd of around 10,000 aimed to finish up with speeches at the Guildhall Square in the heart of the city. They never got there.

Fearful of clashes, the security forces prevented the march from heading into the centre and rerouted it into the Bogside area. Some marchers began to riot against the army at barricades that had been erected. Stones were thrown, teargas and rubber bullets fired in response. Then everything changed. Shots were fired. The 1st Battalion of the Parachute Regiment went over the barricades, ostensibly to scoop up rioters, but actually headed deep into the Bogside. In the space of a few minutes twenty-one of the soldiers fired a total of 108 rounds in an area filled with fleeing marchers and civilians.

By the time firing stopped thirteen civilians lay dead on the streets. Fifteen more were wounded. One died a few months later. It was the worst massacre of British citizens by British troops since Peterloo in 1819 and a landmark low point of the Northern Irish conflict – one of a few seminal moments that escalated a bloody and internecine conflict into a long-drawn-out and sadistic civil war. That conflict, which became known as 'The Troubles', staggered on for another three decades, claiming three and a half thousand lives. Its embers are not yet out.

What happened that day was a source of terrible dispute from the moment it occurred. Army commanders claimed that, on entering the Bogside, British

---

[1] For the purposes of brevity I have used 'Derry' throughout.

troops had come under heavy fire from civilian nail-bombers and gunmen and had shot at them. Community leaders and civilians denied any such thing: innocent civilians had been gunned down in cold blood, they said. In an effort to settle the matter, the British government set up an Inquiry into the events under the chairmanship of the then Lord Chief Justice, Lord Widgery. It broadly found in favour of the army's version of events. This verdict ground dirt into the already existing wound of Bloody Sunday. The idea that the British state, including the judicial system, had colluded with the British army in murdering Catholics became entrenched, vindicating and making alluring for some the claims of the Irish Republican Army (IRA).

Many years after these events a new British Prime Minister stood up to address the House of Commons. Full of hope, and with colossal public goodwill behind him, in 1998 Tony Blair announced that the British government was going to set up another Inquiry into what happened that day. It was to be chaired by another British peer, Mark Saville. By the time Lord Saville started work many of those involved were dead. Many others were to be summoned out of retirement to attempt to recall, and account for, events in their youth. At last the truth would be discovered. And there would be a very different result.

What ensued was a monumental task. The Inquiry was not only the lengthiest and most detailed but also the costliest in legal history and became a huge matter of controversy itself. Saville and the two Commonwealth judges who sat with him were expected to report within a couple of years at a cost of a few million pounds. It fact the report took another twelve years. By the time Saville did report back it was not to the Prime Minister who had set him off on the task. Both that Prime Minister and his successor had left office and it fell to a new Conservative Prime Minister to announce the Inquiry's findings.

Meanwhile, as the costs rose towards £200 million the Saville Inquiry became the object of ridicule and disdain from the media, depicted as a gravy-train for lawyers. As a result of the vast cost and the even vaster quantities of time and documentation involved, much of the wealth of new information that Saville turned up was lost: lost to recriminations over cost, lost to recriminations over time, and lost on a media that, with few exceptions, gave up on the proceedings as they dragged interminably on.

In 2002 the Inquiry transferred from Derry to London to hear from military, political and intelligence witnesses before returning to Derry to hear from the

IRA. Interest had waned, but I started attending daily. Firstly because I wanted to hear the evidence first- hand – to hear from the soldiers and the IRA who were there that day and who had fired. If anybody was going to have the key to the mysteries of what happened that day it would be these men. I wanted to hear if the Republican stories were true. Or if the British army had been maligned. Perhaps nobody was telling the truth? I knew this would be the last chance to find out.

But there was another reason I attended. The hatred and distrust that led to that day and were embedded by that day remain strong. Many British people think that they have heard quite enough about Bloody Sunday. They believe that Irish Republicans and their sympathisers have had quite enough attention directed at this event. As a result, Bloody Sunday has been a tragedy that few non- Republicans have looked into. That should be addressed. Bloody Sunday was not only a Derry tragedy, it was a British tragedy and one with serious repercussions for the way in which the army, the judiciary and the state should operate.

Because the day had become Republican holy ground it had also been manipulated. As the Inquiry progressed it became clear that the British army were not the only army to open fire in the Bogside that day. The IRA and their sympathisers did not want these facts to come out, indeed did everything they could to stop them, but, as this book shows, the real story of Bloody Sunday turns out to be not only more straightforward than the British army would like to admit, but more complex than the IRA have ever said.

The process also deserves attention because for twelve years the most extraordinary, unparalleled, effort was made to get to the truth. What came out of that was more than just an effort at reaching the truth of what happened on that terrible day. It revealed much about how any truth can be uncovered after such a long time – what people remember and what they forget. And what happens when things turn up from the past that might have been easier left undiscovered. For Northern Ireland, like many other places of conflict around the world, the past is always before us, threatening to reopen at any stage. What turned up before Saville was often as much about the present and future as it was about the past: an effort at truth and reconciliation that woke some ghosts just as others were being laid to rest.

The volume of material now in the public domain thanks to Lord Saville's Inquiry is extraordinary. Few minutes in history can be as heavily documented as these now are. From the top of the British state, from the Prime Minister, Lord Chief Justice and chiefs of the army down to ordinary people who got caught up in events, the Inquiry provided the most complete snapshot ever exposed of how a state operates, how its various departments work and what happens when they fail. It reveals a cross-section of how a society operated at a single moment in time, including a glimpse into some of the most covert recesses of the nation. For Saville the UK intelligence services offered up information of a kind that had never before been made available in open court.

The sheer quantity of this information is itself off-putting. Lord Saville's final magnum opus alone is ten volumes long. A monumental piece of legal investigation, its length, however, means that very few people, if any, have read or will read his findings. As a result still too few people are aware not just of what happened, but why. And since Lord Saville's investigation is a legal one, along the way some of the human significance is lost.

At times the reality of what happened that day as well as the intense drama of what happened in court might read like fiction. There were certainly plenty of times when those of us watching proceedings had to blink. And others when we had to look away.

Here the story is approached through a set of major figures involved in the day: a victim, a soldier, a politician, a paramilitary commander and so on. The aim is not just to provide a way into the event, but to show something of the nature of justice.

Since the first publication of this book there has been a development that is worth noting. In July 2012, following a review of Lord Saville's findings by the Police Service of Northern Ireland and the Public Prosecution Service, it was announced that the police had decided to open a murder investigation into the deaths of Bloody Sunday. It was reported that the investigation would require a team of thirty police working on the case for at least four years. The announcement was welcomed by a number of the families of the dead.

Given the time and costs involved, it is possible that the planned investigation will either never start or, if it does, never finish. Some have been critical of the decision to even begin such a process. Three main reasons are given. Firstly, it is assumed that those most heavily criticised by Lord Saville would be those most likely to face criminal charges, and defenders of these men are obviously opposed to any such investigation. Secondly, a number of people have complained on the grounds of public expense. The third cause for scepticism has been that since the release of prisoners in the aftermath of the Good Friday Agreement it is unlikely that any jail time would be served, even if convictions were secured.

The process is in its earliest stages. However, one thing is worth pointing out. The Saville Inquiry never provided immunity for people who lied while giving evidence. The final report identifies a fair number of people who did so, and not only to Lord Saville but to the judicial inquiry that was held before. Given the number of public inquiries now underway, it may well be thought desirable to pursue those who sought to mislead Lord Saville, on a point of precedent as well as principle.

Whether prosecutions are obtained or not, time served in jail or not, it is unlikely that this latest episode in the story of Bloody Sunday will be any less tortuous, difficult or controversial than the many that have gone before.

1

A VICTIM

On 30 January 1972 a 41-year-old man named Barney McGuigan stepped out from a group of people sheltering behind a block of flats in Londonderry. Yards away a younger man was crying out as he lay dying on the floor.

Thirty-one-year-old Patrick Doherty had been shot in the backside as he tried to crawl to safety. The group huddling behind the flats could hear him as he lay dying. 'I don't want to die alone - somebody help me,' a young woman called Geraldine Richmond remembered him shouting out. 'I could also hear him whining', the same witness said, 'and saying, "God help me." The whining would stop and then start up again.' Doherty had been shot by a soldier of the British army. The bullet had entered his body above the right buttock and exited from the left side of his chest causing massive internal injuries. Hearing his cries, the young woman said, 'I wanted to go out to help him but I couldn't move, I was too scared. We all huddled together tighter.'

Some witnesses saw a white handkerchief being waved in McGuigan's hand as he stepped out. Others recalled his hands being empty. Across the road, a single soldier from the 1st Battalion of the Parachute Regiment went down on one knee into a firing position.

The soldier taking up this position was seen by plenty of civilians, but also by army witnesses. Among them was an officer positioned in an observation post on the city walls. Later, in evidence, that soldier (known as '227') described how he saw the kneeling soldier fire 'two deliberate shots... As he did this I saw a man falling.' Soldier 227 was shown photographs of the group huddled together that were taken seconds before McGuigan stepped out from the group. 'I identify the foreground figure as the man I saw fall,' he said, adding, 'I saw nothing in the hands of the man who fell.'

Closer to the scene the man's fall was grimmer.

He had spent that morning at church with his family and then attended a funeral. 'Barney McGuigan, one of the men huddled at the wall with me, was a "community man",' Richmond recalled, 'and was generally looked up to.' During the march a family friend of McGuigan had got into an argument with a soldier. McGuigan had grabbed him by the shoulder and led him away. The friend remembered, 'He said something like "Come away from there, you're going to get yourself into trouble."'

But the dying Doherty's cries carried on for a period that stretched out interminably for those who could hear them. Richmond recalled, 'Mr McGuigan said that he could not stand the sound of the man calling any longer and that if he went out waving a white hanky they would not shoot at him. We tried to dissuade him from going out. We told him they would shoot him. However, he was brave and he stepped away from us holding the white hanky in his hand. Although I cannot be certain I think he held it in his left hand. He walked out slowly sideways in an arc towards where we thought the sound was coming from. He stepped out about 10 to 12 feet away from us. All the time he was walking I could see the left-hand side of his face. We were calling to him all the time to come back. He kept looking back towards us. I could see bullets going past us and Mr McGuigan from all directions.

'I remember hearing two distinct shots. After the first one Mr McGuigan turned back towards us and, although I cannot be certain, I think he turned his whole body and not just his face. I did not see the bullet hit anything, I just heard it. The second shot hit him and blew his head up like a tomato exploding. I saw his eye come out.'

Giving evidence even nearly thirty years later, Richmond had to take a break while recounting these events. She recalled that 'when the bullet hit him, you know, his whole body turned around.'

The bullet entered McGuigan's head at the back, by the left ear and exited from the front at his right eye. Richmond recorded her reaction. 'After Mr McGuigan was shot I went hysterical and couldn't take it anymore. His shooting had seemed to me to be in slow motion and I thought I was going to die. Although I do not remember this I was told later that I was screaming and that Mr McFadden hit me in order to shut me up, as he thought that I was going to get them all killed.'

2

Others also remembered this. One recalled, 'After Barney McGuigan was shot a girl called Richmond went hysterical. A man I now know to be Barney McFadden punched her on the chin and knocked her out. I think he was concerned that her screaming would attract fire.' The same witness testified that when McGuigan, who was only a couple of feet away from him, was shot, 'I think I was looking at him ... but I can't be entirely certain.'

William McDonagh had also been on the march, but after firing started he had managed to get inside the Rossville Flats. When the shooting stopped, shaking from shock, he left the building and saw the body of McGuigan in a pool of blood. He was physically sick.

This battlefield-like scene on the streets was witnessed by a lot of people. And because of the number of memories there were subtle variations on what happened. Hugh Barbour, who was sixteen at the time, recalled McGuigan being 'very animated and waving his arms. I think he was holding and waving a white handkerchief but I may have got this memory confused with pictures that I have seen of Father Daly doing the same.' He remembered McGuigan 'shouting to somebody through the gap who I couldn't see.

He was shouting, "Please, please help – don't shoot me."' Before going into shock he remembered McGuigan lying on the floor, 'the blood spurting from his cheek each time his heart beat'.

Paul McLaughlin was on first-aid duty with the Knights of Malta ambulance corps. He had been sheltering behind the building with McGuigan, seen him walk out and seen him fall. He said that he realised that McGuigan had received a head wound 'because of the amount of blood'.

'At this point, I was so scared I did not know what else to do and started to pray,' he recalled. 'It is not very often that I pray in public, but at that time other people joined in with me.' McLaughlin, like the other Knights of Malta at the march, was expecting to apply plasters and perhaps bandages. But as he said, 'My first-aid training did not prepare me for having to deal with fatal bullet wounds and I felt totally unable to help.'

The reactions of ordinary people in this situation varied and led to some haunting and pitiful attempts to help.

3

One man recalled standing over the body and remembered thinking what a lovely coat McGuigan was wearing 'and that it was destroyed because of the blood'. A friend of McGuigan's took the dead man's shoes off and laid them next to his feet. Someone else asked why he had done that. 'He said it was because the blood would rush to his feet and make them swell.' A man who had known McGuigan described looking at the body and the pool of blood. He observed awkwardly in testimony: 'I knew Barney before he was shot.'

Another man who had known him well was sheltering upstairs in the flats, crawled into the lift and came down to the bottom in it. Not knowing what to expect when he got there he walked out and saw the body. In his own words, he 'burst out crying at the sight of it'.

One other man, who had not known McGuigan, said, 'The sight of the man has stayed with me to this day. Photographs are nothing like the real thing and I will never forget what he looked like. He wasn't covered up and it was just like someone had dropped a pot of jam around his head. It wasn't like any blood I had ever seen before, it was gooey and dark.'

Derry in 1972 was a small community and many of the people who saw people being shot or lying dead were seeing neighbours, acquaintances, friends and also family. One of McGuigan's sons, Charles, was sixteen years old on Bloody Sunday. He had been told by his father that he was not to go on the march. Keeping to the letter though not the spirit of the request, the young man did not go on the march but went to watch it with friends.

A local sixteen-year-old, Róisín Stewart, remembered standing with her male cousin looking at the body of McGuigan, now covered, when they saw his son. She remembered him 'horrified by what had happened... He said he was going straight home as he knew his parents would be worried about him.' After he had gone Stewart recalled her cousin indicating the body and saying, 'I think that's his father.'

A stretcher was called for and McGuigan's body was put on to it. As his body was lifted on to it part of his brain fell out. But even as the shooting seemed to have stopped and people drifted, stunned, back into the open they weren't safe. People remember shouting and a volley of shots. As the shots rang out the people who had lifted McGuigan's body on to the stretcher darted back to cover and left him alone again.

During all of this time, arrestees were rounded up, medics tended to people with light injuries and ambulances began to arrive to ferry the dead to nearby Altnagelvin hospital. For McGuigan all that could be done was a formal identification of the deceased and the carrying out of a post-mortem.

Charles's uncle Paddy went to identify Barney at the morgue. Thirty years later Charles said that his uncle had told him that though he had grown up with Barney the only visual memory he now had of him was as he was in the morgue.

When his body was on the ground, McGuigan was photographed a number of times, both covered and uncovered. In order to work out the exact position of the body and ascertain the direction from which the fatal shot had been fired, photographs of the body came up many times in evidence. But as the victim's son testified, 'I was unable to look at any of the photographs of my father's body. My mother has never been able to look at these photographs. My sisters Alice and Bridie and my brothers Bernard and Garvin have never looked at these photographs either.' At McGuigan's wake the coffin was sealed so that nobody would see the injury.

Thirty years after this incident the soldier who fired the shot that killed McGuigan sat in London, in Central Hall Westminster, to testify to the Saville Inquiry, which had transferred from Derry to hear the military witnesses. Citizens of Derry had remembered this man for a long time – some vividly. Many had last seen him delivering arrested civilians to the police. Others had last seen him seconds after his last fatal shot when he was called to by a comrade, got up off his knee, turned and walked away. Most had only seen him once but, because of the deaths attributed to him that day, Soldier F's testimony was more keenly anticipated than that of perhaps any other witness to appear over five years of hearings.

The public gallery was packed. Many of the relatives of the deceased had attended every day of the Inquiry, in Derry and London. To see Soldier F, the extended families of the deceased came over to watch proceedings or filled the room in Derry where the testimony was being relayed live. Many knew it would be their only chance to see their relative's killer in the flesh. For others it was the best chance they had to see him confess, apologise or otherwise admit what he had done.

5

There was the evidence of another soldier to hear (who had not fired) in the morning and the routine change-over of witnesses seemed rather less routine this time. As his evidence wrapped up, conversation suddenly filled the room. As the witness left and the next entered to take his place Lord Saville told the room that if people wanted to talk they should go outside. The noise stopped. Soldier F had arrived.

A nondescript, short and plain man in late middle age took the oath and then sat down to one side of the judges, in front of the phalanx of lawyers and just a few feet away from the families' seating area. If Soldier F had not been swiftly taken in and out by security at either end of the day anyone in the room might have sat beside him on the bus or tube. Nothing would have caused them to think that this man knew something, and nothing would have caused them to double-take.

For the first of the two days of his testimony Soldier F was painstakingly and methodically questioned about every aspect of the day and his statement, first by Counsel to the Inquiry and then by representatives of the families. Maps and trajectories demonstrating where he had been positioned on that day in 1972 were brought up on the screen in front of him. Witness statements were read to him. The paragraph about McGuigan's head exploding he was asked to read to himself.

But he stonewalled all questions. He had no memory of the day. He knew he had fired his gun that day, but thirty years on he no longer had any memory of 'when, where or why'.

Finally, in the humming air-conditioned room the Inquiry saw a rare and previously protected thing. In all the rolling years of live testimony, one piece of evidence had been deemed too sensitive to show in open court: the mortuary photos of the dead. Every last detail of the day, every photo had been gone over repeatedly – apart from these. At the end of his questioning the QC acting for McGuigan's family asked for the mortuary photos of his head to be shown to Soldier F. He asked that they be kept off the public and press screens. But the photos appeared on the screens of the dozens of lawyers sitting in lines. From parts of the public and families' galleries the photos on the lawyers' screens – the photos being shown to Soldier F – could be seen very clearly indeed. Nobody who saw them would ever forget it.

First came the photo of the back of the head and the relatively neat, incision-like, cleaned and clean wound made by the bullet as it entered. And then – numbered P181 – the frontal mortuary shot of the dead man's face. The clearest feature was the crater where the dead man's right eye should have been, where the bullet had exited, which, as is usual with exit wounds, was far larger than the mark the bullet had made on its way in. The wound where the eye once was gaped – a mess of blood and tissue. Around the room all those who could see it shared a sharp intake of breath, then a moaning and the turning away of faces.

If Soldier F felt any emotion he did not show it. He played the tough soldier to the last, looking at the screen, helpful but impassive. Then the silence was broken by a terrible eruption of sobbing.

McGuigan's widow was in the room, along with the children she had with the man whose head had just appeared on the screen. She had waited a long time for justice and a long time to see her husband's killer. Now, gasping with grief, she was escorted from the room by her remaining family. The Inquiry, which had trundled on for years, caught in the often soporific bureaucracy of trying to get to the bottom of events, was suddenly, finally, reminded of them. There was a pause as Mrs. McGuigan was helped out. After a while, questioning resumed. People in the public galleries wiped their eyes. The smart young woman doing live notes beside the judges tried to keep typing while dabbing tears from her eyes.

During the vast Inquiry some of the riddles of Bloody Sunday were finally answered. And plenty more were raised.

This whole search for the truth had a disadvantage: the problem of time. Hearings for the Inquiry started almost three decades after the events of 1972. The report finally came almost four decades after the day.

A more thorough effort to get to the truth could not be imagined. Yet thirty years on is no time to start getting to the truth. A single, disturbing example relating to the death of Barney McGuigan may demonstrate the problem.

In her Saville evidence a woman who was a married mother of four in 1972 testified that the morning after Bloody Sunday a group of children were playing by the place where McGuigan had been shot. A small boy had been picking bullets out of the nearby wall. He came to her, she said, because he had found something stuck to the wall. 'When I looked I saw that it was part of an eyelid. It was stuck on the side, about half a yard down from the top of the seat. I realised that it must have come from somebody who had been shot and so I put it into a matchbox. Later I gave the matchbox to a priest who said that he would make sure that it was buried. I do not know the name of the priest.'

This might only provide one last grim detail of the shooting of Barney McGuigan. But even on this relatively simple and certainly memorable detail about one of the victims there is no agreement over what had happened or when.

Seamus Carlin testified that on the day of the march itself, after the bodies had been taken away, he saw a blue civil rights banner on the floor steeped in McGuigan's blood, and that on top of that banner was a matchbox. He testified, 'Someone gave me the match- box which contained Barney McGuigan's lower eyelid. I took it away and gave it to my brother who asked a priest what to do with it. The priest told him to put it on the ground.'

John Patrick Friel testified that after the shooting (when the body itself may or may not have still been there, he was not sure) 'someone pointed out to me that Bernard McGuigan's eyelid was stuck to the wall of Block 2. It was about four or five feet above the pavement, directly below the kitchen window of our flat. I had simply never seen anything like it. I will stand over this statement until the day I die. I definitely saw this but I am still confused as to the exact time. It is possible that Barney McGuigan's body had already been removed from the spot where he died. This could have been shortly after my first sight of his covered body or it may even have been the next day.'

Noel Millar said that immediately after the shooting finished, and before the body was covered, 'I could see the body of the man whom I had seen fall, whom I know to be Barney McGuigan. He was not covered by anything at this time. Someone drew my attention to the eyelid and eyelash which was stuck to the gable end wall at about head height. Someone asked whether anyone had a matchbox. I did so I lifted the eyelid off the wall with a matchstick, put it in the matchbox and placed it near Barney McGuigan's head, on the ground.'

James Patrick McCafferty, who spent the day itself trying to tune in to army radio on the airwaves, testified that he went back down to the Bogside the day after Bloody Sunday and there 'noticed about five feet up the wall on my right (the gable end) north wall of Block 2 of the Rossville Flats that there was a perfectly formed eyelid complete with eyelashes stuck to the wall. There was not a tear in the eyelid; it was so perfect.

'The eyelid was stuck to the wall about five feet up and approximately halfway along the wall. I cannot recall precisely how far but believe it may have been a little further towards the car park end of the wall... Blood was splattered all around it.

'I was drawn to the eyelid on the wall, I could hardly believe what I was seeing. A small crowd gathered around and somebody got a matchbox out and put the eyelid in it. Personally I did not think that was the right thing to do, but we did not know what else to do. The box was placed on the ground on the civil rights banner which had been used the previous day but which was now saturated with blood and on the floor near the barricade... Since then I have learnt that the bullet that killed Mr Bernard McGuigan, the father of my school friend Charlie McGuigan, came out of his eye. From this I concluded that the eyelid that I found must have been Mr. Bernard McGuigan's eyelid. Although I have talked to Charlie about that day, I did not tell him what I saw.'

The story has a number of other variants from numerous other sources. Some claimed to have taken the eyelid down themselves. Others claimed that they were with the person who did but name different people. One said her daddy took it down, others a friend. For some it happened straight after the shooting, for others the next morning, some late the next day. Others claimed that they saw two eyelids. No two stories match, and if you named all the number of people who claimed to have been the person or to have been with the person who did this small act, the list would run to more than twenty.

Were any of these people wrong? Certainly. Possibly all of them. But were they lying? Almost certainly not. They were saying what they remembered.

Perhaps one of them was the person who placed the eyelid by the body. Or perhaps whoever it was that carried out this small, stunned act of kindness has been dead for years. In any case very many people transferred something they had either seen or heard about and took it into their own memory. When the call went out for those with evidence about the day to come forward, the day itself was a long way back in memory.

9

In the intervening years some people embellished or invented small parts of what they did on that day. Some consciously. Some entirely unconsciously. Some must have come to the Inquiry and decided that they were not willing to backtrack on a story they had been telling for years. Others may have told the story so often in pubs and at gatherings that the invented or elaborated memory had become a real one – as accurate a description of what was in their mind's eye as anything that they actually saw. Still others may never have intended to mislead anyone. Some witnesses admitted that they feared their memory might have become contaminated over the years by images they saw subsequently on film or television.

If the truth of what happened on Bloody Sunday was already messy, over the course of decades it became far messier. Memories had amalgamated, shifted and in some cases been remade. And of course for some, who had never had any intention to mislead, the subconscious and indeed the conscience played a consoling trick.

There were many people who had helped those who were dying. But under the circumstances not only was there little they could do; for most people, like the Knights of Malta first-aid volunteer tending to McGuigan, there was nothing they could do even when they wanted to. The guilt of those who saw neighbours, family friends and community figures killed before them, and the knowledge that at a central point in their own lives as well as in the life of their city they could not save somebody, meant that their consciences consoled them with facts – even created ones.

One man who was with a local priest who went to the aid of a dying boy said with rare candour, 'I had the normal human instinct to stay and see what I could do to help, but another part of me was telling me to get away to safety as soon as I could. I think that one of the reasons that Father Daly is so remembered from that day is that he stayed with Jack Duddy while he died, and did not think about his own safety. I wanted to get away.' That is a perfectly normal instinct. But it is a rare one to express. Extraordinary acts of bravery by ordinary people were carried out that day, Barney McGuigan's efforts to aid a dying man among them. But most people are not heroes and have to find ways to comfort themselves in the meantime.

The case of McGuigan's eyelid is just one relatively unimportant example. But it is a reminder of something crucial about this search for justice. Even

10

during everyday incidents, people come up with wildly different versions of what they have seen. Place people amid deeply traumatic events, with crowds fleeing down narrow lanes, bodies lying in familiar streets and shots ricocheting in all directions, then try to recreate what people think they saw three decades later, and arriving at a truth becomes, if not impossible, then certainly extremely hard.

Yet this was exactly the task that Lord Saville and his Inquiry had been set. It was their task to sift through the evidence. It would take twelve years to try to find the complex and upsetting truths about what had happened in the space of a few minutes, one day in 1972.

2

THE SCENE: DERRY

In 1972 Northern Ireland's second largest city was a deeply riven and unstable place. The Protestant and Catholic communities lived in different areas and remembered different pasts. Then, as now, the city's divided inhabitants could not even agree on its name. For Protestant Unionists it was 'Londonderry'. For Catholic Republicans, plain 'Derry'.

It had been like this since the beginning of the seventeenth century when the city was a destination for incoming Unionist planters. Since then, from the English Civil War right through the Irish war of independence and beyond, the 'loyalists' had been on opposing sides from the local Irish Catholics. Tensions and fighting between the two flared and diminished but never went away.

In 1920 the Government of Ireland Act was passed in Westminster, dividing six of the northernmost counties from the rest of Ireland. The Protestant-majority North had, like the Catholic-majority South, its own Parliament, and in this new jurisdiction Derry was the largest city after Belfast. By the 1960s, when the latest round of civil unrest began, there was a growing awareness of the fact that Catholics in the area were discriminated against in a range of ways. Manipulation of ward boundaries as well as property qualifications for local government elections meant that Catholics were underrepresented at all levels of governance.

In response to this, and partly in the spirit of the times, a civil rights movement emerged. The one set up in Northern Ireland was wide-ranging not only in its ambitions but also in its membership. Though there were Protestants among its members, the first march of the movement called NICRA (Northern Ireland Civil Rights Association) in July 1968 was countered by some Protestants. Many Protestants in the area viewed the agenda and make-up of the new organisation with suspicion, concluding that it was little more than a front for the IRA, the armed part of the Republican movement. Further marches were also faced with counter-marches, leading to stand-offs between the two sides and local security forces. In October 1968 a civil rights march led to severe injuries to civilians and policemen. The following year saw the Battle of the Bogside – the main Catholic area of Derry – and the embedding of 'no-go areas' in the North, where the police and other forces seen as loyal to the British Crown were stopped by locals from entering.

Throughout this period, and as the early stages of reform ground into motion, the government in Westminster reiterated its position that Northern Ireland would remain a part of the United Kingdom as long as the majority of its inhabitants desired this to be the case. But the situation grew steadily worse. Loyalist marches increasingly became flashpoints as much as did civil rights marches. And by August 1969, realising that the local Royal Ulster Constabulary could no longer cope with the policing role they faced, Westminster agreed to requests from the government of Northern Ireland at Stormont to send in British troops. Initially they were welcomed by much of the Catholic population for the security it was hoped they would be able to bring with them. But for the IRA and other hardcore Republicans the presence of British troops on Irish soil was inflammatory, not least because the IRA thought themselves the protectors of the Catholic communities.

Adding to the confusion, the period also provoked a split within the IRA. The movement divided in two: the Officials and the Provisionals. In-fighting between the movements often seemed as intense as their common hatred for the British, assisting the deterioration of the situation as the movements fought for supremacy.

During this whole period what had once seemed unusual became commonplace. And gradually a society that had always been fractious took one step after another to a situation where the unthinkable became routine.

Regular violent rioting on the streets was one example, as common in Derry as it was in Belfast. Indeed the whole process had become, as one regular rioter put it, 'fairly ritualised'. Rioters would stand in a certain spot near the soldiers or RUC line and, from a certain distance, would hurl stones and other missiles at the troops. The soldiers would respond with rubber bullets, which caused painful bruising. During serious riots the army would use CS gas canisters, which temporarily blinded those who were nearby as well as causing nausea and

14

breathing problems. Water-cannons were often employed against crowds that the security forces wanted to move on.

At the same time the army found itself facing riots in which far worse than bricks and stones were coming their way. The use of home-made nail-bombs and blast-bombs made by the IRA and distributed to volunteers became a feature. These devices, which caused horrific injuries where they did not kill, were behind a number of disputed incidents when soldiers, fearing a nail-bomb was being thrown, had fired in response. Frequently, after the event, civilians would deny that the devices had been present. Northern Ireland was heading towards the point where nobody believed the word of anybody else. As one writer who witnessed events put it, 'In the absence of an agreed reality, truth is whatever you're having yourself.'

In the wake of the Battle of the Bogside and up to January 1972 the lines that the authorities were not allowed to cross were almost formally agreed upon. In Belfast it became army policy to ensure there were no places where the rule of law did not operate. But in Derry there were parts of town that the army could not enter, in particular the low-lying Bogside area outside the city walls. Daily rioting positions – including that known to the army as 'Aggro Corner' – went up around the area.

Much of that rioting has now found itself becoming part of a nostalgic reverie, the wounding and maiming of people paid to keep order reduced to being all just part of the fun. In some cases time has coloured the fighting against security forces as a demonstration of revolutionary anti-imperialism. In others, harmless high spirits. But behind the rioters, as the army was becoming increasingly aware, were people intent on a lot worse.

One habitual rioter put it in evidence to Saville that 'there were occasions during the rioting when the IRA would shoot at the British army, but these were rare. We were not pleased when the IRA became involved because it would disrupt our rioting – the soldiers would fire at us rioters and we would have to stop rioting.'

That firing became the subject of considerable dispute, as did the firing that the army responded with. But among crowds of civilians it was often exceedingly hard to identify targets, let alone hit them without harming unarmed rioters. The number of disputed occasions grew. The army said that a gunman or a nail-bomber had been hit while others among the crowd of rioters were said to have spirited either the gunman or his gun (or both) away and either denied the incident took place or claimed that the person hit was an innocent passer-by.

It had become normal for soldiers to fear for their own safety when they faced hordes of stone-throwing, petrol-bombing and, possibly, armed locals. A distinguished reporter of the Troubles, Peter Taylor, estimated in his book on the British in Northern Ireland that, in the three months before Bloody Sunday alone, some 2,000 shots were fired at soldiers in the city of Derry. It was in these circumstances that the government in Stormont in Northern Ireland introduced internment without trial in 1971, in an effort to stop the IRA, and finally, in a desperate move, imposed a ban on marches.

Much that emerged in recent years played down the fears of the military in the city. Indeed one of the lawyers for the families at the Saville Inquiry, Michael Mansfield QC, made the submission that in January 1972 the Bogside and Creggan had been 'havens of non-violent civilian protest'. There certainly was civilian protest, but as a mounting toll of death showed, an increasing amount of that protest was very far from non-violent.

The first of the many hundreds of soldiers to die in Northern Ireland was a member of the Royal Artillery shot dead in North Belfast on 6 February 1971. He was killed by an IRA sniper using a Thompson submachine gun. Gunner Robert Curtis's unit was under attack from a large crowd of rioters armed with petrol- and blast-bombs. The shots reportedly came from the direction of the rioters. Gunner Curtis was twenty years old, his wife three months pregnant with their first child.

On 25 May 1971 the first member of the Parachute Regiment was killed by the IRA. Michael Willetts was killed when the IRA threw a suitcase-bomb into the reception of an RUC station in West Belfast. Several Catholic civilians were sitting in the room, including a 27-year-old electrician with his young daughter and a mother with her four-year-old boy. Realising what was about to happen, Sergeant Willetts thrust the children into a corner and shielded them from the blast. He was killed instantly. Seven police officers, two soldiers and eighteen civilians were injured in the explosion. The two children survived thanks to Sergeant Willetts's action. But he was killed by a shard from a metal locker thrown across the room by the explosion. The citation for his posthumous award of the George Cross read that 'he risked – and lost – his life for those of the

16

adults and children. His selflessness, his courage are beyond praise.' As ambulances arrived to ferry Sergeant Willetts and those injured in the blast a crowd of local youths gathered. As the dead Para's body was taken out the crowd began to shout, hurling obscenities and insults at the soldiers. The lieutenant-colonel accompanying Willetts's body said, 'My reaction was one of total disbelief that anyone could be so inhumane.'

Two months later during a riot two civilians, an engaged 28-year- old called Seamus Cusack and a nineteen-year-old called Desmond Beattie were shot dead by members of the Royal Anglian Regiment in disputed circumstances in Derry. The army claimed that they were armed but civilians present denied this. Cusack was shot in the top inside of his left leg. The crowd urged a man with a car to take him across the Irish border to hospital instead of to the local one. Cusack lost a substantial amount of blood on the way and died minutes after arriving at the Irish hospital after a twenty-mile drive. Over the ensuing weeks and months soldiers were repeatedly killed by snipers knowingly or unknowingly given cover by crowds of rioters. In Belfast, Derry and along the border the death toll mounted. A Para was shot by a sniper in Belfast on 14 July 1971, a Royal Horse Artillery soldier in Derry in August, while a growing list of others were killed by routine sniper and bomb attacks on army observation posts and patrols.

In October a 24-year-old married soldier in the Royal Green Jackets was shot by an IRA sniper in Derry city centre during a Saturday afternoon riot. Rifleman Joseph Hill was one of the soldiers facing the rioting youths in William Street at the edge of the Bogside. Rifleman Hill was shot in the head by a single bullet fired by an IRA sniper as he stood in Columbcille Court. As the military ambulance carrying the dying soldier turned from William Street into Little James Street it was within view of a large crowd of a hundred or so youths who were in Rossville Street. When they saw the military ambulance the crowd 'cheered and clapped their hands'. Yards away crowds were shopping on Waterloo Place. The normalisation of savagery was under way.

In November the IRA planted a bomb in the Red Lion pub beside an RUC station in South Belfast. The planting of bombs in civilian areas became almost as normal as the picking off of soldiers by snipers. A soldier from the Queen's Regiment, a native of the Irish Republic, was killed by the IRA while on a trip to the South to meet with his fiancée to discuss wedding plans.

As the violence spread it managed not only to grow in depth and reach. Every

17

atrocity by a particular side or splinter-group of a side could be the subject of retaliation by any of the rival or opposing groups. Into this mix came the unsettling realisation that now anybody could do anything to anyone, and anybody at all could be responsible.

In December 1971 a bomb was placed in McGurk's bar in North Belfast. It went off just after a quarter to nine in the evening killing fifteen people. Although it is now believed to have been planted by loyalists, the IRA were early suspects for placing the bomb. Immediately after it went off, rival gangs began hurling stones at each other. Gunfire followed. The army moved in to try to separate the various factions and Major Jeremy Snow of the Royal Fusiliers, father of two, was shot in the neck by an IRA sniper and died four days later in hospital, his wife at his side.

On one of the last days of the year, a soldier from the Royal Artillery was killed by an IRA sniper in Bishop Street in Derry. He was aged twenty.

The bloody year of 1972 got off to a bloody start. A soldier was shot dead on 5 January and another blown up on 21 January. On 27 January two RUC officers aged twenty and twenty-six were shot dead by the IRA as they drove along the Creggan Road in Derry.

The weekend before Bloody Sunday, an anti-internment march at Magilligan Strand in County Derry broke down in disarray as members of the Parachute Regiment bussed in from Belfast went in to arrest marchers and ended up batoning many and chasing others into the freezing sea. It was an action that boded ill for the regiment's imminent deployment to police the anti-internment march in Derry the next Sunday.

On the morning of Bloody Sunday, Major Robin Alers-Hankey of the Royal Green Jackets died in hospital. He had been shot by the IRA in Derry four months earlier. A 35-year-old father of two, Major Alers-Hankey was shot as he deployed his troops to protect a group of firemen who were being pelted with stones by a crowd. The firemen Alers-Hankey was trying to protect were being targeted as they battled to put out a fire in a timber yard at the end of Abbey Street in the Bogside. One of the civilians present on Bloody Sunday recalled that when the news came through on the television that evening that 'some soldier' had died just before the march 'everyone cheered'.

18

But then came Bloody Sunday, the bloodiest year of the Troubles, and another thirty years of blame, counter-blame, murder and counter-murder.

3

WHAT HAPPENED?

One of the few things that everybody who was present at the march in Derry on 30 January 1972 was in agreement on was the weather. Almost to a man and woman they remembered it as a cold and crisp day covered with a clear blue sky.

Hovering in that clear blue sky was an army helicopter. And in it was a young surveillance officer known to the Saville Inquiry as INQ 2030. From this vantage point he could see over the whole of the Bogside. Years later he recorded what events looked like from up there. 'I can recall seeing lots and lots of people on the ground, perhaps as many as five or ten thousand. They appeared to be congregating in one particular spot. All of a sudden, there was a burst of activity. People began running in all directions and the crowd effectively scattered. I can think of no better way to describe it than the effect that dropping a stone on an ants' nest would have. It was almost as if the people on the ground had disappeared although I could see them hiding behind walls and buildings.'

Down on the ground that reality was not only much less serene, it was full of terror, contradiction, bravery and cowardice: some people demonstrating the best of human nature and others down there the worst.

Despite the ban on marches the planned march against internment left from the Creggan area of the city early in the afternoon. Young and old were on the march, and the huge crowd showed not just how strong the opposition to internment was but also how many people were willing to break the government's ban. The thousands of marchers wound their way through the nationalist area of the city and into William Street. Originally the organisers had planned for the march to finish in the Guildhall Square with speeches on top of the lorry that was leading the march.

But the security forces were intent on avoiding clashes with loyalist groups in the centre of the city and ensured that the march did not get to the Guildhall Square. They set up an army barrier across William Street called Barrier 14. As the march got to the corner of William Street and Rossville Street it rerouted down Rossville Street past the high Rossville Flats towards Free Derry Corner, where speeches would now take place. But sections of the marchers, predominantly young men, went a little further along William Street to face down the army barrier and begin rioting. Stones and bricks were thrown. Teargas was fired in return. Similar rioting broke out in Little James Street and Sackville Street at the army's erected Barriers 12 and 13.

Rubber bullets were fired, CS gas canisters were thrown back at the soldiers and eventually water-cannons were brought into use to dispel the rioters.

Meanwhile, members of 1st Battalion Parachute Regiment prepared to go in on an arrest operation ordered by General Ford, the Commander of Land Forces. The battalion had arrived in Derry from their base near Belfast early that morning. The Commanding Officer of 1 Para, Colonel Derek Wilford, placed the support company by the Presbyterian church in St James' Street. Wilford had briefed the soldiers the night before about the arrest operation: if rioting broke out they were to be used as a snatch squad to go in over the barriers and arrest the rioters. Many of the soldiers had seen action recently. Not only the action against marchers at Magilligan the previous week, but much more serious action, not only in Belfast but also in Aden. One of the soldiers who was to play a major role in what followed had been flown back from training in Cyprus earlier that morning.

At around 15.55 two things happened very nearly simultaneously. Two members of the Parachute Regiment with their rifles trained on the rioting crowd in wasteground in front of them spotted somebody who they said they believed was about to throw a nail-bomb. Soldiers A and B fired their rifles. Damien Donaghey, aged fifteen, and John Johnston, aged fifty-five, fell, the former (who was the target) shot in the thigh, the latter hit by fragments of the bullets aimed at Donaghey.

And either shortly before or shortly after this the army in the same position received an incoming round. Soldiers believed that the direction of the bullet showed that it had come from the Rossville Flats. In fact it almost certainly came from the same direction, but closer, from Columbcille Court, from which Rifleman Hill had been shot three months earlier. The single round was fired at

21

soldiers at the Presbyterian church. It hit and shattered the drain- pipe on the side of the church. Though many denied it, this round could not but have affected the army's impression of what lay before them when they went over the barricades.

As Soldier O said in evidence years later, 'After we had heard this shot, the mood in the churchyard became more serious. We realised that the prospect of the Rossville Flats being used by snipers had become a fact. We knew that there was someone in there, or around there, with a gun. This was the first shot I heard that day. This shot which hit the church had a significant effect on the operation. Up to that point, all we thought we would be doing was going in to arrest people. We would have gone in to make the arrests with most of the men just carrying batons, a few having rubber bullet guns, and one or two having self-loading rifles [SLRs] as protection. As we now knew that there were gunmen operating in the area, most of the men carried SLRs and one or two carried rubber bullet guns.' The man who fired the shot at the soldiers and the man with him claimed years later that the shot had been intended as a reprisal for the shooting and wounding of Donaghey and Johnston. But it happened so close to the shootings that if it did not precede them then it happened so swiftly afterwards that the gunman was obviously already in position to fire at the army before the army had fired a shot.

Shortly after the drainpipe shot, Colonel Wilford decided to order 1 Para Support Company to go into the Bogside on their arrest operation not on foot but in armoured personnel vehicles known as Saracens or, colloquially among the troops, 'Pigs'. At 16.07 Brigadier MacLellan gave the order for a company of 1 Para to go through Barrier 14 in William Street but added that there were to be 'no running battles down Rossville Street'. By this point many of the peaceful marchers had headed towards Free Derry Corner and, the hope was, could therefore be separated from the rioters.

Colonel Wilford did not simply send one company through Barrier 14, he sent another company, Support Company, through Barrier 12 in Little James Street. As they went through the barriers the voice of General Ford, whose decision it had been to use 1 Para, was picked up on a recording being made by a journalist: 'Go on, 1 Para, go and get them and good luck.' He said years later that he considered these to be 'normal words of encouragement being given to soldiers about to go into a dangerous situation'.

As the army vehicles went through Barrier 12 and down Rossville Street the crowds before them began to run and then flee. The first vehicle, carrying, among others, the soldier who was to become known as Soldier N, turned left into the wasteground of Eden Place. The second, carrying, among others, Soldier O, ended up in the car-park in front of the Rossville Flats. On the way this vehicle hit and wounded two civilians, Alana Burke and Thomas Harkin. A small number of arrests were made and rubber bullets were fired. Rioters here, within the Bogside itself, were now throwing missiles at the soldiers. And then something happened.

Soldier N – who had got out of his 'Pig' – had found himself caught in an alleyway between Eden Place and Chamberlain Street. He fired two rifle shots over the heads of the crowd. In evidence decades later he said that he thought this was the only way he could prevent the crowd from attacking him and his fellow soldiers. Saville rejected this, concluding that N 'probably fired these shots because he decided that this would be an effective way of frightening the people and moving them on'. This firing was clearly in contravention of the rules of the army's Yellow Card, which explained to soldiers the situations in which live rounds were and were not allowed to be fired. But once Soldier N fired these shots, though they only hit a building, everything changed. It is very likely that at least part of what happened next did so because of the sound of N's firing. With the Derry city walls on one side and the high Rossville Flats in front, the crack of these rounds must have echoed all around the Bogside. In the echo-chamber created by the high walls in the area it is likely that one of the other soldiers who were now about to start firing mistook these warning shots of Soldier N's for live incoming rounds. The warning shots had become catalyst shots.

Some of the soldiers from the Mortar Platoon began to fire from their positions in the Rossville car-park area. A local priest, Father Daly, and a seventeen-year-old boy called Jackie Duddy were among those running for cover towards the flats. The priest was ahead of the boy when he heard a shot ring out. 'The young boy', he remembered, 'gasped or groaned loudly.' When the priest looked around he saw the boy had fallen on his face, his head pointing towards the Rossville Flats. During a temporary lull in the firing Father Daly went back out into the car-park. Another man had turned the boy over and blood was clearly oozing from his shirt. Father Daly tried to stop the bleeding with his white handkerchief and was joined by a Knight of Malta, one of the first-aid helpers on the march, who knelt beside him.

Duddy had gone on the march with friends and was looking forward to

23

hearing Bernadette Devlin speaking. But a bullet fired from a soldier's SLR had entered his body from the outer part of the right shoulder. It travelled through his body, damaging both his lungs, breaking his windpipe and exiting from the upper part of the left chest. With his breathing impaired and his lungs bleeding, death would have occurred, according to the autopsy, within a few minutes. As he knelt over him Father Daly realised the boy was dying and he gave him the last rites. He escorted a group of civilians who carried the dead or dying boy's body through the Bogside, past army lines, in footage that would become some of the most iconic and upsetting of the Troubles.

At the same time the only woman to be wounded by a gunshot that day, Margaret Deery, aged thirty-eight, was shot in the same car-park as Duddy, as were Michael Bridge (25) and Michael Bradley (22). Two other men, Pius McCarron (30) and Patrick McDaid (24), were hit by debris caused by the firing. A forty- year-old in one of the Rossville Flats, Patrick Brolly, was probably injured by the same firing.

Michael Bridge, who had previously been throwing stones at the soldiers at Barrier 14, was probably holding a half-brick as he shouted in rage at a soldier after the shooting of Duddy. 'Go ahead and shoot me,' he was heard to shout. And a soldier did shoot him – in the leg.

Meanwhile, soldiers from the Anti-Tank Platoon of the Para Company reached the ramp at Kells Walk, on the west side of Rossville Street. About eighty yards in front was a rubble barricade that had been put up by civilians to prevent army vehicles going further into the Bogside. Almost immediately on reaching the low wall that faced the rubble barricade the soldiers opened fire.

Michael Kelly (17) was shot and mortally wounded. A group of civilians came to carry his body away. Soldiers shot and killed five more people around the rubble barricade: Hugh Gilmour (17), William Nash (19), John Young (17), Michael McDaid (20) and Kevin McElhinney (17). As William Nash lay dying his father, Alexander Nash (52), went to tend to him. As he was bent over the body of his dead or dying son a bullet passed through his raised left arm.

Either after, or in the final moments of, this shooting, four soldiers from the Anti-Tank Platoon started running from the Kells Walk ramp into Glenfada Park North, a courtyard of flats to the side of Rossville Street. As they entered the courtyard civilians were running away to escape from them.

24

Immediately on arrival in Glenfada Park the soldiers opened fire. They shot and killed William McKinney (26) and James Wray (22), and shot and wounded Joe Friel (20), Michael Quinn (17), Joe Mahon (16) and Patrick O'Donnell (41). Daniel Gillespie (32) was also injured as the result of army fire. Among the dead, James Wray was shot twice, the second time, as Saville concluded, probably as he lay dying on the ground.

Among the soldiers who did the shooting in Glenfada Park, one, Soldier G, went into the neighbouring residential court of Abbey Park and there shot and killed 35-year-old Gerard McKinney. Some witnesses said he had his hands in the air and was shouting, 'Don't shoot, don't shoot.' The bullet that passed through his body also went into the body of, and killed, Gerald Donaghey (17).

Shortly afterwards, some among the soldiers who had been firing in Glenfada Park and Abbey Park got to the bottom corner of Glenfada Park overlooking the back of the Rossville Flats. Soldiers, or a soldier, firing from this position shot across Rossville Street at four men between the Rossville Flats and Joseph Place. The casualties there included Patrick Doherty (32), who was mortally wounded. As he lay dying he cried out. Bernard McGuigan (41) went to his help and was shot in the head, dying instantly. Two other men, Patrick Campbell (53) and Daniel McGowan (37), were wounded by bullets in the same area.

Though there was other gunfire during the course of the day, these shots constituted the main body of firing. It took only ten minutes from the moment that the soldiers drove into the Bogside to the shooting of these final casualties. A total of thirteen people lay dead and another fifteen had been wounded. One, John Johnston, wounded by the first shots of the day, died five months later. His family blamed the trauma of the shooting.

Ten minutes was all it took, but those ten minutes were going to be scrutinised in the most minute detail over the next three decades and beyond. As the smoke began to clear from the Bogside, terrified civilians who had been gathered together in huddles came back out into the open. Many civilians were arrested for rioting and taken in groups to Fort George detention centre.

As ambulances came in to take the dead and wounded to hospital and as the Bogside cleared, the army were already telling their version of what happened to press from around the world who had been covering the march. Early accounts of casualties were confused, with journalists and army putting numbers to each other that bore no relation to the final death toll.

Later General Ford complained about the pressure of having to respond to the media immediately. But in Northern Ireland the army had learned one of the lessons of modern war. As Ford said, if the army did not provide information to the media straightaway then they would find that that media had picked up the IRA's 'self- serving' version of events and would find the press reporting this as fact. The army had to respond to the media straight after any situation, he said, but responding promptly was, however, 'a problem in itself '.

Colonel Wilford and General Ford were in front of the cameras within minutes of the cessation of firing. Colonel Wilford, his face still blacked up, said that at this stage it seemed that there were five casualties. He conceded that the figure 'is quite large in these circumstances'. But he stressed that his men had been fired on, had been petrol-bombed and had acid thrown on them. 'Local people are saying that you used excessive force when you went in,' the interviewer said to him. Colonel Wilford's response was a strange and in the circumstances rather detached, philosophical, one. 'Well, what is force?' he asked, continuing, 'If you're being fired at you return fire. They know that perfectly well.'

By 17.30 the soldiers were back at the Clarence Avenue position that they had left from earlier in the day. There many, though not all, of the soldiers who had fired in the Bogside were called in by Major Loden, the commander of Support Company. They squeezed into the back of his small command vehicle. There with the light fading and with the help of a grid map Major Loden attempted to get each soldier who had fired his rifle to explain where he had fired and what he had fired at. He then handed this list to the regiment's headquarters. Only a manuscript copy taken by the young Captain Mike Jackson survived.

This list provided the first version of what happened. It was a list of engagements with targets very different from those who had fallen on the ground. It talked of nail-bombers hit, of petrol-bombers hit, of a 'gunman with pistol hit' and so on. It was the directory of a serious set of engagements with armed assailants. It was the record of a company that had gone into the Bogside and encountered substantial armed opposition.

26

Back at base later that night and in the early hours of the following morning the soldiers who fired were interviewed more thoroughly by the Royal Military Police. There they started to account in detail for the shots they had fired. Again, the accounts related engagements with armed men. Soldier R – who probably shot Jackie Duddy – claimed that he had fired at a man about to throw a nail-bomb. Though he probably had a stone in his hand at the time he was shot, neither Duddy nor any of the other victims was in the act of throwing a nail-bomb or any other device when shot. Other soldiers who fired in the area of the Rossville Flats car-park claimed to have been firing at nail-bombers, petrol-bombers or gunmen.

The soldiers who fired from the Kells Walk ramp towards the direction of the rubble barricade on Rossville Street said similar things. Corporal P said that he had fired at a man with a pistol, Lance Corporal J that he had fired at a nail-bomber. Corporal E said he had fired at a man with a pistol in the Rossville Flats. Private U said he had fired at a man with a handgun. Private L and Private M said that they had seen two people with rifles crawling away from the rubble barricade and shot them.

The soldiers who fired in Glenfada Park, Corporal E, Lance Corporal F, Private G and Private H, told a similar story. They said they had encountered nail-bombers and gunmen. Yet the men who had been shot were in each case facing away from the soldiers when they were shot. The entrance wounds of the bullets were in their backs. All the soldiers who had been in Glenfada Park denied shooting anybody while they were on the ground.

Private G, who was shown to have fired in Abbey Park, denied that he had fired there. But one of the men he shot, Gerald Donaghey, who was killed by the bullet that had already passed through Gerard McKinney, was unique among the dead. Seventeen-year-old Gerald Donaghey was, it later turned out, a member of the Fianna, the youth wing of the Provisional IRA. Donaghey was the only member of any such organisation killed or wounded on the day. When his body was on its way to hospital it was found that he had four nail-bombs in his pockets. The Saville Inquiry concluded that though he had these on him when he was shot, he was not in the process of throwing a nail-bomb. In any case, Private G, who was responsible for shooting him, could hardly have intended to shoot him by doing so through another, stationary, innocent person.

The remaining casualties, behind the Rossville Flats, were shot in an area

27

most likely shot in only by Lance Corporal F. Initially he did not mention anything in statements about firing into the area behind the Rossville Flats. When he eventually did, he said that he had fired at a man who was either holding or firing a pistol. Four people in the area were shot: two killed, two injured. Of the two men who were shot dead Patrick Doherty was shot in the buttock as he tried to crawl to safety. The man who went to aid him in his dying moments and was himself shot in the head, Barney McGuigan, had not been carrying anything more deadly than a handkerchief.

But the soldiers had their stories. They varied in probability and some of them began to vary in details. On the one hand there were experienced soldiers who had fired a small number of shots at, they said, highly specific targets. At the other end was an inexperienced soldier called Private H who seemed to be able to account only very poorly for at least nineteen of his twenty-two shots.

A set of mysteries already existed. If the soldiers had indeed found themselves in a hostile environment full of nail-bombers and gunmen, why had no soldier from Support Company been injured? A couple of the soldiers suffered slight injuries probably caused by acid thrown down on them in bottles from high up in the Rossville Flats. But there were no blast or bullet injuries.

But if there were no gunmen, no bombers, no hostile fire, why had the soldiers of Support Company behaved as they had? Among those who fired were not only inexperienced privates, terrified by fears of entering an IRA den. There were also experienced soldiers who had seen action elsewhere and whose training prepared them for telling when to fire and when not to fire their rifles. If there were no gunmen or bombers at all in the Bogside, why had so many of the soldiers of 1 Para fired their guns, some for the first time? Could they all have been mistaken? Could all of them have made it up? Could there have been such a complete breakdown of discipline across the whole company?

Perhaps there were gunmen in the Bogside. But if that was the case, then why had no gunman firing or nail-bomber in the act of throwing actually been hit? Why were the accounts coming out straight after the event of people shot while running away or with their hands raised in the air?

And if the army had run amok, as people were claiming from the moment they started firing, why had the targeting been so precise? Even among trained soldiers a dead-to-wounded ratio of almost exactly one to one demonstrated very careful shooting. As did the fact that only one woman had been hit by a bullet and that the majority of the casualties, even within those areas milling with crowds of people, were young men.

Had the army walked into a trap or had it committed a massacre?

These and very many more questions began to be asked not just in the mourning city of Derry but around the world in the months and years after those ten minutes of firing. And over the course of forty years a picture began to build that was at once simpler than many people thought it could be and more complex than people thought it would be.

It included many rival claims and opposing claims. It included the testimony of many people who under oath said they did things that nobody saw, who saw things that nobody did, and those who said they had seen and done nothing. As the smoke lifted on the Bogside a fog of contradictory claims descended over that ten- minute period, and a swirl of lies and counter-lies began to be spun that would take decades to unravel. The first effort to unravel it began within days, but on this occasion swiftness turned out to be the enemy of truth.

4

THE FIRST INQUIRY

The Bogside had been full of journalists. Some were behind the army barriers and had captured footage of the Paras as they went through. Others had been with the march throughout its progress and recorded footage from the other side of the barriers. Some newspapers had their correspondents in army watchtowers. Others were on the ground. During the crucial minutes many had come tantalisingly close to photographing or filming events that if captured would have solved the mysteries of the day immediately. Others caught important footage that would be replayed and reshown for years and went much of the way to solving parts of the riddle. Not least, photos helped decipher the sequence of events: people at the rubble barricade; crowds clearing in Glenfada Park; huddled figures behind buildings with people among them living who would soon be dead. The press could not answer the questions. But they could certainly pose some of them, and footage of what they had managed to capture soon went around the world.

Army commanders had been in front of the cameras and had given their side of what happened. But civilians and civic leaders were already relaying an entirely contradictory message. Their stories were very different from those of the soldiers, stories that if true would bring the protest and condemnation of the world down on the British army and the government that had sent them into Northern Ireland in the first place.

The Prime Minister of the United Kingdom, Edward Heath, was at his grace-and-favour country house, Chequers, when he received the news. He had spent the day discussing the approaching sailing season with his boat crew. Among the phone calls he received that evening was one from the Taoiseach, the Irish Prime Minister. Heath remembered the phone conversation being 'tense'. The Irish government recalled its ambassador to London.

The day after Bloody Sunday, on Monday 31 January 1972, the Home Secretary, Reginald Maudling, addressed the House of Commons. During a fiery and contentious exchange anger turned to violence. The Speaker tried to keep calm but it was clear that inside as much as outside the House there was a demand that something should be done.

Edward Heath's government was already aware that some action was needed to counteract the public relations catastrophe that it now had on its hands. In the Commons on 31 January the Home Secretary announced the setting up of an Inquiry into the events in Derry. That evening the Prime Minister and the Lord Chancellor, Lord Hailsham, met with the Lord Chief Justice, Lord Widgery. He agreed to chair an Inquiry into the events, and the three discussed the remit and conduct of that Inquiry. It was agreed that it would be best if Widgery limited his focus to the period of the shootings rather than the whole period of troubles up to and including the events. The government already had bad experience of judicial inquiries that had been too wide in their remit and protracted in their delivery. The report that had been commissioned from Lord Scarman into the violence that had erupted in Northern Ireland in 1969 had still not been published.

Lord Widgery was eager to draw lessons from this delay by sitting alone. This suited the Prime Minister. The army was still deployed in Northern Ireland, and the troops, including the regiment of those who fired, would be expected to continue serving there. Heath wanted the investigation concluded while the events were 'fresh in people's minds, and so that the troops would be able as soon as possible to carry on with their duties'. And in a phrase that would come back on him decades later, Heath also asked the Lord Chancellor to bear in mind that in Northern Ireland the British were fighting 'not just a military war, but a propaganda war'. There was considerable concern over where the hearings should be. Robin Chichester-Clark, the Unionist Member of Parliament for Londonderry and brother of the former Prime Minister of Northern Ireland James Chichester-Clark, reported his fears of the Inquiry sitting in his city. In the days after Bloody Sunday shops and banks in Derry had shut and the IRA had been strengthened and emboldened. The whole city was described as being 'in the grip of terror and intimidation on a scale it has never before known'. In this situation there was, as Heath recalled, considerable concern that 'revenge' attacks would be carried out by the IRA if the Inquiry were to sit in Derry. And so it was decided that the Inquiry should sit elsewhere, with the choice eventually landing on the town of Coleraine, twenty-four miles north-east of the site of the shootings.

31

The appointment of Lord Widgery was announced by the Prime Minister the next day. He said, 'The House will be glad to know that the Lord Chief Justice of England, Lord Widgery, has consented to undertake the Inquiry. He will sit alone.' But the debate that followed gave a flavour of the problem already arising. The day before, the government had given, in the House, its own version of what had happened on the march. It had done the same again that day. How could the Lord Chief Justice carry out an independent investigation into the events if the government that appointed him had already presented, as the truth, its version of what happened? The Liberal leader, Jeremy Thorpe, made this point repeatedly. And he was repeatedly interrupted – by a Conservative MP, Sir Harry Legge-Bourke. 'If there is one thing which should unite the whole House,' Thorpe said, 'it is the statement that we should dispassionately and impartially establish the true facts about what happened on Sunday last.' Legge-Bourke broke in, 'And back the army.' Thorpe tried again. Legge-Bourke broke in again. 'No, in the meantime we should certainly not remain impartial,' he said. 'In the meantime, let us back the army.'

The Labour Party leader, Harold Wilson, asked if the government was aware that 'however speedy, consistent with a fair report, it may be, the Northern Irish situation will not wait for an Inquiry.' He reminded the House that 'we have not had the Scarman Report yet to deal with events from 1969.' The same concern was expressed by Chichester-Clark. He spoke for many when he expressed the fear that the Inquiry by Lord Widgery might take too much time. That, at least, was a fear that was not realised.

The funerals of the victims took place the day after the Widgery Inquiry was announced, on 2 February. In the Irish Republic a day of national mourning was observed. Over several days crowds of thousands protested outside the British embassy in Merrion Square, Dublin.

In his memoirs, *Dublin from Downing* Street, Sir John Peck, the British ambassador to Dublin at the time, described what happened: 'Bloody Sunday had unleashed a wave of fury and exasperation the like of which I had never encountered in my life, in Egypt or Cyprus or anywhere else. Hatred of the British was intense. Someone had summed it up: "We are all IRA now."'

At the height of the protests in Dublin an estimated 35,000 people demonstrated outside the British embassy. Outside the post office in O'Connell

Street a *Guardian* reporter saw balaclava- wearing members of the IRA collecting money from the crowds. There were around 4,500 police in the county of Dublin and at the height of the rioting, petrol-bombing and looting, half of the police force of Dublin were drafted to Merrion Square. In the words of the ambassador, 'They fought on as long as they could, and many were burnt by bottles of burning petrol.' But eventually the crowds overwhelmed them. The petrol-bombs caught and finally, in front of a cheering crowd of thousands, the British embassy burnt to the ground. People in the crowds cut the water-hoses of the firemen who were trying to put out the blaze.

Twelve days later Lord Widgery arrived in Coleraine to conduct a preliminary hearing. A week later the full hearings began. Over the course of less than a month, between 21 February and 14 March, Lord Widgery heard the evidence of 114 witnesses. These included thirty civilians, twenty-one members of the media and seven priests as well as forensics experts, pathologists, doctors, policemen and of course the soldiers. Five officers testified, including General Ford and Colonel Wilford. Also in the witness stand were all of the soldiers who had fired a shot and a dozen other soldiers who had relevant evidence.

The soldiers were helicoptered in to give testimony and entered the court wearing dark glasses to protect their identities. Every soldier who testified, whether he had fired or not, was also given anonymity. Only commanders whose names were already in the public sphere were named. The Widgery letterings remained in the succeeding years and indeed through the succeeding Inquiry. They had a simple and standard army order. The soldiers who fired the earliest shots, at Damien Donaghey and John Johnston, were named Soldier A and Soldier B. And so on. The soldiers who went into Glenfada Park were Soldiers E, F, G and H. This was normal army practice at the time and went some way to allaying soldiers' concerns over testifying.

Among the citizens of Derry there was also concern about testifying, but a concern of a quite different kind. In the run-up to the Inquiry there was intense scepticism that a British Lord Chief Justice could get to the truth of events. Many were nevertheless persuaded to give evidence. But the prospect was a daunting one. For Lord Saville's Inquiry a number recalled their experiences at the Widgery Tribunal.

Joseph Doherty, who saw Barney McGuigan and others shot, recalled testifying at Widgery. 'Some people did not want to co-operate, but I did. I wanted to tell the Tribunal what I had seen and heard. I can remember sitting fairly close to Widgery and looking at the model.' To assist the Inquiry a model of the crucial area of Derry had been made and was laid in front of the judge.

'However,' recalled Doherty, 'I came away with the distinct impression that he was not interested in what I had to say and that he simply wanted to get through the witnesses as quickly as possible. He showed no real concern or interest and he did not come across to me as a man who wanted to find the truth. I felt he had a preconceived idea as to what had taken place and I felt that the outcome was a whitewash.'

Others agreed. Geraldine McBride (née Richmond), the woman who had been beside McGuigan when he was shot, recalled that she was initially 'delighted' when she heard about the Widgery Inquiry. 'I thought it would put everything right,' she said. But the experience of testifying in a strange town was made worse by the fact that, as McBride remembered, 'there were protestors outside calling us names and I was very frightened. I had never been in a police station or a court before in my life and I didn't realise that I would be cross-examined, never mind by three different people. I just wanted people to know that those who had been killed on Bloody Sunday did not carry weapons. In the cross-examination they kept pressing me and coming back to me for more and more detail. I was shown a model but I do not think it was correct as the gable end of Block 1 of Rossville Flats, where the telephone box was, was not on the model. I found giving evidence horrible and felt terrible when I came out.' She, like other civilians, felt that the set-up of the Inquiry meant that she was made to be 'on the defensive all the time' when she had done nothing wrong.

During the course of the Inquiry there came a strong reminder of the urgency of the situation. In the days after Bloody Sunday a number of soldiers and others were shot dead, and on 22 February the Official IRA managed to hit the Paras where they assumed it would hurt, carrying out a car-bomb attack on the Parachute Regiment's Aldershot headquarters. The device was retaliation for Bloody Sunday, the Official IRA announced, and it wrecked the Officers' Mess. But though there were twenty people inside the mess at the time, only one member of the Parachute Regiment was killed – Gerry Weston, the 38-year-old Catholic chaplain. Setting a pattern that was going to persist for decades, a much larger number of people who were not the direct targets suffered most from the act. Six other people, all civilians, were killed in the blast. Five were domestic staff working on the base as cleaners. The sixth was a local gardener, John

Haslar, who died from a fractured skull.

What the opinion was of the soldiers who were called to give evidence to Widgery nobody truthfully knows. But one man (though his testimony would be questioned on other counts) relayed a view that certainly rang true here. The 'whistleblower' soldier, 027, told Saville that though he did not testify, among his fellow soldiers 'there was a feeling about the Widgery Inquiry that we were being put on trial by our own government. There was indignation; it was an affront in some way.'

Soldiers flown into Coleraine in Sioux helicopters faced, he said, an 'intimidating prospect'. He said that soldiers were under the impression that 'half the IRA's supporters were supposed to be in the public gallery.'

On 24 March, four days after Lord Widgery's final hearing, with a continuously deteriorating security situation, the Stormont Parliament in Northern Ireland was finally dissolved and direct rule was imposed from Westminster. On 10 April Lord Widgery handed the report of his Inquiry to the Home Secretary. It was published eight days later, on 18 April, and the anger and hatred caused by the actions of the Parachute Regiment on 30 January was embedded into the citizens of the city. For many, the Widgery Report showed that the legal establishment had joined with the military and political establishments in condoning the murder of British citizens.

It was officially titled 'The Report of the Tribunal appointed to inquire into the events on Sunday, 30 January 1972, which led to loss of life in connection with the procession in Londonderry on that day by The Rt. Hon. Lord Widgery, O.B.E., T.D.' and it covered a considerable amount of information in its 104 paragraphs. It made sense of many of the complex and contradictory events, and who was shot in each sector and so on, but it arrived at conclusions about these events that, while apparently satisfying to the government, were not satisfactory to anybody else.

First the report criticised the march organisers, saying that 'there would have been no deaths in Londonderry on 30 January if those who organised the illegal march had not thereby created a highly dangerous situation in which a clash between demonstrators and the security forces was almost inevitable.'

Widgery also concluded that 'none of the deceased or wounded is proved to have been shot while handling a firearm or bomb. Some are wholly acquitted of complicity in such action; but there is a strong suspicion that some others had been firing weapons or handling bombs in the course of the afternoon and that yet others had been closely supporting them.' In this regard Lord Widgery was not helped by the forensic evidence of the time. In 1972 the test for gunfire residue was a paraffin test. On the results of these tests a number of the dead, including Barney McGuigan, had garments or portions of their body that showed the person had been in proximity to the firing of a gun. In McGuigan's case this was made even more complex. At some stage after he was killed somebody put a scarf over his body. The scarf, which his widow testified was not his, had residue that suggested the wearer had been close to the firing of weapons.

Other victims had similar or more damning verdicts. The likelihood was, Widgery concluded, that John Young, shot dead at the Rossville Street barricade, had been firing a gun. Widgery wrote that 'when his case is considered in conjunction with those of Nash and McDaid and regard is had to the soldiers' evidence about civilians firing from the barricade a very strong suspicion is raised that one or more of Young, Nash and McDaid was using a firearm. No weapon was found but there was sufficient opportunity for this to be removed by others.' Tests carried out on the clothes and body of James Wray, shot in Glenfada Park, concluded that he was also likely to have been carrying a firearm.

This element of Lord Widgery's report probably did more damage to its credibility than any other. The fact that some of the dead had their reputations posthumously tarnished in this way added terrible insult to fatal injury. In the succeeding years the paraffin test that Widgery had relied on was shown to be desperately flawed. It transpired, as the ballistics experts to Lord Saville's Inquiry noted, that being near a car starting up, among other ordinary, everyday events, could leave the kind of residue that had been determined by Lord Widgery's tests as betraying evidence of weapons-handling. Residue from the gunfire that killed them could also have caused this, as could the poor laboratory conditions in which the tests were carried out. The tests, in fact, were worthless, though Widgery was not the only legal authority to be misled by the alleged forensic evidence in such a case.

But aside from the spreading of guilt on to the deceased the Widgery Report was probably most notorious for its descriptions of the actions of the soldiers.

On the vital question of who fired first Widgery concluded that he was

36

'entirely satisfied that the first firing in the courtyard was directed at the soldiers'. He also said that 'in general the accounts given by the soldiers of the circumstances in which they fired and the reasons why they did so were, in my opinion, truthful.' And in a passage that would make many gasp he declared that 'those accustomed to listening to witnesses could not fail to be impressed by the demeanour of the soldiers of 1 Para. They gave their evidence with confidence and without hesitation or prevarication and withstood a rigorous cross-examination without contradicting themselves or each other. With one or two exceptions I accept that they were telling the truth as they remembered it.' But those one or two exceptions were important.

In the years since his findings were published many people have seen Widgery as a pure whitewash, but in fact the findings are far more interesting and, in the final analysis of why the army and government did not pick up on this, surprisingly damning. For in the body of the report Widgery certainly did find fault with the soldiers. The warning shots fired by Soldier N over the heads of the crowd to disperse them had, like the firing of Soldiers P, T, O and V, breached the terms of the soldiers' Yellow Card, he said. But he found that these actions 'do not seem to point to a breakdown in discipline or to require censure'.

For the soldiers who fired the most shots Widgery had tougher words. He noted that 'at one end of the scale some soldiers showed a high degree of responsibility; at the other, notably in Glenfada Park, firing bordered on the reckless.' And in the case of at least one soldier, Widgery made it clear that he did not believe a word he said. Widgery dismissed Soldier H's claim that he had fired nineteen rounds at a gunman behind a window that did not shatter. He said that 'it is highly improbable that this cycle of events should repeat itself nineteen times; and indeed it did not. I accepted evidence subsequently given, supported by photographs, which showed that no shot at all had been fired through the window in question. So nineteen of the twenty-two shots fired by Soldier H were wholly unaccounted for.'

And of the death of Patrick Doherty, Widgery concluded that 'the probability is that he was shot by Soldier F, who spoke of hearing pistol shots and seeing a crouching man firing a pistol from the position where Doherty's body was found. Soldier F said that he fired as the man turned away, which would account for an entry wound in the buttock. Doherty's reaction to the paraffin test was negative. In the light of all the evidence I conclude that he was not carrying a weapon. If Soldier F shot Doherty in the belief that he had a pistol that belief

37

was mistaken.'

Soldiers firing 'recklessly', having nineteen shots 'unaccounted for' and shooting and killing people in the 'mistaken' belief that they were armed: ordinarily this criticism should have led somewhere. Couched as it was in a necessary blanket of legalese, it should have been enough to encourage the government and army to take action against those soldiers who the Lord Chief Justice said he believed had fired in a reckless manner and whose evidence on oath in the witness stand he had said he did not believe.

But nothing happened. In July 1972 the RUC sent the Director of Public Prosecutions a file on the Bloody Sunday deaths. The Attorney General replied to it on 1 August. He said that he had concluded that there would be no prosecutions of any members of the army relating to the day. And that would have been that and the matter dealt with: the Lord Chief Justice had delivered a swift and judicious report. However, from the delivery of the Widgery Inquiry, another set of inquiries got under way, propelled by individuals with a desire to see a terrible wrong righted.

In August 1973 the formal inquest into the deaths was held. The coroner, Major Hubert O'Neill – a Unionist – went absolutely against the conclusions reached by the head of the judiciary. He stated of the day that 'this Sunday became known as Bloody Sunday and bloody it was. It was quite unnecessary. It strikes me that the Army ran amok that day and shot without thinking what they were doing. They were shooting innocent people. These people may have been taking part in a march that was banned but that does not justify the troops coming in and firing live rounds indiscriminately. I would say without hesitation that it was sheer, unadulterated murder. It was murder.'

This certainly summed up the feelings of the Catholic citizens of Derry and many others around the world. But the outrage in many places died down and what anger there was either subsided or was lost amid the ensuing years and the endless rounds of anger that endless rounds of violence either fired or dulled. But in the city of Derry fury at the Widgery conclusions did not abate. The report immediately became known in the city as the 'Widgery whitewash'. As Father Daly – who had escorted the body of Jack Duddy past the army lines – said succinctly of Widgery: 'He found the guilty innocent, and the innocent guilty.'

For those like Father Daly who had testified and trusted Widgery to get to the truth the report was a catastrophe. For many it was a personal as much as a societal one. One of Widgery's other witnesses summed up her feelings thirty years later. Geraldine McBride – the young woman who went into hysterics when she saw Barney McGuigan shot in the head beside her – was brave to turn up and testify to Widgery, but she had done so because she believed that he might get to the truth. Her reaction to his verdict was painful. She said: 'When the Widgery Report came out I could not believe it. He had seemed a nice man when he talked to me and I thought that he would sort it out. I could not believe that all those fellows had not been cleared. I was hurt, and was hurt for the people who had died as I felt I had let them down. I also felt that the law had let us down and there was not much future for us if that was the law.

'I did not talk about the events of 30 January 1972 for twenty years. That was my way of coping, although I didn't cope very well for years afterwards.'

On the first anniversary of Bloody Sunday the families gathered to remember the victims. Soon it became a tradition each anniversary to retread the progress of the fatal march. It kept memories alive and provided a focal point to the families and campaigners who wanted the wrong of the day as well as the wrong of Widgery acknowledged.

It was a long march. And as the Troubles continued and the numbers of dead on all sides grew and grew, keeping the focus on the atrocity of Bloody Sunday was not easy in a city and a society that became used, if never immune, to atrocity.

In 1974, in an effort to close the matter, the British government agreed to pay compensation to the relatives of those killed on Bloody Sunday. The sums ranged from £250 to over £16,500. The Ministry of Defence said that the payments had been given 'in a spirit of goodwill and conciliation'. But the families wanted exoneration of their relatives, not cash.

However, as the war continued amid recriminations from every side towards every side, and as the list of paramilitary atrocities mounted, there was never any real likelihood that the one among all the events to be reopened for investigation would be the one that had already had one judicial Inquiry – by the Lord Chief Justice, no less. And even less chance that – with many terrorists not captured and so many atrocities going unpunished – an Inquiry into the activities of 1 Para in 1972 would be a priority for governments still fighting a military as well as a propaganda war. By 1984, when the IRA nearly succeeded in wiping out the British government and killed and maimed MPs and spouses in the Brighton bomb attack, a hearing for the Bloody Sunday relatives was the last thing that could have been envisaged.

In fact it took more perseverance than anybody could have imagined, and the beginning of the IRA's ceasefire, for the campaign of the Bloody Sunday families to look as if it might finally be rewarded. In 1992, on the twentieth anniversary of Bloody Sunday, the British Prime Minister, John Major, said in a letter to the Social Democratic and Labour Party leader, John Hume, that 'the Government made clear in 1974 that those who were killed on "Bloody Sunday" should be regarded as innocent of any allegation that they were shot whilst handling firearms or explosives.' And he said that 'I hope that the families of those who died will accept that assurance.'

But they did not. Calls for a fresh Inquiry into the day were bolstered by anniversary articles and broadcasts. Then in 1997 a new government came into power in Westminster. The new Labour administration was keen on starting with a clean slate on a range of things, not least on Northern Ireland. As Tony Blair, the new Prime Minister, pushed for a peace settlement, it became clear that one of the things in his gift that he thought would go furthest to satisfying Republican demands would be to agree to a new Inquiry into Bloody Sunday.

Also around this time, as the twenty-fifth anniversary of the day approached, new information came to light. A soldier of the Parachute Regiment appeared to have broken ranks and come out with a version of events that sounded all too believable to those who had tried for years to get to the truth of what 1 Para did that day. This and other evidence compiled by the Irish government as well as by the families of the victims was presented to the new government in Westminster.

Finally, on 29 January 1998, the day before the twenty-sixth anniversary of the day itself, Prime Minister Blair stood up and told the House that a long campaign was about to come to an end. 'With permission, Madam Speaker, I will make a statement on the events in Northern Ireland on 30 January 1972, which has become known as Bloody Sunday,' he said.

> Lord Widgery produced a report within eleven weeks of the day... The timescale within which Lord Widgery produced his report meant that he was not able to consider all the evidence that might have been available. For example, he did not receive any evidence from the wounded who were still in

40

hospital, and he did not consider individually substantial numbers of eyewitness accounts provided to his Inquiry in the early part of March 1972.

Since the report was published, much new material has come to light about the events of that day. That material includes new eyewitness accounts, new interpretation of ballistic material and new medical evidence.

He paid tribute to the security forces and stressed that painful lessons had been learned over the years. But he was careful to underline why Bloody Sunday and not the myriad other atrocities of the Troubles was now once again being singled out.

Bloody Sunday was different because, where the state's own authorities are concerned, we must be as sure as we can of the truth, precisely because we pride ourselves on our democracy and respect for the law, and on the professionalism and dedication of our security forces.

This has been a very difficult issue. I have reread Lord Widgery's report... I have been strongly advised, and I believe, that there are indeed grounds for such a further inquiry. We believe that the weight of material now available is such that the events require re-examination. We believe that the only course that will lead to public confidence in the results of any further investigation is to set up a full-scale judicial Inquiry into Bloody Sunday.

And so he announced that under the Tribunal of Inquiry (Evidence) Act 1921 a new Inquiry would be set up, with the power to call witnesses and search for all available evidence. The resolution was tabled as follows: 'That it is expedient that a Tribunal be established for inquiring into a definite matter of urgent public importance, namely the events on Sunday, 30 January 1972 which led to loss of life in connection with the procession in Londonderry on that day, taking account of any new information relevant to events on that day.' He announced that Lord Saville of Newdigate, a Law Lord, had agreed to chair the Tribunal, that this Tribunal would have three judges and that he would therefore be joined by two judges from the Commonwealth.

Pre-empting, though not enough, some of the criticism that was going to come his way, Blair also conceded that it was impossible to say how long the Inquiry would take, but he stressed that it must be given the time to investigate thoroughly. Nobody, it was clear, wanted another Widgery. Blair spelt out what was another important argument if he was going to ensure cross-party support for his proposal:

41

Let me make it clear that the aim of the Inquiry is not to accuse individuals or institutions, or to invite fresh recriminations, but to establish the truth about what happened on that day, so far as that can be achieved at twenty-six years' distance.

'It will not be easy,' Blair said. And on that he was certainly right. But neither he nor anybody else involved, least of all the judge that had just agreed to lead the effort to pick up what Lord Widgery had left, could have appreciated how gargantuan the task was going to be. The wheels of justice had finally ground into motion. But the mere fact that they were finally moving did not mean that they were going to move swiftly.

5

THE CONSPIRACIES

Edward Heath and his government had hoped that the Widgery Report would dampen concerns over the conduct of the Parachute Regiment and the conduct of the British army as a whole in Northern Ireland. But the verdict Widgery reached, in fact, did not just fuel condemnation of certain soldiers or a particular regiment but contaminated the whole of the British state with what members of 1 Para had done in the Bogside. It embedded one of the most pervasive ideas of all – that the whole of the state was involved in a conspiracy: one to which somebody somewhere would one day produce, or find, the key. The 26-year gap between the Widgery verdict and the announcement of a new Inquiry provided ample opportunity for the original suspicions to fester into something much bigger and apparently deeply significant.

Every necessary element was there: the involvement of the army, the intelligence services, leading politicians and a leading judge. And it was not just the civilians of Derry or sympathisers around the world that fostered such elaboration of the day's mysteries. Rumours came from every side and spread in all directions.

Some of the more fanciful either drifted away or fed into the general pool of grievance. A man who had been a seventeen-year- old schoolboy on the day said that he had taken film with his cine-camera that, when he took it to be developed, was returned as 'undevelopable'. This had never happened before or since. Was this significant? Were Kodak in on the plot?

Other rumours that came up had slightly more substance. And of course rumours of unimaginable army malfeasance found a particularly receptive audience in a city that had just seen the most unimaginable army behaviour. Stories abounded of soldiers telling people, or telling somebody else whom somebody knew, about what they had done or meant to do that day. One Derry local claimed to have received a phone call, after the event, at his family's shop from what he took to be a soldier involved in Bloody Sunday. He claimed that the caller, identifiable by the English accent, said something like 'We shot those fuckers for the two policemen,' taken to refer to the two policemen shot dead in Derry by the IRA three days before Bloody Sunday. Others claimed to have met soldiers who warned them off in similar tones. These and other small-scale rumours fed into an atmosphere of much grander conspiracy.

From the day itself right throughout the evidence-taking stage of Saville, senior Republican and their cheerleaders claimed that the actions of 1 Para on Bloody Sunday demonstrated a conspiracy – to murder people and then to cover up the fact – that had emanated from the very top of the British government. Perhaps from Edward Heath himself. Rumour turned into accepted fact. When the Saville Inquiry was set up the scene was meant to have been set for a magnificent exposé – a final revelation of the great scandal at the dark heart of the British state. What transpired turned out to be not only much less grand, but far more human.

The Saville Inquiry held the first of its preliminary sessions in the Guildhall in Derry on 3 April 1998. The symbolism of the Tribunal sitting in the hall where the Bloody Sunday march had intended to arrive in 1972 was not missed. But this was not the completion, but rather the beginning, of a process. It began with the chairman introducing himself to the city.

> My name is Mark Saville. I am an English Law Lord, one of the judges who sits in the House of Lords as the highest court of appeal in the United Kingdom. I am presiding as Chairman of the Inquiry. I have two colleagues sitting with me.

He then introduced his fellow judges from the Commonwealth, one of whom was replaced early in the Tribunal after retiring for health reasons. He also introduced Christopher Clarke QC, who as Counsel to the Inquiry would ask questions on behalf of the Tribunal, and he then introduced the other administrative and legal staff. He was clearly aware of speaking to a city that had reason to be wary of trusting a British judge appointed by a British Lord Chancellor. But Saville was quiet, unassuming and called simply for all those people with knowledge of what happened on Bloody Sunday to come forward and provide evidence to the Inquiry.

Over the course of almost two years the Inquiry continued with preliminary

44

hearings to overcome myriad difficulties. To ensure that witnesses did not fear telling the truth about what they did on the day the Attorney General gave the assurance that no written or oral evidence provided by witnesses to the Inquiry could be used against them in any later criminal proceedings. This did not mean that criminal proceedings could not come from the Inquiry, but that the evidence people gave to it could not be used against them. It was the best chance the Inquiry had of receiving full disclosure from witnesses – however damaging.

Other lengthy hearings and ancillary cases were conducted on whether the soldiers could retain their anonymity. And then of course there was the task of collecting evidence: around 2,500 witness statements were taken by the Inquiry's solicitors. Lord Saville also began the lengthy process of acquiring all relevant materials from the relevant government departments, including the Ministry of Defence and the Security Service. Among the information that was turned up was some that exploded some of the most cherished myths about the day and other revelations that created, temporarily, new myths of their own.

In 2000, during its trawl of government documents, the Saville Inquiry unearthed a memorandum written on 7 January 1972, three weeks before Bloody Sunday. It was written by General Ford (and thus became known as the 'Ford memorandum') to his boss at army headquarters in Lisburn, General Harry Tuzo. In it Ford said that he was 'coming to the conclusion that the minimum force necessary to achieve a restoration of law and order is to shoot selected ring-leaders amongst the DYH (Derry Young Hooligans), after clear warnings have been issued'.

The DYH were in Ford's definition the 'gangs of tough teenage youths ... who have developed sophisticated tactics of brick and stone throwing, destruction and arson'. The challenge for the army, he said, was that they were 'virtually incapable' against the DYH because snipers operated among them and their presence hindered the ability of soldiers to deal with such gunmen and bombers. Ford did not advocate that the ringleaders should be killed, but the memorandum when it came to light nevertheless provided what looked like the 'smoking gun'. Here was the commander of the British forces writing to his superior suggesting the shooting of Derry citizens. For a time the discovery of the memorandum was the best hope that Republican sympathisers had of proving that the shootings on Bloody Sunday had indeed been ordered 'from the top'.

And there were two other pieces of evidence that seemed to support the notion. The first was a comment, not a policy decision, that had gained some notoriety when it became public in a book published by Tony Geraghty in 1998 called *The Irish War*. In the course of researching the book the author had heard from the Chief of the General Staff at the time of Bloody Sunday, Field Marshall Lord Carver, who had told him that a 'legal luminary' at a cabinet meeting around the time had suggested 'under some medieval statute' that anyone 'who obstructed the servants of the King, acting in the course of their duty, was by that very fact one of the King's enemies and therefore liable to be shot by the King's soldiers'. Subsequently Lord Carver revealed that the 'legal luminary' had been Lord Hailsham, the Lord Chancellor.

The third possible smoking gun that emerged in the years after the Widgery Inquiry involved a meeting between the same Lord Hailsham, the Prime Minister and the Lord Chief Justice, Lord Widgery, on 1 February 1972. The meeting came to light on 4 August 1995 thanks to the discovery of a letter in the Public Record Office. It referred to the fact that, while speaking to Lord Widgery about the nature of the Inquiry he was about to conduct, the Prime Minister had felt it appropriate to remind the Lord Chief Justice 'that we were in Northern Ireland fighting not only a military war but a propaganda war'. Was this a nod to Widgery to find in a particular direction?

Were any of these things evidence that the deaths on Bloody Sunday were ordered or approved from the very top of the British government and British army? As the Saville Inquiry began its work, truth and conspiracy were gradually, as they had to be, separated out.

Among the myths about the day that had grown in prominence through the 1990s was the claim that as well as the shootings carried out by members of 1 Para in the Bogside, there had also been firing by members of the British army stationed on the city walls. Over the years journalists investigated and promoted the idea that shots had been fired from the walls, in, for instance, a 1997 Channel 4 programme and several books. The idea was given apparently expert backing by a New York ballistics specialist who was called in by some journalists. What was most convincing, and had been across the years, was the testimony, repeated in written statements for Lord Saville, of a huge number of people who were absolutely convinced this was true, and some who even claimed to have seen it.

As the Inquiry proceeded one thing that became clear was that even to the trained ear of soldiers, let alone to the untrained ears of most civilians, the

46

Bogside on that day was one huge echo-chamber in which it was, if not impossible, then certainly extremely hard to tell where firing was coming from. A person caught in the middle of this could be convinced that firing had come from any direction. In this situation, dozens of civilian witnesses were so convinced that they testified on oath that firing had come from the city walls. In some cases it became clear that this conclusion had been come to not by observation but by assumption and deduction. For instance, one witness insisted that because of where two of the casualties were shot they could only have been shot from the city walls and claimed to have heard 'specific shots' from there. Another, a local headmaster, stated that 'it was my definite impression … that the fire was coming from the City Walls or buildings behind them.' Others who were convinced that some firing had come from there included journalists and also the civil rights leader Ivan Cooper, who was 'pinned to the ground' as bullets flew above him in front of the speakers' platform. Cooper described in his written statement how he 'was convinced at the time that shots were being fired from the City Wall. I am not clear as to why.' In oral evidence he related simply that 'it was an impression I had… That was the feeling that I had.'

In fact, as Paul James McLaughlin, a Knights of Malta first- aid man who had been huddled by the telephone box with Barney McGuigan, said in testimony: 'In my view, it would have been impossible for any lay person to indicate which way the shots were being fired, unless they had specifically seen the soldiers who fired them.' But for others it was not merely an impression or a suspicion of something they thought had happened, but something they positively swore that they had seen.

Thomas Mullarkey said in his statement to Saville that 'while I thought that all the firing was coming south along Rossville Street, I did notice soldiers on the City Walls near the Walker Monument… I watched the soldiers sighting their rifles, which was something they did all the time, even in non-violent situations. However, I remember seeing at least three puffs of smoke from the mouths of the rifle muzzles. I realised that soldiers were firing from the City Walls.'

William Lindsay said in testimony that 'there were about half a dozen men in all, possibly in their fifties. They were lying on my side of the wall and shouting, "Get down, get down, they will fucking kill you. Get out of the fucking road." I looked up behind them (to the east) to the City Walls and could see several flashes as shots were fired from the City Walls. I recall that there were about seven or eight flashes which appeared to be coming from the area on the City Walls. I was aware of bullets bouncing all around me. At the time, I was the only person standing up – there was an empty space around me – everyone else was taking cover. I realised that the shots were aimed at me and so I ran towards the wall and dived for cover to join the men already lying there.'

Pauline McDermott claimed that one point during the firing 'something caught my eye. I would say it was a flash of something but I couldn't give any more description of it than that. I just know something in the same direction as where the gunfire was coming from caught my attention. The noise and the flash which caught my eye seemed to come from a high position on the City Walls somewhere between Butcher's Gate and the Walker Memorial. The sharp staccato noises seemed to go on for a long time and the cracking sounds seemed to echo all around me.'

As it turned out, all of the above were wrong. No soldier fired from the walls that day. No bullets were unaccounted for among those soldiers in observation posts along the city walls. Did people's ears deceive them? Certainly. But could their eyes have deceived them too? In the end, it appeared, yes. Again the reaction of people unused to firing situations led after the event to analysis that turned out to simply be wrong. The McDermott 'flash' for instance was probably something commonplace – the flash of binoculars in the sun or the transplanting of one visual memory on to a different location.

Lord Saville concluded that 'we are sure, from what we regard as convincing evidence from those on the Walls, that there was no firing by soldiers from there' and that 'in the confusion, fear and noise following the incursion of soldiers of Support Company into the Bogside and the substantial amount of firing by those soldiers that followed, people mistakenly came to believe or suspect that soldiers on the Walls had fired into the areas under discussion.'

But there was a reason why the idea that soldiers fired from the walls that day became a popular narrative. People believed it because it confirmed the worst suspicions of the Bogsiders: that, caught in the low-level ground of the Bogside, its inhabitants were being picked off one by one, like animals in a trap. More colourful still, this was being done by figures of authority who were themselves at a safe distance. In the aftermath of the day the understandable levels of paranoia in the area fed this and many other rumours. While some conspiracies about the day had no basis in fact, it appeared at times that others certainly did.

48

Of these, one of the most potent concerned the army guns that had been fired.

Though only twenty-eight guns were fired, twenty-eight SLRs and one converted sniper rifle were, in the immediate aftermath of Bloody Sunday, sent to the Department of Industrial and Forensic Science (DIFS) in Belfast for testing. This testing would be crucial in revealing the origin of some of the shots fired that day. It was only thanks to ballistic testing that certain of the dead could be identified as having been shot by certain soldiers, for each bullet carries a unique imprint of the gun that fired it.

In 1999, in its earliest stages, the Saville Inquiry asked the them too? In the end, it appeared, yes. Again the reaction of people unused to firing situations led after the event to analysis that turned out to simply be wrong. The McDermott 'flash' for instance was probably something commonplace – the flash of binoculars in the sun or the transplanting of one visual memory on to a different location.

Lord Saville concluded that 'we are sure, from what we regard as convincing evidence from those on the Walls, that there was no firing by soldiers from there' and that 'in the confusion, fear and noise following the incursion of soldiers of Support Company into the Bogside and the substantial amount of firing by those soldiers that followed, people mistakenly came to believe or suspect that soldiers on the Walls had fired into the areas under discussion.'

But there was a reason why the idea that soldiers fired from the walls that day became a popular narrative. People believed it because it confirmed the worst suspicions of the Bogsiders: that, caught in the low-level ground of the Bogside, its inhabitants were being picked off one by one, like animals in a trap. More colourful still, this was being done by figures of authority who were themselves at a safe distance. In the aftermath of the day the understandable levels of paranoia in the area fed this and many other rumours. While some conspiracies about the day had no basis in fact, it appeared at times that others certainly did. Of these, one of the most potent concerned the army guns that had been fired.

Though only twenty-eight guns were fired, twenty-eight SLRs and one converted sniper rifle were, in the immediate aftermath of Bloody Sunday, sent to the Department of Industrial and Forensic Science (DIFS) in Belfast for testing. This testing would be crucial in revealing the origin of some of the shots fired that day. It was only thanks to ballistic testing that certain of the dead could be identified as having been shot by certain soldiers, for each bullet carries a unique imprint of the gun that fired it.

In 1999, in its earliest stages, the Saville Inquiry asked the Ministry of Defence in London if they had any information about the rifles. Did they still exist? Were they in the army's possession? How could the Inquiry get hold of them? A sense of what has been described as a 'lack of enthusiasm' for Saville's 1999 request can be garnered from an internal MoD email that read: 'The Bloody Sunday inquiry are after records (if any) of what happened to the Bloody Sunday weapons ... on Tuesday the Battle of Hastings inquiry will want to find the longbow which put Harold's eye out!'

Though it was thought that a number were abroad, in 1999 the Ministry of Defence reported that only five of the twenty-nine SLRs previously held at its Donnington storage complex in Shropshire were available for testing. Fourteen had been destroyed after the introduction of the new models and the other ten had been sold abroad.

The five SLRs that remained in the MoD's hands were, it transpired, due to be destroyed. Saville acted immediately, issuing an order that everything possible be done to stop the destruction of the guns. But two of the rifles slated to be destroyed were among the 4,000 SLRs a month that were destroyed anyway.

An Inquiry source was reported saying that when Saville heard the news, 'His Lordship blew his top.' Aside from the investigative setback Saville must have been aware how bad this could look. Conscious of this, a joint investigation into the destruction of the two rifles and a search for the remaining three was launched by the MoD police and the West Mercia Constabulary under the codename 'Operation Apollo'. Like everything else involved in the Inquiry even this operation swiftly metastasised.

First it transpired that the army record system was a mess, and that not only could the serial number of a rifle change, but some of its components, including the barrel, could be replaced without any record of the change on file. It also turned out that the serial numbers of twenty of the twenty-nine guns had been assigned twice, to different SLRs, meaning that the number of rifles that could now possibly be of interest to Saville was around sixty.

The search stepped up, and soon went global. Representatives of the Saville Inquiry arrived in Sierra Leone in the middle of the restarted civil war in 2000. They had flown in in an effort to retrieve a single SLR thought to have been part of a multi-million-pound arms package given by the British government to Sierra Leone's armed forces. In a tense situation, as rebel forces closed in on the airport they had come into, the Saville team were ordered to leave the country. But in May 2000 the rifle was located by Sierra Leone's security forces and repatriated by military aircraft to RAF Northolt. The search for the other rifles took the investigative team to, among other places, Germany, Belgium and Canada. In America one of the rifles of interest to Lord Saville was traced to a gun shop in Arkansas only for it to be discovered that it had recently been sold at a gun-fair to an unknown buyer. Another rifle of possible interest, with the lower part of the original firing mechanism still in place, had been bought by a man in North Carolina. It was repatriated and the gun-owner offered a replacement. Three other Bloody Sunday rifles were tracked down to the barracks of the internal security forces in Beirut, Lebanon. Via the records of a defunct Belgian firm, two more rifles were found in Belgium. The investigation was painstaking but it turned out to have all been to no avail.

The Operation Apollo team discovered that the two destroyed rifles that had started their search would not have been any use in any case. The investigative team managed in the end to trace fourteen rifles in addition to those at the MoD. But it transpired that the 1972 record of the guns only carried the last part of each gun's serial number. This meant that it was impossible to say, even with the recovered guns, that they were definitely the guns used on Bloody Sunday.

One single gun – the sniper rifle sent in to the DIFS in 1972 – had a unique number that meant it could confidently be said to have been in use, but after all this the Inquiry discovered that 'no useful scientific evidence was obtained from it.'

In the end, Operation Apollo itself cost nearly half a million pounds. And though its findings finally proved little more than their thoroughness, they did at least show the futility of one of the latest chapters of the conspiracy claims. Lord Saville concluded that 'the Inquiry's inability to trace and examine the 29 rifles turned out to cause no disadvantage to the Inquiry. The Inquiry's ballistics expert concluded that the lack of ballistics evidence from 1972 (including the absence of most of the bullets known to have been fired), coupled with the likelihood that the rifles had been used, refurbished or rebarrelled over the years, would have made useful ballistics evidence impossible to obtain.'

It was exceedingly easy, when the news of Operation Apollo emerged, to put the worst construction on events. Republican journalists and others did exactly that, seeing in these latest actions of the MoD a sinister agenda of obstruction intended to cover up wrongdoing. John Kelly, brother of Michael Kelly, told the Sinn Fein paper *An Phoblacht* that it was 'beyond any doubt whatsoever that there was a conspiracy by the MoD to cover up', going on to explain, 'I believe this goes all the way up the chain of command at the MoD. I would be very surprised if Geoff Hoon [then Defence Secretary] knew nothing about this, or did not have a hand in it somewhere.' In fact as the investigation – just one of the many byways of Saville's larger investigation – showed, human failure, in this case an MoD cock-up, rather than grand conspiracy turned out to be once again at the centre of this episode. The Apollo team's final report stated that they had found no conspiracy to destroy weapons or conceal evidence. 'What occurred was a combination of mistakes, human errors and negligence.'

The Saville Inquiry's investigations not only set about to debunk some of the conspiracy theories held by civilians. They also refuted some of those that turned out to have great appeal to members of the armed forces and others. The conspiracy mindset had spread in all directions – albeit for different reasons and with clearly different psychological and political motivations.

A glimpse of one such conspiracy was given to Saville by a civilian witness to the Inquiry, Alan Harkens, who recorded it in his statement. Harkens related that in the year following Bloody Sunday he got talking to a soldier who had been there on the day. The soldier, from Dublin, said that he had been positioned at Butcher's Gate on the day and had been one of those who stopped and checked ambulances on their way to the hospital. 'He said', claimed Harkens, 'the bodies in the ambulances were dirty and smelly and it was obvious that they were the bodies of IRA men who had been killed and their bodies hidden down manholes. From the way he was talking my impression was that he was referring to men who had been shot before Bloody Sunday and it had now been decided to remove them from the manholes. I was not sure from my conversation with the soldier whether he genuinely thought this to be true or whether it was something that he had been told.'

There were plenty of people with similar stories and a considerable number of variations on the rumour. One such variation held that the bodies taken to the hospital on Bloody Sunday were not killed that day but had been dead for some time and that the IRA brought the bodies out then to blame their deaths on the British army.

But like most conspiracy theories the story could go any way. For in another version that went off in the opposite direction it was said that the number of casualties had not been lower, and the body-count supplemented by IRA corpses, but had actually been far higher than reported.

Lieutenant 026 of 1 Para testified that in the army mess immediately after Bloody Sunday 'all the officers I spoke to were adamant that those who had been shot were terrorists. There was also a feeling that the actual number of casualties was higher and that some of the bodies may have been taken away and not accounted for.'

A more colourful version of the same rumour was volunteered by Captain Conder, the battalion public relations officer and intelligence officer of the Royal Anglian Regiment (whose evidence Saville finally found to be 'of no assistance'). Conder claimed that several days after Bloody Sunday he was speaking with a member of the RUC, whose name he could not recall, who told him that several members of the IRA had been killed on that day, in addition to the thirteen known victims, but that, in order to disguise the fact that IRA members had been killed, the bodies were taken over the border to Buncrana and buried in secret.

Elsewhere there was an even more unreliable testimony. Soldier 1766, serving in the Royal Anglians, thought that early in the day he had seen two balaclava-wearing men carrying rifles by a barrier. Before he could shoot them, he claimed, somebody else did. According to 1766 'as the fourth [shot] struck both of the men exploded. They were blown to pieces. The barrier disintegrated and one of the houses nearby partially collapsed.' Soldier 1766 also thought members of his regiment must have fired from the walls.

It is no surprise that this soldier gives one of the most colourful versions of the unidentified casualties story. He said in his statement:

> I am sure that more than thirteen people were killed on 30 January 1972. I remember two days after Bloody Sunday being ordered to go to Craigavon Cemetery, with a section of men. We were ordered to dig up the fresh graves which we found there, which we did. The order to search the graves was given by Lieutenant UNK 33. We found about seven or eight unmarked, fresh

53

graves. All of them contained the bodies of men, all of whom had apparently been killed by gunshot wounds. This find was never recorded by the army. I do not know what happened to the bodies after we found them. None of them were in coffins.

Soldier 1766 did not give evidence in person to the Tribunal to answer questions on his outlandish statement.

What all the many variations of the 'missing IRA dead' stories had in common was that they were stories members of the army would have wanted to believe. The suggestion that the army had not actually killed all thirteen Bloody Sunday victims must have had its attractions, not least among those army people who had done nothing themselves and witnessed nothing but wanted to think well of their colleagues. Many would not have believed that members of the British army could have gunned down innocent people on British streets and it was this, among other things, that clearly gave the 'missing casualties' rumour such impetus. And though a straightforward desire to believe the rumour certainly gave it legs, there was, as with most conspiracies, usually only the slightest grounding in reality.

In the wake of Bloody Sunday a number of civilian witnesses claimed – and testified – that they had seen bodies in places where no casualty was recorded. To take just one example, a woman called Eileen Collins claimed in a 1992 media interview that she identified a dead body outside her window on her balcony in the Rossville Flats. Ten years later, giving evidence to Saville, she denied that she had ever said any such thing. When questioned it became clear that the only dead body she had seen on the day was that of Kevin McElhinney, who after being shot was carried into the doorway of Block 1 of the flats and then carried up the stairs. The claims in the earlier interview, Saville decided, were probably the result of misunderstanding by the journalist, a degree of exaggeration by Collins 'or a combination of both these things'.

Many of the other cases of allegedly unidentified casualties can also, on inspection, be explained by the same process. In many cases the reported 'missing' casualties bear striking resemblances either in appearance or in reported injury to the known dead. In other cases the unidentified bodies were most likely people lying wounded rather than dead. Or indeed 'playing dead'. A number of civilians (one Noel Moore, for instance) lay on the ground in positions such that a passer-by, particularly one who might already have seen another dead body, could have mistaken them for casualties.

Again, this does not mean that any of the people who reported seeing mysteriously misplaced casualties were lying, or that they were wrong in what they reported. Some of them will have seen someone who survived. But most will have discovered that immediately after shocking and traumatic events, particularly after seeing a dead body on their streets or outside their home, the details, the description, even the location morphed and switched. Bodies moved, not because anybody transported them or spirited them away for secret interment, but because the mind, in the immediate aftermath, and the memory, later on, mixed what the person had seen happening and what they subsequently heard had happened, and added to this a dose of conjecture and exaggeration.

At one early stage of the Inquiry, Edwin Glasgow, acting for many of the soldiers, provided a list and map of these missing casualties. It listed thirty-four accounts, solely relying on civilian witnesses, where people saw wounded or dead people in places where no casualty was found or otherwise recorded. They included unrecorded casualties being carried away from the rubble barricade. As well as a young man propped up in a stairwell in the Rossville Flats, there were numerous extra casualties in Glenfada Park, and others clustered by the area where Patrick Doherty was shot behind the flats. The map of missing casualties put together by Glasgow (available on the Bloody Sunday Inquiry website at 0S7.0034) must have provided some hope for those in the military who wished to see the story of Bloody Sunday turn out differently.

On Day 51, before any witnesses had appeared, Glasgow explained that although he and his team would not contend that any of the known deceased were nail-bombers or gunmen, there were civilian gunmen operating on the day and 'we positively make that assertion as an issue for you [the Tribunal] to consider, that gunmen and bombers were killed on Bloody Sunday.' If that had been the case then the families and friends of those men, probably in the same town – a close-knit community – would have had to agree to a conspiracy of silence: not just an IRA conspiracy of silence but a city-wide conspiracy of silence. Was that likely? In his verbal evidence the proposal was put to Father, by now Bishop, Daly. Would it have been possible, he was asked by a representative of the families, that private burials of unknown gunmen could have taken place after Bloody Sunday? Were there secret burials in Derry that he knew of? Daly was firm: 'No.' Had he ever heard any such suggestions? Again, 'No.' And after thirty-one years of service as a priest to the Derry community was the suggestion even remotely credible? Daly was sharp. 'I think it is

55

offensive nonsense,' he said. Another local priest, Father O'Keeffe, described it as 'inconceivable', stressing that in Republican ideology the dead are meant to be 'honoured' at their funeral, not buried in secret.

These opinions were enough to persuade the Tribunal, which unequivocally rejected the submission that there were any unidentified casualties on the day, ruling that 'we do not believe that the local community would have considered it desirable or acceptable to try to conceal such deaths, nor do we believe that it would have been possible to conceal them.'

Bloody Sunday was fertile ground for conspiracies. And the analytical glare of a decade-long Inquiry exposed many of them. But all of these rumours and conspiracies, from every side, had their common basis in a series of horrific events. As civilians and soldiers began to testify, they provided the best possible reminder that nothing needed to be made up. What had really happened was extraordinary enough.

6

THE FIREBRAND:
BERNADETTE DEVLIN

For two years, from 2000 to 2002, the Saville Inquiry sat in the Guildhall in Derry and listened to the stream of civilian witnesses who had come forward to speak about what they had seen that day. At one side of the neo-Gothic building sat the three judges of the Tribunal. To their side was the box for witnesses and in front of them the dozens of lawyers who represented the various parties. There were lawyers representing the families. Most were represented by one team, but some families had separate lawyers. There were also legal teams representing the soldiers, and, again, while one team represented the majority of them, some soldiers had their own legal teams. There were also representative teams for NICRA and other interested parties.

In front of the witnesses, each member of the Tribunal and each lawyer there was a computer screen. Technical teams ensured that every document being referred to could be summoned up in a moment and displayed on each screen in the hall. Colossal versions of these screens also hung in front of the public and press galleries to keep everybody there in touch with each document as it was referred to. When maps came up witnesses could draw with a pen on the screen where they had gone or mark the area in which they had seen something. The pen marks could be seen on all the other screens and would then be saved as a screen-grab to go into the bundle of evidence for the Tribunal's reference. It was hardly surprising that, as the months and years went on, the files of evidence constituted a larger and larger wall behind the judges.

The civilian witnesses who testified in front of the Inquiry varied hugely in the quality of the evidence they gave. Some were proud to be able to give evidence about their presence on the day. Others were shy or embarrassed at having so much attention focused on them by so many people for intense periods. For some the experience was too much, and breaks would be called to allow a witness time to recover. Lord Saville made sure that the days did not stretch on, allowing not only witnesses but his fellow judges time to absorb all of the evidence that was accumulating day by day.

In its first years the Inquiry heard from many people who were only too keen to help it get to the truth of that day, as well as a smaller number who refused to assist on matters they did not want to. But few performances in the witness box were so impressive and belligerent as that of a woman who had been out of the public eye for many years by the time she testified in May 2001, but could hardly have been more notorious and prominent during the period in question.

On the evening of Bloody Sunday Bernadette Devlin left Derry and headed to Westminster. Three years earlier she had been elected to Parliament as the youngest-ever female MP. Having attempted to address the crowds as shooting started on the platform at Free Derry Corner she now intended to address the House of Commons. But her next speech was thwarted like her previous one. And though this time the circumstances did not include bloodshed, they certainly included violence.

It was on the day after Bloody Sunday that the Home Secretary, Reginald Maudling, rose to address the House of Commons on 'the disturbances in Londonderry'. He told the House that the army had returned aimed shots in reaction to fire aimed at them. Devlin was seated in the chamber. She attempted to intervene. She was told by the Speaker that she could speak at the end of the statement. 'Is it in order for the Minister to lie to the House?' she said, breaking parliamentary etiquette by making a direct accusation of lying against a minister. The Speaker called for 'Order'.

The Home Secretary reiterated to the House that the army had been fired on first and furthermore stressed that when people attack soldiers 'with bullets and bombs, they must expect retaliation'.
Devlin was furious. 'On a point of order, Mr Speaker. That is the second time the Minister has stood up and lied to the House. Nobody shot at the paratroops, but somebody will shortly.'

'That is not a point of order,' cried the Speaker, trying to keep control. Another member tried to intervene by reminding the Speaker that the Member for Mid Ulster 'was the subject of a murderous attempt on her life yesterday on a platform at Derry and that she has not been allowed to speak in this short exchange'. The Speaker insisted that he must remain in control of proceedings.

'I am the only person in this House who was present yesterday,' screamed Devlin, 'when, whatever the facts of the situation might be said—' She was interrupted. 'Shut up!' she yelled. 'I have a right, as the only representative in this House who was an eyewitness, to ask a question of that murdering hypocrite.'

Members joined the Speaker in shouting for 'Order!' and as they did so Devlin crossed the floor of the House of Commons and punched the Home Secretary in the face. Years later Devlin recalled walking down calmly to the middle of the House, bowing to the Speaker, catching Maudling by the throat and giving him 'a smack in the gob'. She said that a Tory MP had hit her, at which point another MP had hit him, knocking him on to the lower bench. 'I left quickly,' she recalled, 'leaving a whole pile of MPs literally boxing on the floor of the House.'

The official record of the House, Hansard, recalls it rather differently. An array of accusations and recriminations flew every way. Some members tried to explain the conduct of the Member for Mid Ulster. 'She was provoked by a murderous attempt on her and by your attempt to silence her,' the Labour MP Paul Rose cried out to the Speaker. The Conservative MP Tom Boardman, speaking for the other side, asked provocatively, 'What is the position of an hon. Member who, having taken the oath, incites others to break the law?' 'Sit down,' other members shouted at him. 'I refer in particular to the hon. Lady the Member for Mid Ulster,' he continued, 'who must bear a very heavy responsibility for yesterday's tragic events.' Michael Foot stood to object that this was 'thoroughly out of order'.

Another Conservative MP, John Biggs-Davison, spoke out. 'On a point of order, Mr Speaker. Is it really in keeping with the practices of the House that an hon. Member who has made a violent attack upon other Members of the House should remain seated within the Chamber?' 'I did not shoot him in the back, which is what they did to our people,' was Devlin's response. In any case, the session ended.

Questioned outside the House by reporters, Devlin was quoted saying that not only did she refuse to apologise for her actions, she intended to repeat them.

And a furious Devlin said something else too. White with rage she declared, 'The Official and the Provisional IRA have each said they will kill thirteen paratroopers in vengeance for those who died on Sunday. That is twenty-six coffins coming home to England, and I won't shed a tear for any one of them.'

Bernadette Devlin was elected to Parliament in 1969 when at the age of twenty-one she stood as an independent Unity candidate in Mid Ulster. A rousing public speaker, and fresh and almost flirtatious enough to be picked up by the British press, Devlin became an iconic figure in the Troubles that followed.

She published her memoir, *The Price of My Soul*, in August 1969, the same month that the 'Battle of the Bogside' broke out, a grandiose title for three days of rioting. It had started when a planned loyalist march caused fighting to break out between the two sides. The police attempted to separate them by pushing residents of the Bogside back into the area. Residents responded by throwing petrol-bombs and stones at the police. For three days police fired teargas and tried to arrest rioters while coming under constant bombardment. Young Derry residents stood on the roofs of the high Rossville Flats and from there rained down petrol-bombs on the police, dozens of whom were seriously injured.

During one point in the riots the newly elected MP for Mid Ulster asked police to let her through to address the rioters. They allowed her to do so. Devlin took the opportunity to advise the crowds that the RUC's shields were too small to protect their whole bodies, and that the rioters were not organised in their throwing. Devlin told them to break up into two ranks so they could simultaneously hurl their missiles at the lower parts of the policemen's bodies as well as their heads. When the police realised what Devlin was doing they charged the crowds again.

Correctly identified as one of the ringleaders of the riots, Devlin was arrested, convicted of three charges of incitement to riot and one charge of rioting and sentenced, along with others, to six months in jail. When the news of her arrest got out, rioting began again in the Bogside. She was unrepentant, explaining, 'I was involved with people in defending their area. They were justified in defending themselves and I believe I was justified in assisting their defence.'

But she was out of jail and back in Parliament by the time she came to address the crowds from the lorry at the head of the march on Bloody Sunday.

61

One of the members of the NICRA executive, Bobby Heatley, explained a complex, shifting movement:

> Bernadette Devlin's group, the People's Democracy, wanted socialism here and now and that was their interest in the civil rights campaign. When I appeared on the scene the People's Democracy had more or less decided to go its own way as NICRA was not interested in street demonstrations. By 1971 the People's Democracy had little use for NICRA. The turning point for NICRA getting involved in street demonstrations was internment.

By January 1972 the hardline Devlin was one of the undisputed leaders of the civil rights movement and somebody who epitomised its problems while being one of its most eloquent spokespeople. From the time of her election Devlin had declared that she was sympathetic to the IRA. By Bloody Sunday the IRA had bombed numerous bars and killed its first British soldiers. While being a focal point of Catholic and Republican grievances Devlin was also a focal point for the growing outrage at the actions of the IRA.

What she actually said on the float by Free Derry Corner on Bloody Sunday and when she said it were not agreed upon by many of the witnesses who testified about the events thirty years later. But the outlines were.

One of the NICRA organisers remembered arriving at Free Derry Corner and parking the lorry facing the city walls. He remembered hearing what he took to be rubber bullets being fired in the background. As Devlin began speaking, he remembered, people started to run down Rossville Street towards the lorry. The NICRA organiser said, 'I remember Bernadette calling to the crowd not to panic and to hold their ground − that they outnumbered the army by fifteen to one. Suddenly there was a volley of high-velocity shots and everyone dived to the ground. I dived to the flat bed of the lorry where I lay for approximately five minutes, keeping as flat as I could.'

Another NICRA executive remembered getting to the lorry and seeing Devlin on the vehicle with her fellow Parliamentarian Lord (Fenner) Brockway. 'Devlin had the microphone in her hand. People were still arriving at the lorry as I placed my hands on the platform and placed one foot on the wheel of the lorry to hoist myself up on to it. As I was doing this something made me look up at Bernadette Devlin. Perhaps the chat on the lorry came to an abrupt halt. Whatever it was, I saw that Bernadette's face had frozen and that her eyes were as wide as saucers. She then roared at the people to get down. As I did, a whistling noise flew past

62

me from behind.'

Leo Friel had already seen someone shot by the time he got to the lorry and saw Devlin trying to rally the crowd. 'She was calling people in and saying something like "They can't shoot all of us!" The words were barely out of her mouth when the shooting started again, although this time it was ten times worse than I had heard before.'

Another civilian remembered the first part of the speech and that Devlin had said, 'If the Brits want to stop us having a legal meeting, let them try. There are fifteen of us to each one of them.' But before she could get any further there were screams and shouts of 'They are coming in' and 'The paras are coming'. And then, he remembered, 'I heard the noise of a large amount of people panicking. People around us were shouting out things like "Stand your ground", "Let them come – don't panic!"'

A regular of the civil rights marches recalled the crack of rifles and Devlin 'shouting through a loudspeaker from Free Derry Corner that everyone should stand their ground. She was saying that the army were not going to come in and that there were forty of us to every one of them, or words to that effect. Others were shouting, "They're shooting people." Looking back, Bernadette Devlin could have got us all killed.'

Devlin herself remembered hearing several individual shots from up towards Rossville Street. Slowly, as the next firing came, she remembered seeing the faces of the crowd change, from a state of calm to one of panic. 'I can hear myself effectively telling people to stay on their knees,' she remembered. 'I can hear my own voice with my own ears as if neither ears nor voice belonged to me. Inside my head my own voice without any connection to my mouth instinctively silently repeating the prayers for the dying.' She got under the platform, how she could not remember, but she recalled that even as she huddled there and urged people to move away, she was still holding the microphone in her hand. She remained convinced that some of the firing had come from the army firing down from the city walls.

After the tumultuous encounter with the Home Secretary on 31 January 1972, a fuller debate on events was scheduled the next day. This time Devlin was given the floor to speak and she certainly used it.

In the session, by turns formal and bitter, Lord Balniel, the Minister of State for Defence, reiterated the claim that the army had 'fired in self-defence or in defence of their comrades who were threatened'. He deplored the 'slurs' that had been made on the Parachute Regiment. Even by the House of Commons' standards, the debate swiftly became angrily antagonistic, with interjections, heckling and growing shouts of anger. Hovering over proceedings were not only the dead of Derry and the mounting death toll in Northern Ireland from that month alone. There was also a sense of urgency: another illegal march was due to be taking place in Northern Ireland, at Newry, that coming weekend.

A number of leading Parliamentarians spoke: Jeremy Thorpe for the Liberals, Merlyn Rees for Labour, as well as the MP for Londonderry, Robin Chichester-Clark. Then Bernadette Devlin.

How, she demanded to know, could the government promise to set up an independent Inquiry when, she pointed out, the Defence Minister had already put forward the views of the army as fact? Everything the minister said she challenged and denied. 'He was not in the city of Derry on Sunday. I was. I therefore make no apology for putting my side of the story beside the story of the people who took part in the march and for questioning a number of the facts put forward by the Minister today.'

Devlin's version was certainly very different from that put forward by the minister. From the size of the crowd to the direction which the army claimed to have been fired on, she disagreed with every supposed fact the minister had just put before the House. She attacked the government's claim that four of the dead had links with outlawed organisations, demanding to know which of the dead the minister thought they were. Reminding the House of the human tragedy of what had occurred she read out the names of the thirteen victims. Then she announced that she, and many others, would once again break the law that coming weekend. 'This is not our first bloody Sunday at the hands of the British army. But we will be in Newry on Saturday and we will be marching.' Some members cried out, 'Shame.' It only spurred her on.

> We have been kicked and batoned by the police, we have been imprisoned and interned and finally we have been slaughtered by the British army. But we have yet to be defeated. I would say, not so much to the British government on the benches opposite, but to the people who strengthen their nerve and stiffen their resolve at home and to their friends in this country, that the paratroopers may have had their day on our bloody Sunday, but we have a

64

saying in Ireland that there is another day coming.

Next up was the Reverend Ian Paisley. Devlin had accused the government of having no concern for the loss of human life. But Paisley pointed out that there 'should be no discrimination in the value of human life'. And so he quoted back to Devlin her comments that had been reported from yesterday in that day's press: that she had said that she would not shed a tear for the twenty-six army coffins coming to England. He read the quote in full. Members of the House shouted, 'Disgraceful!'

Paisley must have known this punch would also land. 'All of us who heard the hon. Lady today', he continued, 'will realise that we have seen on the floor of this House something of the hatred and real terror with which Northern Ireland is being gripped.'

While he did not hold that the army were all 'angels', the army had been, he stated, 'seriously maligned', the Parachute Regiment 'slurred and slandered'.

Norman St John-Stevas issued a dismissive review of a speech in which he declared that 'The hon. Member for Mid Ulster did not make a very helpful contribution to our discussions today but it was a significant contribution,' he granted, 'because it is only by listening to her words that one can plumb the depths of bitterness and hatred that are rampant amongst the minority in Northern Ireland today.

'In his own way, the hon. Member for Antrim North [Paisley] was equally significant – his was a rather more skilful speech because he is a more sophisticated politician than the hon. Member for Mid Ulster.'

Gerard Fitt for Belfast West was interrupted as he declared that thirteen people had just been gunned down in the back as they were running away. 'Nonsense,' shouted Nicholas Winterton for the Tories. Fitt referred to the 'fools' on the government benches.

Harold Wilson – who had been the Prime Minister who had first sent the troops into Northern Ireland – made the most thoughtful speech of the session, taking responsibility for that decision and managing to calm proceedings, welcome the Inquiry and provide a warning:

We have reached a point now where reality is not what is but what is believed to be. Londonderry, 30 January 1972, in that sense has passed into history and

65

will itself play its part in determining the unfolding of future history.

Yet this House realises that thirteen deaths in a few minutes are also to be set against week after week where equal numbers have been killed regardless, as was last Sunday, of guilt or innocence, whatever that may be, of Catholic or Protestant. More have been killed over a number of incidents in a single week or less. More have been killed in one tragic explosion in a bar in Belfast. There have been the murders of British soldiers off duty, of Defence Regiment members, of police and public men, in some cases brutally struck down in the presence of their families. This tragedy is now becoming greater than the actors who play their willing or unwilling role in it.

That sentiment was certainly confirmed by what followed.

The Home Secretary took to the dispatch box to give his speech. He opened by observing that even as the debate had been going on another British soldier had been shot dead in Belfast.

All that I will say about the role of the army in Northern Ireland – I say it because time and again it has been said that the army is a tool of a corrupt political regime in Stormont, which is utterly untrue is that it is not there at its request. Our soldiers do not want to be there. They did not ask to be there. They are performing a duty which has been imposed on them as part of their loyalty to the Crown. They are there to protect law and order – (Interruption.) and the army is brought into action only when law and order are threatened.

The march had been illegal and the banning of such marches had been agreed by both sides of the House, he said. The security forces, ordered to prevent breaches of the law, had done their job with 'the minimum use of force'. Devlin attempted to intervene. Maudling refused.

There was never any suggestion, he insisted, that the time had come to 'teach the people of Bogside a lesson'. He stressed that any further marches would also be illegal. And he warned the Member for Belfast West, Gerard Fitt, against organising further marches. Fitt objected. 'Why not shoot him now?' another member jibed at the Home Secretary. 'Give way,' Devlin was shouting.

Maudling tried to finish his point. 'I am putting a simple proposition. I am simply saying that those who organise a breach of the law bear a heavy responsibility for what follows that breach.'

Devlin was outraged. 'Atrocious,' she shouted. Other members cried, 'Disgraceful.' Maudling persevered. Returning a year earlier from his first visit to Northern Ireland on becoming Home Secretary, he had been overheard by press as he got on to the plane home saying, 'For God's sake bring me a large Scotch. What a bloody awful country.' Two years later he was injured when the IRA sent him a letter-bomb.

The years between Bloody Sunday and the beginning of the Saville process were not kind to Devlin, nor she to them. The birth of a daughter out of wedlock, Róisín, in 1971 lost her considerable support among Catholic voters. Attempts to gain re-election in 1974 and afterwards were unsuccessful. However, though her role at the centre of Northern Irish politics declined she remained active in various Republican movements including a breakaway movement of Sinn Fein.

In 1981 she and her husband were shot by a group of Ulster Freedom Fighters who broke into their home. Devlin was shot nine times and left for dead. But members of the Parachute Regiment were in the local area and were alerted. The Paras caught the attackers and got Devlin as well as her husband to the local hospital in time for their lives to be saved.

In 1994 Devlin and her daughter Róisín, along with Martin McGuinness, carried the coffin of the Republican paramilitary Dominic 'Mad Dog' McGlinchey. Though she later claimed that McGlinchey had simply been a family friend, in her address at the funeral Devlin hailed McGlinchey as 'the finest Republican of them all'. McGlinchey had by his own reckoning been involved in around thirty murders in his career including that of a 77-year-old postmistress in County Antrim called Hester McMullen.

That same year Devlin strongly criticised the IRA's ceasefire call, claiming that it demonstrated that 'the good guys lost.'

In 1996 Róisín was sought by the German authorities for extradition on suspicion of being part of an IRA gang which had mortar-bombed an army barracks in Osnabrück. Devlin and her daughter fought the extradition. Questioned about the case in the press the following year, Devlin was quoted saying that 'I have said that I find the use of violence understandable. That would go for Róisín, too. Frankly, I can think of more traumatic things than finding out that my daughter is a terrorist.'

67

She opposed the Good Friday Agreement and the entry of Sinn Fein into government in Northern Ireland.

It was certainly a slightly wearied if not chastened Devlin that appeared before Saville in the spring of 2001.

Her statement was among other things fiercely hostile to the Inquiry itself. And it was filled with the confusion that most people had over the passage of time. She had forgotten that she spoke to the Commons two days after Bloody Sunday. Her contribution was in Hansard, but like many things in Devlin's memory, as in so many others', what was true and what might be wished to be true, or true by repetition, got mixed together to the point that they were indistinguishable.

She said at the outset that it was her belief

> without prejudice to the individual integrity of those currently conducting and participating in this Inquiry, that no inquiry established, funded and controlled by such a powerful, vindictive, deceitful, ruthless and experienced perpetrator of terror as the British state can reasonably be expected to bring in an honourable verdict of 'guilty as charged' against that state.

Devlin said that after all these years she had an 'unreliable memory'. For instance she had some recall of issues being discussed in relation to a demonstration around the time of Bloody Sunday. But she couldn't be sure if it was to do with Bloody Sunday or the demonstration after the Cusack/Beattie killings or whether it had become amalgamated and thus become 'part of the legend of Bloody Sunday'.

Again and again paragraphs of Devlin's statement began with 'I have no clear recollection', 'I cannot recall' and 'I have no recollection'. But she also, it became obvious, saw conspiracy where there was none. Her reaction on being asked about interviews that she had given in 1972 was telling. On being shown a copy of a *Sunday Times* interview that differed from her current recollections her initial reaction was that the interview's content 'emanates from the British Army Press Office' and she said, 'I would have more than a passing suspicion that its author worked for the British army.' Later she dismissed the notes of the interview as bearing 'an uncanny resemblance to the quality of document you might get in an intelligence report'. She claimed that the notes represented 'the culmination of many years' work of dubious quality compiled by people of little intelligence and dubious integrity'. Despite admitting the substantial holes in her own memory of the day, anything she couldn't remember was debunked as the work of 'intelligence agencies'.

The *Sunday Times* and other contemporaneous interviews with her quoted her saying that after the shooting she saw a crowd of sixty-year-old women 'demanding guns' from a known IRA leader, pressing him up against a wall and shouting 'Where were you?' and 'Give us guns, we'll do it fer ye.' But in her statement for Saville she said that although she had a memory of an IRA leader being surrounded and being barracked by people wanting guns, 'I am unsure as to whether that is a memory which relates to 1969 or 1972.'

At another point while in the witness box she complained that 'you are asking a woman of great many words to recall a half a dozen issued over thirty years ago.' She also fiercely denied the Inquiry's own account that she had initially refused to co-operate with it. Impatient and truculent, at one point she scolded Counsel to the Inquiry for asking her about details – what she described as 'all this nitty-gritty'. Unable to remember what individuals had said and where people had gone, she broke out repeatedly against the whole proceedings. 'It is part of my problem with the whole procedure,' she said. 'This has no bearing on the real issue, which is that a crowd of unarmed civilians were fired on by Her Majesty's Armed Forces on Her Majesty's Government's orders and whether I said "Oh, why are you taking the lorry away, Rory?" is neither here nor there.' For this rebuke to the Tribunal's proceedings, Devlin was rewarded with clapping from the public gallery.

She was scornful of the inability of others to remember things, and complained that the memories of others that she disagreed with were misinformation. But when parts of her own inaccurate accounts were put to her she had trouble justifying them. A *Times* piece from the Tuesday after Bloody Sunday reported a speech by Devlin to an Anti-Internment League event in London the previous day in which she had claimed that the army had shot an eight- year-old boy during the march: 'One young boy was found only this morning. He had been shot in the back and he was only eight years old.' She claimed that there had been an extra two casualties to those known about.

'Do you know how it came about,' Counsel asked her, 'that you were describing and being reported as describing the discovery of a young boy eight years old on the Monday after Bloody Sunday, shot in the back?'

'I have no clear knowledge,' she said. Perhaps, she said, she had heard it from somebody who had heard it from somebody. Perhaps 'in the telling he got younger,' she speculated. 'Terrible deeds', she stressed, can get more terrible in the telling.

But there was also film of her the day after Bloody Sunday claiming that the body of a young girl was carried out of the Bogside that morning, having been shot in the back. She was asked if the young girl shot in the back that she referred to in that ITN interview was 'supposed to be a different person to the young eight-year-old boy'. 'No,' said Devlin, 'probably exactly the same non-existent person.'

She was asked if she had been at all aware of an understanding having been reached before the march with members of the IRA about what they would or would not be doing on the day. Devlin said in her statement that she had no knowledge of any deal being made to keep the IRA away from the march: 'I had and have no personal knowledge of any arrangements made in connection with the anti-internment march of Jan. 30th.'

During questioning a number of points were put to her of evidence suggesting she had indeed been aware of such negotiations. She fiercely denied it and challenged the principle behind the question. 'The reality is that there is no history from '68 on, there is no history, or from '72 after, there is no history of either or any Republican armed grouping organising armed activity in, out, through, during or in conjunction with the marches.'

As the questioning progressed on this she got irritable. As one quotation in particular was put to her she complained, 'I do not see the point of me spending an afternoon going through a statement that I do not think is attributable to me.' Saville intervened soothingly, saying, 'The details in themselves quite often do not matter,' but that she had to have quotations that were attributed to her put to her, and that the Tribunal would use all of this, accept or reject it, in order to come to a final assessment. 'Having the advantage of you here this afternoon will give us an aid in trying to discover where the truth lies; that is why we are doing it,' he explained.

This sent Devlin off into a speech about her belief that the British government was behind all this, that a public Inquiry could not get to the truth and that the UK government should instead be taken 'through the proper procedure' to the

International Court of Justice at The Hague. 'We are going around contaminating each other's proper memory to no good purpose,' she complained.

'I would ask you, if you would, to bear with us,' said Lord Saville. 'We are doing the best we can.'

'Well, I would really prefer not to be here,' said Devlin, complaining that she was being drawn further and further in 'to matters of no consequence'. Repeating her claim that the government of the day had ordered the army to shoot civilians she went off into another speech:

> That to me is all that matters and I have no doubt that that is what happened and I actually do not care, and I do not think that it matters, and I do not think it is irrelevant if the entire Brigade of the Provisional IRA, aided and abetted by the Official IRA and any of CRA [Civil Rights Association] and anybody else that they could gather up for the occasion were conspiring to take on the British army on that day... Even if all of it was true, none of it adds up to justification of the armed forces of the state firing on the unarmed citizens. I do not care what they thought, I do not care how they felt.

Here she checked herself.

> I do not mean that in that I do not care, I mean that it is irrelevant what they thought; it is irrelevant what they felt; the matter is they were there to do the bidding of the government.

> If they were not fit to do the bidding of their government, they should not have been there. If they were fit to do the bidding of their government, and I believe they were, they did it, and the rest of this, to me, is just clouding that issue, and I appreciate that is not a criticism of the Inquiry. I appreciate those are your terms of reference, which is why I do not believe this should be happening. This should be somewhere, this should be somewhere else where the accused is not running the party.

For this speech Devlin got another ovation from the public gallery.

> This is not against the Inquiry, you are doing your best and so am I and when I get out of here today, I will not be back. I do not care where it goes or what Mr – whoever turns up or what his recollections are, whatever I have to say today is said and then I am home and all the High Court writs in Christendom will not be getting me back after this day.

After this speech Lord Saville asked calmly of Counsel to the Inquiry, 'Shall we try and finish the day as soon as possible, Mr Clarke?'

Counsel said that there were only two remaining topics he had to ask the witness about. Unfortunately one of them was a crucial one. Did Devlin know the identity of some of the members of the Provisional IRA who were on the march?

In her statement Devlin had claimed not to have known McGuinness in January 1972 and claimed not even to have known of him. But she had admitted that she had known another IRA man identified by the Tribunal, in fact knew him 'reasonably well and held him in high regard'.

Counsel started to put his question to her and brought up part of a video on the screens for Devlin to look at. He was going to ask her about the person identified by her in her statement and asked if she could identify him as the person on tape in an interview on Ireland's national broadcaster, RTE.

But before the photo was even up on the screen Devlin had interrupted Counsel. 'I think it is only fair to say before you show it to me, whether I could or not I am not going to tell you.' Even silence from her could be interpreted in a particular way, she said, so she would not even look at the screen. 'I am not getting into identifying persons,' she repeated. 'I have never assisted Her Majesty's Government in identifying a citizen of this country other than myself. I do not propose to start now.'

Was that 'because there are some people who you do not want to identify?' she was asked. 'There may be people, yes,' she confirmed. It was hard to see what more help Devlin would be able or willing to give to the Inquiry. But after being thanked by Lord Saville for appearing she took the opportunity to make one further speech.

It might have been one of the most important she ever gave. 'Before that day,' she said, 'although people were being shot here and had been shot, I did not have a belief that death was an integral part of the equation of seeking justice in this country and after Bloody Sunday I believed that it was.'
She reflected on the encounter with the Home Secretary.

> I do clearly recall after striking Mr Maudling... I said that I did not want a public inquiry, I would not participate in a public inquiry. I understood that both wings of the IRA were ... at that point promising to avenge every death,

72

which was set at thirteen.

I have a clear recollection on that day of saying something I never believed I would hear myself say, which is 'that makes twenty-six soldiers and I will not shed a tear over one of them'; it was an unbelievably cruel thing to say, and I meant every single word of it... I am not justifying what I said, I am setting it out there simply because that – twenty-four hours before that, never mind what anybody else was doing ... twenty-four hours before that, me and my rhetoric were arguing against extending the collective defence of areas against localist and British attack, me and my rhetoric were arguing against secret and armed organisations and after Bloody Sunday and the making of that statement, I never, for thirty years, raised my voice against the arming and taking of the war to the British government. I did not participate in the war. I was never a soldier. But for thirty years, as a consequence of Bloody Sunday – and it matters only to me – my policy was, death is part of this equation and the government made it a part of this equation and because I took that positioning myself, and I take responsibility for it, I am not prepared, not this side of this Inquiry, or anything else, to participate in any way in the identification or the minimising of anybody else who may have gone beyond that.

To my mind, whatever was happening before it, the British army declared war on the people seeking justice in this country on that day and everything that I did in regard to the war and the British government after it related to that and I cannot change that now. My most abiding memory is that it happened, and my other most abiding human memory is not that I hit that waster in the House of Commons, but that I stood outside it and said that I would not have a tear to shed if twenty-six other coffins were to follow. Three thousand and more coffins followed and years of imprisonment and torture and pain and sorrow followed and it is highly arguable that without Bloody Sunday where we are today, we would have been in 1972; that which we have today would most likely have been agreed to by all the parties, except me, in 1972 and I cannot forgive the British government for that, and this public inquiry cannot sort that out, but I would like to thank you. I have not wanted to come here and I would very much like to express my appreciation to those who worked this morning to ensure I did not go back down the road, but I will not be back.

Within hours of the Saville Report being released, Devlin wrote a piece for The Guardian in which she declared that the UK government, rather than individual soldiers, should be put on trial in The Hague for war crimes.

7

THE SHOOTERS

After hearing from civilian witnesses in Derry's Guildhall from 2000, in 2002 the Inquiry moved to Central Hall Westminster, London. At a cost of an estimated extra £15 million the computer technologies, screens, libraries of evidence and other equipment were transferred to London to ensure that the soldiers and other sensitive witnesses testified in safety and did not need the even more elaborate security that would have been provided had the hearings been in Derry. Once again the vast screens hung over new press and public galleries and the vast array of desks for the vast array of lawyers stretched over the expanse of floor before the three judges of the Tribunal and the witness stand. Back in Derry members of the public who wanted to watch the proceedings were able to go to the Guildhall still and watch a live relay of the evidence being given in London.

In London the soldiers were ferried in and out of Central Hall by a back entrance, whisked in and whisked out – the more sensitive witnesses hidden by a tunnel that was brought out right up to the door of the waiting dark cars to keep them from being photographed or seen on the pavement between the door of the hall and the door of the waiting car.

The elaborate security procedures and the cost of transferring the Inquiry to London allowed the Inquiry to hear from some of its most crucial witnesses – the members of the army who had been in the other city on that day; most especially, those soldiers who had fired. As they began to give evidence, it swiftly became apparent that in the battalion that Colonel Derek Wilford had commanded on Bloody Sunday were soldiers of the most varying abilities.

At one end there was the man then known as Captain Mike Jackson. Adjutant of 1 Para on the day of Bloody Sunday, by the time he came to testify about his role in it he was Chief of the General Staff, the highest position in the British army.

When he came to testify, General Jackson's memory was, like that of many witnesses, vivid but no longer detailed. He was one of the small group of soldiers who had to stick beside Colonel Wilford. He remembered being in position before deploying into the Bogside, that the view from the building they were in was clear, and that he went over to one of the windows to get a better view. He remembered Wilford 'calling sharply to me and saying, "Get back from that window, you bloody fool – you will be shot."'

And he remembered some of what happened when he had deployed. 'It was Derek Wilford's practice to be forward amongst the troops to see what was going on for himself,' he recalled. He remembered clearly entering the Bogside by running with Wilford 'like fury' down Rossville Street and across the wasteground. 'As I sprinted across the wasteground I had an absolutely firm impression that I was being shot at. What I thought was: "Some bugger is firing at me." I could hear the crack of incoming rounds but cannot describe this further or distinguish it in my memory now from the noise that was all around. I did not see the strike of rounds. Around me the soldiers that I saw had the postures of men who were under fire, who had been under fire or thought they were going to be killed.'

He also said, 'I can recall "losing" Derek Wilford for a while. It seemed he was with me one minute and then gone the next. Eventually he came back. I think he went across the road towards Glenfada Park, but I did not see what he was doing.'

By the time Jackson testified to the Saville Inquiry on 7 April 2003 he was involved in the recently started Iraq war. After a morning of questioning Lord Saville asked if he would prefer to stop for a short lunch-break as normal or whether a ten-minute break was better. 'We understand you are probably quite busy,' Saville observed. 'My diary is more or less clear, knowing that I was going to be here,' the general replied amiably.

Jackson was a soldier in Wilford's battalion who rose to an exceptional position. Though their identities remain a secret and though little is known about what they did in the years after, few of those who served alongside Jackson and under Wilford that day had careers, or lives, that won similar esteem.

76

Wilford himself testified only in the mornings for eight days. One of his former soldiers who followed him in appearing before the Inquiry one afternoon reminded people of some of the human beings behind the ciphers. Asked the formality of verifying that his statement to the Inquiry was true, Soldier 112, who had not fired, confirmed, 'They are, sir. Um, there is one other thing I would like to make attention to, it is the fact that I am an alcoholic and I have been for a long, long time and a lot of my memory is blurred and a lot of the things that occurred on that day, intermingled with other things that have happened on previous riots.' Counsel to the Inquiry thanked him and said that the Tribunal would bear this in mind.

Just like the civilians, others were clearly intimidated when they appeared before a room packed with confident and sharp lawyers. Soldier A, a corporal on the day, was being questioned by Arthur Harvey QC on behalf of the families when he was asked about his use in his statement of the term 'hyped-up'. In the box he said perhaps this was the wrong word to use. Perhaps he had meant 'apprehensive'. Harvey pounced. '"Hyped-up" is different from "apprehensive", is it not?' 'I do not know,' the soldier said forlornly, 'I am not that educated, with respect.'

Though their actions had banded them together and though their ciphers joined them in anonymity, the soldiers who had fired on the day were exceedingly different in personality. Some seemed truculent, some helpful, some honest, some very clearly not. But of the soldiers who had survived the thirty years since Bloody Sunday, few could have been more sad, even pathetic, than one who was known as Soldier L.

Soldier L was the only black soldier in his company. Whether being so relatively identifiable in photos and evidence of the day had been a contributing factor or not, it became clear when L appeared that he was mentally ill, paranoid and delusional. L had been meant to appear at the Tribunal in September 2003 but failed to show up. Lord Saville began the process of High Court contempt proceedings against him – something that could have seen him go to prison. Eventually, with careful mediation from his lawyers, Soldier L agreed to testify the next month, providing that he was screened from the view of the public and family galleries and only the Tribunal and questioning lawyers could see him. The Tribunal were given medical reports that satisfied them that he could only testify under these conditions. He was a pitiful witness.

As well as being contradictory, his evidence included the wildest and most implausible claims. He claimed that he had seen Father Daly putting two rifles under his coat by the Rossville Flats. He claimed that he had seen another soldier repeatedly shooting into the body of an unarmed man who was lying on the ground until the body split in half. No such wounds occurred in any of the dead. Had Soldier L later seen or later heard of something similar? Though most of what he said was clearly untrue, it was hard to discern which memories were once based in fact and which were only ever built on fantasy. His statement began by talking about his poverty-stricken situation before joining the Paras, how he and his family had lived in one room, how he had lost a daughter, and how 'one of our childhood games was to chase the rats.'

When he finally appeared behind a screen in Central Hall, Soldier L was obviously very distressed about the possibility that he could be seen or recognised. But the colour of his skin did matter. Because a number of incidents on the day related to a black soldier, L's movements during the day were as a consequence easier to follow than those of almost any of his colleagues.

Therefore, at the opening, Counsel for the Inquiry asked him, since the public could not see him, to confirm his skin colour. He was told that he was about to hear a description of his skin colour that had been agreed and was permitted under the anonymity rule. The description was that he was 'of mixed race, being Afro- European'. Counsel also added that 'you say I can say your skin tone is in fact similar to that of the very well-known sportsman Mr Rio Ferdinand.' The LiveNote system that transcribed every word spoken at the Inquiry was not expecting this. The system, more used to language relating to Derry in the 1970s than to current football stars, produced early transcripts with a version of the footballer's name written up as 'real fur, Northern Ireland'.

Though Private L had given lucid enough evidence at Widgery, by the time he came to give evidence to Saville it was clear that he was going to be little use to the Inquiry. He stuck adamantly to parts of his story that were provably untrue. And he added episodes in his statement and in evidence that appeared to show him in a heroic light. In particular he was fixated on Martin McGuinness, who had clearly stuck in his mind. He claimed that during an earlier operation in Belfast he had had McGuinness in his rifle sights, that McGuinness was throwing bricks and bottles and that he had been awaiting an order to shoot him. He also claimed that on Bloody Sunday it was his intention to get McGuinness 'dead or alive'.

78

Was it possible, he was asked, that his memory had become less accurate over the passage of time? 'Well, it is something I have to live with,' he answered, 'and I have constant nightmares about it, yes, you know, and the nightmares are vivid as anything.'

None of this would have had any importance, and the pain of the hearing could have been spared, but for the fact that Soldier L had fired his rifle four times on Bloody Sunday. He claimed that two of these shots were aimed at two men crawling at the rubble barricade cradling what he claimed to think were rifles in their arms. As Saville was to conclude, L was one of only two soldiers (the other being M) who could have shot and killed Kevin McElhinney, a seventeen-year-old civilian. McElhinney had no weapon, but L was questioned about why he thought he should shoot someone who was crawling away even if he had a weapon. L's manner of answering questions was certainly unorthodox:

> A: He has got a rifle, he may escape to the top of the flats and then pick us all off as a sniper. Hey, you cannot allow that to happen. Are you crazy or something?

> Q: So were you prepared to shoot at any man that you saw with a weapon, whatever he was doing with that weapon?

> A: Exactly, yes.

> Q: Even if he was not taking any offensive action against you?

> A: That is right, weapons are not allowed to be put in civilian hands in British society, as far as I know, and anybody with a weapon is endangering somebody else.

Questioned by a lawyer for the families some of L's obviously very disturbed inner life came out. He was asked:

> Q: You say that you have had nightmares in relation to this. A: Mmm.

> Q: Is it just in relation to this you have had nightmares or is it in relation to other areas of your service?

> A: Mainly with this.

> Q: Could it be that the nightmares have become more real to you than what

79

happened on the day?

A: Oh, yes, definitely, yes, I agree with you there.

When he was asked about his claim that he had seen Father Daly put guns up his cassock it was explained to him that the priest he was talking about was not at the scene and could not have been in the place he was saying, guns or not.

Q: Could that be just part of your nightmare?

A: No, he does not really come into it as such, no.

Q: You see, the priest that you have identified was not there. A: I say he was.

Questioned by another lawyer for the families he confirmed that he had suffered for many years from post-traumatic stress.

What in L's memory was true and what was false? He had helped to pick up the bodies at the rubble barricade after the shooting. But what else had he seen? His memories included Soldier H pumping bullets into a dead body on the ground. Either G or H had fired a single shot into Jim Wray as he lay wounded on the ground of Glenfada Park. But had L really been able to see this? Had his movements been such that he had actually seen a much less exaggerated, albeit still fatal, version of this happening? Or had he heard of it and adopted it into his memory afterwards? Certainly he had not remembered this earlier. And of course no body had been found – including Jim Wray's – with anything like the wounds described.

He was offered a chance to break the consensus of his former comrades by ditching the claim that there were any gunmen, but L did not. He was adamant that he had seen them, just as he was adamant about a lot of other things. Questioned on the veracity of his memory he swiftly became upset. Indeed it was arguable, given the state of the witness, that some of the questioning from the families' lawyers went too far.

Q: Are you on any drugs that would cause you difficulties with your recollection or memory?

A: No. I do suffer from post-traumatic stress disorder.

Q: And the nightmares that you have, are those recurrent nightmares?

80

A: Yes, yes.

Q: Do they distort reality for you?

A: I do not think they distort it, they bring it out more visibly, details I missed before, you know, sometimes seem more vivid.

Q: In other words do you have a lot of recovered memories, things that did not seem to be so at the time, but when you have your nightmares, they fall into place for you?

A: Yes.

Q: Whatever the reason for the evidence you are giving now, I want to suggest to you, firstly, a substantial proportion of it is inaccurate, whether you believe it or not.

A: Okay.

Q: What I want to suggest to you is that your problem is that you had started to lie from the very moment after you fired your shots because they were unjustified.

A: Okay.

Q: Has that happened to you before?

A: Not that I know of, no.

One of the lawyers representing the families asked Lord Saville if there was anything he should know about the medical history of the witness before continuing. He was told not. He proceeded and, among other things, attempted to offer L a way out. 'You can retract it,' he was told. 'I just want to give you the chance because there are not too many more chances left. I want to give you the chance to start retracting.' But L was adamant that what he was saying occurred had occurred. As he protested:

A: To my knowledge they occurred. If you say they did not, they did not because if all my statement is a bunch of codswallop and all that, why am I here? I did not want to come here, you know.

81

Q: I appreciate you did not want to come here.

A: I did not want to contribute to another whitewash like the last time. I was under orders last time, I am not under no orders this time. If it is a load of rubbish, please dismiss me, let me go on my way and you get on with what you need to do. I do not want no part of it.

Q: You know that the object of this exercise this time is to seek the truth and if you know—

A: They told me that last time at the Widgery Tribunal.

Q: I appreciate, I do not want to make comparisons—

A: I do, because you expect me to believe you now, I believed you then, you know.

Was this a glimpse of a truth? Of something that had happened? In between the delusions were there hints of things that had indeed occurred and that other soldiers had colluded in and kept silent on? Or was Soldier L simply saying what he thought people wanted to hear? There were certainly times when he did. At one stage he started answering questions and allegations put to him by simply saying 'Okay'. The lawyer questioning him snapped, 'Please do not agree just for the sake of it because you want to go home.'

He described himself as the 'black sheep' in the Para family. But it became obvious that to some extent he was trying to use his outsider status to avoid something. On occasion, for instance, he seemed willing to support the idea that there had been a degree of collusion among soldiers in trying to get their stories right after events. Again, had it happened, was it an invention or – although convenient – did the story nevertheless have a particle of truth in it? He claimed that 'people were trying to claim different things and then I would come in and I disputed with these contradicting things and it is like, um, shut my mouth and get to the back of the class, type of thing and...'

Q: What sort of things were there disputes about and you were put at the back of the class?

A: Well, like, as you said, no one here can verify about what is the name, the man with the pistol, the man getting shot in half, the man with the explosives. Nobody wanted to know nothing about that and especially not from me.

Q: Are you saying there were discussions about all these things in the days after Bloody Sunday and everybody told you to shut up?

A: And, yes – indirectly, yes. I was left out of the loop – 'Do not include him, leave him out of it.'

Q: Why did they want to leave him out of the loop?

A: Because I am a stupid nigger and I go and fuck up everything.

Q: Is it because people realised you were not capable of telling the truth?

A: Okay, maybe that as well.

In the end there was little that Soldier L could help on. His testimony was so unreliable that the Tribunal could only work out his actions from his 1972 statements. But he was certainly a reminder of the illness that many people suffer from after leaving the forces. Others of his former comrades provided equally complex pictures of their relationship with the truth but also of the careers that some of the Bloody Sunday shooters had gone on to.

As the questioning of the crucial shooting soldiers progressed it became clear that a notable number of them had after Bloody Sunday gone into careers in Britain's Special Forces.

One such was Soldier S, who fired twelve rounds on Bloody Sunday. During his testimony a rare glimpse of the man behind the cipher emerged. Rarely enough for a shooting soldier, Soldier S even volunteered an apology at one point. 'I am a Christian person, sir,' he said. 'I have Christian beliefs, I live by a Christian standard myself. This is a tragedy, it is a tragedy for everybody, I realise that and I am sorry that innocent people got killed on that day, I am very, very sorry for that, but for my action on the day, my particular action, I believe was justified in what I did.' But later in questioning another detail about him came out.

He was asked by a representative of the families when he had left the Parachute Regiment. He said that he had left shortly after Bloody Sunday.

Q: Why was that?

83

A: I went to serve with another unit.

Q: You have said that you were injured in a firefight in the Middle East. I am not going to probe this in such a way as to require you to expose details of Special Forces, but you describe being involved in a separatist war. Can we take it that you were not involved in a separatist war as a mercenary?

A: Yes, you may – yes.

Q: But as a member of the British army?

A: That is correct.

Q: And you were involved in firing thousands of rounds in total?

A: Yes.
Q: Do you know how many people you killed?

A: (Pause).

Lord Saville was forced to intervene. 'We have to be a bit careful of this,' he pointed out to the questioning lawyer, Mr MacDonald, 'for reasons you are well aware. Perhaps we could ask him whether, in the course of firing those rounds, he killed one or more people.'

Mr MacDONALD: In the course of firing those thousands of rounds, did you kill one or more people?

A: Yes.

Q: Have you in fact killed lots of people?

A: (Pause).

Q: Have you?

A: Yes.

He said it calmly, quietly and with no relish.

At least Soldier S had entered Special Forces and done his killing under the auspices of the state. Not all of the Paras who were with him that day and went

84

on to fight abroad had such comparatively clean records.

The identities of the soldiers throughout the whole year of their evidence of course remained hidden. Anything that threatened to tread close to revealing their true identities had to be carefully avoided in questioning. The most revealing facts that would emerge about them were rarely more than the date or rank with which they had left the forces. Only very occasionally would even a hint emerge of a life outside Bloody Sunday. In the main the soldiers remained fixed in that moment, named and preserved in memory for only that one day.

One of the exceptions, and by no means in a good way, was somebody whose slight fame or notoriety gave a glimpse into one of the types of person who could be attracted to a life in the Parachute Regiment.

Born in Cyprus to Greek-Cypriot parents in 1951, Costas Georgiou moved to London with his family as a child and was a member of 1st Battalion Parachute Regiment under the command of Colonel Wilford on Bloody Sunday. What role he played is unknown because of his anonymity. But Georgiou's name came into the public domain not because of what he did on Bloody Sunday but because of his role in an even shadier conflict and an even bloodier massacre three years later.

Georgiou was dishonourably discharged from the British army after Bloody Sunday when, along with a fellow member of the Parachute Regiment, Mick Wainhouse, he was found guilty of robbing a Northern Irish post office using army guns. Returning to London, jobless and without prospects, Georgiou connected with a man recruiting foreign mercenaries for the Angolan civil war. Georgiou went out to fight for the FNLA (National Front for the Liberation of Angola) with a number of former colleagues including Wainhouse and a cousin of his girlfriend's, who was also an ex-Para. For the campaign Georgiou styled himself 'Colonel Callan' after a character in a popular television series. The highest rank 'Colonel Callan' had reached in the real army had been corporal.

Despite having no officer training, in Angola 'Callan' commanded a disparate and disorganised group of foreign fighters. The account of his activities in Angola recorded by one of his fellow mercenaries is a story of the most appalling brutality and sadism.

During the campaign, 'Callan' was involved in numerous killings, torturings

85

and massacres. He enjoyed torturing people even when there was no information he could possibly extract. He tested the effectiveness of a particular gun by putting it in the mouth of one of his Angolan soldiers and firing. He repeatedly machine-gunned dozens of Angolans under his command and when a number of his own fighters tried to desert, at an incident known as the Maquela massacre, 'Callan' executed his own men. Fourteen of them. Among them, it seems, former Paras. As one of the soldiers who was with him and survived observed, 'There was some injustice in relation to who got shot.'

'Callan' and some of his mercenary comrades were eventually put on trial in Luanda in June–July 1976 by the victorious rivals of the FNLA, the MPLA (Popular Movement for the Liberation of Angola). At the trial 'Callan' was described as 'a man of despotic power and Satanic terror'. With twelve of his 'soldiers' he was convicted of murder and torture of civilians as well as the crime of fighting as a foreign mercenary. He was one of four men sentenced to death, and was executed by firing squad. His body was repatriated to England.

There is then a question over which soldier Georgiou was. Soldier 202 (who was Company Sergeant Major of Support Company) in his statement refers to 'Callan' as 'UNK 180' and 'quite a controversial character. There is always the odd eccentric who is a cause for concern.' But 202 separates 'Callan' from others of the men. He says that 'Soldier F and Soldier G were maverick types and, although they were not maverick to the same extent as UNK 180, they were enthusiastic soldiers. They were not in the same category as UNK180. If that had been the case I would have done something before the day to rein them in.' Interestingly the CSM puts Soldier H in a different category. 'Soldier H certainly did not fall into the UNK 180 category and I was really surprised when I heard of his actions on the day,' he said.

Meanwhile, a civilian who had been shot at on the day, Noel Kelly, said in his statement that some years after Bloody Sunday he was approached by the *Sunday Times* Insight research team. They showed him photos of various Paras hoping he could identify the one who had shot at him.

> They showed me some pictures and I picked out the one who shot at me. The photograph was strangely familiar at that time. I said that I recognised him from somewhere. I was told by the team that the Para in question had been one of a number of British mercenaries who had been in the news because, during the civil war in Angola, they had killed and wounded many innocent civilians in a village. They had been tried, found guilty and executed. I was

86

shown a picture of a man wearing a surgical gown and on crutches. I was told that this was the same paratrooper. He was a Greek Cypriot nicknamed Colonel Callan... This may have been the Para who shot at me, maybe not.

Did Kelly pick out a photo of someone he had seen in a newspaper more recently than the day itself ? Or had he picked out a shooter? Interviewed by the scriptwriter Jimmy McGovern, Joe Friel, who was wounded on the day, gets close to tying up some of the other strands. Knowing the identities of various of the soldiers, and with the names once again redacted for the public, Friel mentions that Soldier G should be in trouble but is now dead. McGovern didn't know that E and G were dead. 'The only two soldiers left is F and H,' Friel told him. McGovern replied, 'Is that the guy who died in Angola, G?'

Friel's comments reveal a lot about what the families had been able to work out for themselves over the years.

> See this, this is the thing they put out to us. They put out, see the time Colonel Callan ... we were led to believe that one of the soldiers was killed... We were left to believe this boy had died in Angola. So Paul Mahon chasing up, he got the names of all the soldiers, you know. Apparently Callan killed a number of his own soldiers first and then he was brought up on the charge of killing them. He was executed. He was the boy who... Colonel Callan was actually something like X or something, he had a Greek name. He was Colonel Callan but we couldn't tie in any of the soldiers we know. The soldiers in Glenfada Park is X, X, X and X. X, X, X and X, that is the four. That is the four shooters.

> We know for definite that X is Soldier H, we know that for definite. E we are more or less convinced is X. It is F and G we can't determine who is who. All we do know is X had a distinct London accent.

Georgiou's trial and execution in Angola certainly brought his career as a Para in Northern Ireland into question. As well as raising the possibility that he was one of the Bloody Sunday shooters it is also possible that he himself had in fact executed one of the Bloody Sunday shooters.

The army had at least disciplined Georgiou and thrown him from its midst. When it came to others who had been in Wilford's regiment that day a much more pressing question arose: why had certain soldiers, including those with most obvious guilt, never suffered any career setback at all from the day?

87

Whatever the other soldiers' names were, there were four of them who everyone knew would hold the answers to the majority of killings on the day. Among them was the one who was perhaps most notorious over the years between Widgery and Saville. That was Soldier H.

H stood out for one reason in particular. Of all the soldiers who fired on Bloody Sunday he had fired the largest number of shots: twenty-two. Almost twice as many as the next largest shot total. It was H's evidence that Widgery had described as 'highly improbable', concluding that nineteen of H's shots were, in Widgery's final opinion, 'wholly unaccounted for'.

The story of Soldier H was recognised, both by Widgery and by everyone else, to be the weakest and most obviously untrue of all. Everybody, including the special lawyer assigned to him, realised before H arrived to give evidence to Lord Saville that of all the soldiers he was likely to be the one in the most trouble.

The man who eventually appeared in the witness box was not a terrifically impressive figure. Awkward and nervous, he was also, it was clear from the outset, not very bright. Questioning got off to a bad start. As was the usual procedure with all witnesses, H was invited by Counsel to look at his statement on the screen in front of him and confirm it was his. H, now slightly stooped and short sighted, had to put his reading glasses on. As Counsel was asking him a question H interrupted. 'Excuse me, I have a slight problem here, my glasses have fallen apart.' At Lord Saville's suggestion the Tribunal rose for five minutes so that H could fix his glasses.

But Soldier H was not much more help with his glasses on. He simply stuck to his old story, insisting that he had run into Glenfada Park wearing his gasmask and there had fired two shots at a nail-bomber and then nineteen aimed shots at a gunman behind a window.

A twenty-year-old private on Bloody Sunday, he had never before, he said, fired at a live target. In his statement he said that 'over the years I have tried hard to forget what happened on Bloody Sunday and I have not thought about it for a long time.' He also recounted that he had been frightened as he drove in his 'Pig' through the Bogside. On entering Glenfada Park he remembered being terrified, and his knees 'trembling'. 'The knocking of my knees is one of the clearest memories I have of the day,' he maintained.

88

But as to what happened, he stuck doggedly to his story. Even in the face of unanimous incredulity. He stuck to the story that he had shot a nail-bomber and then a sniper. After going through the reasons why his story was impossible, Counsel to the Inquiry asked H plainly if it was not the case that he had fired a number of shots he could not account for and had then made up his story in order to explain what had happened to the shots. Was that truly the position? he was asked. 'No, I think if I was making up a story, sir, I think I would have made up a better one than that,' he replied with a type of candour.

Most of the time Soldier H's testimony was almost embarrassing. Counsel to the Inquiry, Christopher Clarke QC, was clearly as frustrated as everybody else and at times, entirely uncharacteristically, it began to show.

Q: An SLR bullet travels with enormous force, does it not?

A: It does, sir.

Q: At an immense speed?

A: It does, sir.

Q: And it can go a couple of miles and kill somebody at the end?

A: I do not know about that, sir.

Q: Nineteen bullets fired at the same window, at a 50 yards range, would shatter it, would they not?

A: I do not know, sir.

Q: Are you seriously inviting the Tribunal to accept, as a realistic possibility, that nineteen bullets fired at that window would not cause it to shatter?

A: I am stating what I know, sir.

Q: What do you know?

A: I know that I wrote these statements in good faith when I wrote them and I answered the questions at the Widgery Tribunal in good faith when I answered them and if that is what I put down there, that must be correct, sir.

It was carefully explained to H that a rifle in a window would either have to be supported or be held in place. It was also explained to him that either way, every time the gunman stepped back after H fired at him he once again, and repeatedly, put himself back in the line of fire. Counsel persevered.

Q: Right. So he disappears after you fire the first shot, so you must obviously have missed him; is that right?

A: Yes, sir.

Q: He then reappears and you fire again and miss him on the second shot?

A: That is correct, sir, I was sticking to the proper rules of the Yellow Card, firing one shot.

Q: Well, nineteen shots, in fact? A: No, sir, one shot each time.

There was something of a pause and an intake of breath as people tried to work out whether H actually thought this attempt at casuistry could work on Counsel. It was certainly not a meeting of equal minds. Counsel continued.

Q: Right. Rather unlucky that you should have missed him on nineteen separate occasions, is it not?

A: Do you want me to answer that, sir?

Q: Yes, of course I do.

A: Yes.

Q: And you were a first-class shot, were you not?

A: Yes, sir.

Q: Able to shoot with accuracy a standing target at 300 metres?

A: Yes, sir.

Q: So he disappears and the process is repeated so that it occurs nineteen times in all?

A: Yes, sir.

Q: If that account is right, the upshot must be that the gunman, having been shot at once, must have intentionally moved into the same position of mortal danger, in line with a soldier with an SLR, who had just tried to kill him, on eighteen further occasions.

A: Yes, sir.

Q: That is rather incredible, is it not?

A: Yes, sir.

Q: And on eighteen occasions, at least, you fired at and missed him?

A: That is correct, sir.

Q: Doubly incredible really, is it not?

A: Do you want an answer to that, sir?

Q: Sorry?

A: Do you want an answer to that?

Q: Yes, please.

A: Yes.

Counsel then came straight to the point.

Q: Is the explanation for those facts that in fact they are not true?

A: No, that is not right, sir. The statements I made at the time were true to the best of my knowledge and I would stick to those statements.

Q: Soldier H, what happened when you fired your nineteenth shot?

A: I thought I saw the, um, the person, silhouette, whatever you wish to call it, fall and the muzzle did get retrieved as well.

But there was yet another fact that Soldier H did not know.

Q: Were you aware or did you become aware that the inhabitants of number

57, which is the middle house into which you say that you fired, were a couple in their seventies, a Mr & Mrs McCartney?

A: I did become aware at the Widgery Tribunal, yes.

Q: You presumably became aware that Mrs McCartney gave evidence to Lord Widgery; did you?

A: I did not know she gave evidence, no.

Q: Let me tell you what happened. Mrs McCartney gave evidence that she and her husband were in their house on the afternoon of Bloody Sunday when she heard the deafening noise of a single shot which, as she discovered moments later, had gone through the clear glass of her bedroom, which is the third window along from the left from the door; do you follow?

A: I follow, yes.

Q: And according to her evidence before Lord Widgery and according to other evidence from her family before this Tribunal, the bullet made a single hole in the window and went through the curtain and a wardrobe in the bedroom. Could we have on the screen EP35.11? That is a picture, which is said to have been taken of the bedroom. You can see the curtains, here, and the single hole through which a shot went. Is the position that only one shot was fired at a window in the middle house in the south of Glenfada Park by you?

And so it went on. A bafflingly transparent story, without doubt the weakest that any of the Paras who fired that day came up with. And there must have been some hope – the story being so palpably absurd – that H himself would over the course of his two days of questioning, himself tire of it, give it up and come clean.

A: By me, no.

Q: It is not, of course, possible, is it, that having fired one shot making a hole such as we see on the photograph, that the following eighteen shots all went through the same hole?

A: Very, very unlikely, almost impossible, I agree.

And so it went on. A bafflingly transparent story, without doubt the weakest that any of the Paras who fired that day came up with. And there must have been some hope – the story being so palpably absurd – that H himself would over the course of his two days of questioning, himself tire of it, give it up and come clean.

But it got nowhere. H's story was fantastical. He admitted it himself. But he stuck to it. It was the only story he had. Yet as he was questioned repeatedly, as he had to be, on each essential detail each time there lingered the thought that this time he might crack.

Here was the man who held the secrets to most if not all of the deadly shooting that went on that day. Even H began to get frustrated – though not as frustrated as the lawyers and observers hoping to get a straight and honest answer out of him. Told that there was no window in the Bogside which had been fired at in the way he said, H continued to maintain that his shots went through a frosted window. 'I appreciate it is quite easy just to repeat it,' one lawyer scolded him. 'I am only repeating the truth, sir,' protested H. 'I do not wish to lie and you are trying to tell me to lie. I am telling the truth. The truth is my nineteen shots went through a frosted window.' And so it went on. It seemed almost comic at times. A bumbling account from a figure who through his lies had grown notorious over the years but who, when he finally emerged, turned out to be weak and in the end rather silly.

Silly he may have been. But the facts about him remained: that at least nineteen, perhaps all twenty-two of his shots remained – and remain – unaccounted for. Soldier H is still a primary suspect in the killing of the men by the rubble barricade as well as those in Glenfada Park and Abbey Park. Bumbling he may have been, terrified perhaps, but H was also almost certainly a killer – of exactly whom it will probably never be known. This was most likely the last chance to find out.

Counsel for the family of James Wray put it to H at its clearest. Wray had likely been shot on the ground where he lay. The lawyer read H civilian accounts of this event. One described two soldiers 'no more than eighteen years old' with descriptions of their features that seemed to be a good description of G and H. 'The cameo glimpse of a taller and a shorter soldier standing over Jim Wray's body is', it was put to H, 'a glimpse of you and G, standing over the body of a man who had just been executed.' H denied it. But the lawyer went on: 'You and E and G and F were not acting as a brick [a pack] that day; I suggest, Soldier H, you were acting as a death squad.

Finally H was asked whether he had ever even known that Widgery had in 1972 said that his firing could not be accounted for. 'Nobody drew it to my attention,' he claimed. He also confirmed with enormous reluctance, having first refused point-blank to answer the question, that he had stayed in the army 'for a considerable amount of years' after Bloody Sunday and that he had left the army as a senior NCO (non-commissioned officer). He confirmed that he had never been shown Widgery's conclusions, had never been disciplined over the conclusions and had never been criticised for them. 'That is correct, sir,' said H.

8

THE COLONEL:
WILFORD

The man who led his men into the Bogside that day was Colonel Derek Wilford. Commissioned into the British army in 1951, he had served early on in both Aden and Malaya and then with both the SAS and US Special Forces. After a spell at staff college, he joined the Parachute Regiment as a company commander in 1969. He had arrived with his company for a first tour of duty in Northern Ireland in Belfast in 1970, a rising star in the army with a promising career ahead of him. On 21 July 1971 Colonel Wilford took on the role of Commanding Officer of the 1st Battalion the Parachute Regiment and found a regiment that was well disciplined with high morale. Wilford recalled 1 Para in Belfast being involved in the local community, building playgrounds, taking disabled children to the swimming baths and even running playgroups. He described 1 Para as having 'excellent community relations', so much so that he was invited to give a talk on the subject by Brigadier Frank Kitson, the British counter-insurgency guru.

Swiftly, however, the situation changed. The troops that had been invited in to protect Catholics began to be targeted by them as anger around internment grew and the capabilities of the IRA increased. Troops that had been welcomed by many as protectors now found themselves turned on as aggressors. And they responded in kind. In Belfast and Derry rioting became endemic. Barricades sprang up across the streets. And although in Belfast there was a commitment to ensure there were no 'no-go areas' in which the rule of British law did not operate, Derry was a different matter altogether.

These were the things that Colonel Wilford remembered, but a number of incidents involving the Paras before Bloody Sunday suggested their role was rather more aggressive than that of the playgroup-running peacekeepers he described. With a longstanding and proud reputation as the army's attack-dog, the Paras soon developed a reputation for 'no-nonsense' actions in Northern Ireland.

In August 1971 they were involved in an arrest operation intended to scoop up people involved in paramilitary activity in the Ballymurphy housing estate in West Belfast. The Paras shot dead eleven civilians, including a priest. The army claimed that they were fired upon first. The military police were called in but no soldiers were disciplined. Among the soldiers involved in Ballymurphy were the soldiers of 1 Para soon to be deployed in Derry.

Then on 23 January 1972 a large crowd took part in a banned march along Magilligan Strand outside Derry to protest against internment. The march was moving towards the internment camp that was the focus of their protest when, according to the *Daily Telegraph* reporter present, soldiers of 1 Para emerged from behind the sand dunes and attacked the crowd with truncheons and rubber bullets, driving many marchers into the sea. The *Telegraph's* correspondent observed that some of the Paras failed to stop even when their commanders ordered them to and that in some cases officers started using their batons on their own men to beat them off protestors. At Saville, Wilford claimed that the 'press' had used events at Magilligan as 'part [of] a process of demonisation of 1 Para'.

The march on Sunday 30 January was recognised in advance to be a likely flashpoint. The aim of the army and police forces was to allow the march to pass off as peacefully as possible and for a snatch squad of soldiers to arrest any lead rioters if, or rather when, rioting broke out. The city and indeed province were on a fragile cusp. There could not have been a worse moment to decide to send in 1 Para for their first mission in Derry.

In the immediate aftermath when Wilford was asked to speak to the media, the tone was set for his next thirty years. On the BBC's World at One it was put to him that civilians had been shot in the back while running away. Wilford made it perfectly plain that he did not believe it.

> A lot of us in fact do think that some of their people were shot by their own indiscriminate firing. I hesitate to call anybody a liar but I'm afraid in this matter they are lying because I was forward with my troops and my company commanders and my sergeants and my platoon commanders saw people and had shots fired at them and I personally had shots fired at me... It was also highly inaccurate and indiscriminate firing from the other side. I believe in

96

fact they lost their nerve when they saw us coming on. My compassion is of course for those people in fact that were killed but my compassion is moderated by the fact that it might have been some of my soldiers.

Wilford went on to testify at the Widgery Inquiry alongside his soldiers. He defended them completely from the allegations that were already being made against them. Over the years details of his memory, like everyone else's, were lost. Things that he had seen or heard on the day and since made it hard to sort out what was first- hand experience and what had grown on over time. But this was not unusual. By the time that he testified before Saville in 2003 Wilford could certainly no longer remember all that he had remembered before Widgery. But on the central points of where he was that day and the fact that he and his men had been fired upon that day he did not budge. One thing above all remained in Wilford's account: an unwavering, some would say blind, devotion to, and desire to protect, the men who had served under him. Whatever 1 Para had done, their commander would think nothing bad of them.

In 1992, for the twentieth anniversary of Bloody Sunday, the BBC made a commemorative documentary about the day. One of the interviewees was Colonel Wilford. The outline of what his soldiers had done that day was by then fairly widely recognised. But Wilford, it was clear, was having none of it. He was asked, for instance, if he accepted that those who were killed were in fact innocent civilians. 'No', he said, 'I can't accept that because that would be to accept that my soldiers were wrong – and I don't believe they were wrong. There might have been some – er, wrong, things wrong in the sense that innocent people, people in fact who were not carrying a weapon, were shot and wounded or even killed, but that was not done as a deliberate malicious act, it was done as an act if you like of war.'

Even twenty years on Wilford remained a tough, no-nonsense Parachute Regiment commander. It was evident that he still thought it profoundly humiliating that soldiers facing rioting crowds at places like 'Aggro Corner' in Derry should have been expected to simply stand there and take abuse from the crowd and be on the receiving end of missiles hurled by rioters. He recalled watching regiments other than the Paras who just stood and took this. 'This to us was really quite horrifying,' he remembered, 'because it was clear that the soldiers never went forward and just stood there like Aunt Sallies. I had actually said in public that my soldiers were not going to act as Aunt Sallies – ever.'

When 1 Para went into the Bogside they did not go in as 'Aunt Sallies'. They went in as a fighting force, many fresh from foreign operations. They were brought into Derry to join what was meant to be a policing operation of a civil rights march. In reality it could have hardly been any such thing.

As Soldiers from 1 Para were readying to go in, other units were standing at the barriers taking the flak and missiles from the rioting crowds. The army barriers were to be lifted for the 1 Para snatch squads to go through, but 1 Para broke through the barriers, not on foot, but racing through in their armoured 'Pigs'. For a soldier fresh from a warzone, emerging on the streets of Derry from an armoured car, behind enemy lines, hyped up and expecting incoming fire, the stage was set for something likely to turn much more violent than a mere scooping up of brick-throwing hooligans.

'I wanted my soldiers to stay alive,' said Wilford, in 1992. 'I actually said to them, "You will not get killed."'

For Wilford, the moment that set the tone for his day was some minutes before his men went in, before 16.00, when he was near the early shot known as 'the drainpipe shot'. From that moment any pretence that what was about to come would remain a policing operation had been shattered with the drainpipe. Wilford remembered it clearly: 'One of my senior officers who was standing with me at the time said, "That shot was aimed at us, sir."'

Asked by Peter Taylor of the BBC in 1992 about the significance of the drainpipe shot, Wilford said: 'Well, the significance was that there was at least one weapon on the other side, and if there was one weapon then there were probably others. If someone starts shooting at you, you can behave in a variety of ways. You can run away – which of course on the whole soldiers don't – and certainly my battalion would never run away. You could take cover behind your shields and just sit in an area until it all passed over. Or you could do what of course my battalion were trained to do and that is to move forward and seek out the enemy.'

Seeking out the enemy was exactly what Wilford must have thought they were doing. But in the process he disobeyed his orders – not least the order that that there should be 'no running battles down Rossville Street'. He always attempted to argue it, but 1 Para driving down Rossville Street, pursuing rioters and opening fire, more than constituted a running battle. He refused to acknowledge this. They hadn't gone very many yards down Rossville Street, they hadn't run – Wilford's attempts to navigate his way around the central problem were obvious. He had ignored the order he had been given. And, in turn, some of his soldiers were soon to ignore the orders he had given them.

Wilford watched the vehicles containing Support Company go through Barrier 12 before following the carriers in with his signaller. As Wilford's men got out of their armoured cars and scanned out across the Bogside they began firing, engaging targets in the Rossville Flats car-park and at the rubble barricade. Wilford dashed across the wasteground in Bogside as he heard shots from what he said was an M1 carbine. He saw some of his men behind the small wall at Kells Walk and ran towards them. As he joined them he said that he saw one of the men with his rifle at his shoulder fire a shot. Wilford asked him what he was firing at and the soldier said he had engaged a target behind the rubble barricade. At some stage media picked up Wilford shouting: 'Stop firing unless you can see a target.'

Others also recorded the voice of an officer calling out, 'Cease firing, cease firing.' But some of 1 Para did not cease firing. Indeed, as four of them went out of Wilford's sight into Glenfada Park some of them had only just begun.

Over the next twenty-four hours Wilford appeared in television and other media interviews from Britain and Ireland, explaining what had happened, why his men had behaved well, and what the response they had encountered in the Bogside had been. Though the army's story about how many people had been killed, where and how inevitably changed as the situation reports came in, a set of Wilford's points never shifted. That the dead were, if not guilty, then in any case not innocent, that his men had been fired on first, and that none of his men had done anything wrong. These core aspects were ones Wilford would never shift from. In his 1992 BBC interview he complained to his interviewer, 'You keep using the word "innocent". There is no innocence in a riot.'

He was told that Lord Widgery had used the word. 'Yes, of course he will, because you know that's a civilian word and riots actually sort of breed the idea that there is some innocence and some not so innocent.'

Q: But you don't sign your death warrant by taking part in a demonstration.

A: Some people do.

Wilford remained unrepentant, most of all because he was convinced that his men had done, and could do, no wrong. But for himself? Was there anything he could have done better? About himself Wilford was willing to be a bit more candid, and in that 1992 interview he opened up for a moment. The BBC's Peter Taylor asked him, 'What has Bloody Sunday done to you?' The question clearly came as a bit of a surprise and showed a more ruminative side to Wilford.

> Oh (sighs) – what has it done to me? It's, er, it's an event of course which is in my subconscious all the time and occasionally it – it comes to the surface. Erm (pause) and I suppose in fact it's made me if anything rather anti-war but it's made me also I think anti-politicians and anti a hierarchy which allows a situation to go on. I would like to have thought that out of that tragedy – which it was, a tragedy, however way you look at it – that something more positive could have happened. Instead it just became negative, it was something that went into the, the history books – went into a Widgery tribunal.

So 'Did Bloody Sunday achieve anything?' he was asked.

> Nothing at all except tragedy. Nothing, and that I think has to be the worst thing of all about it, that there was a tragedy and nothing good came out of it.

By the time Peter Taylor interviewed him for the BBC, Wilford was in retirement and was, in Taylor's description, 'a disillusioned man'. Six months after Bloody Sunday he had received an OBE. But with this one exception it had been downhill all the way after Bloody Sunday. He had spent another nine years in the army in a series of desk jobs from Whitehall to Nigeria. But his career was clearly at a dead end. As a young officer he had hoped to follow in the footsteps of Frank Kitson, had hoped to go to Oxford, write a thesis and become, like Kitson, a respected counter-insurgency expert. But his career did not pan out that way. He retired from the army early, in 1981. But Wilford's career in the army had in truth been over well before he left.

After leaving the army he moved abroad, took up painting and experienced something of a personal crisis. Interviewed by Taylor, he reflected on his career path. 'There has to be a scapegoat and I was the one. I'm not bitter about it. The only good thing about being a scapegoat is that you protect other people. I adored my soldiers and I protected them because I believed they were right.'

> Q: Are you still protecting them twenty years later?

> A: I suppose so.

There, in sad and disillusioned retirement, Colonel Wilford might have stayed had not, after the 1997 Labour Party election victory, talk begun of an apology from the British government for the events of Bloody Sunday and even the setting up of a new Inquiry. Wilford suddenly came out of retirement. A combination of rage, hurt and betrayal came together: betrayal by his superiors, rage at the injustice of focusing again on Bloody Sunday and above all the fiercest and most unquestioning loyalty to his men. For the British government and the British army the re-emergence of the man who had been given the moniker 'the butcher of the Bogside' must have been the least desirable of all immediate outcomes. But Wilford was no longer answerable to anyone else. In a number of blistering media appearances Colonel Wilford made it obvious that he was willing to cast blame anywhere else but on to his men. They were interviews that he – as well as many other people – ended up with much cause to regret.

Late in 1997 *Channel 4 News* ran a story about the new government's plan to issue an apology for the Bloody Sunday shootings. Speaking to Channel 4 'exclusively' – though not for long – Colonel Wilford was brought out to give his response. 'Mr Wilford', it was announced, had 'decided to speak out.' Among the civil servants Wilford had left behind in Whitehall, the announcement could not have been welcomed. Just as the British government was preparing to apologise and make reparation, here was Wilford on the screens again, more belligerent than ever. Questioned about the behaviour of his men that day he said, 'My troops behaved magnificently. My troops did the job for which they were trained and which I expected.' Had they not simply run amok? Colonel Wilford appeared to miss the opportunity to make things better. 'If my troops had run amok there would have been far more than thirteen people killed … you would have been counting the dead in dozens … many dozens.' Which didn't quite play into the spirit of reconciliation that was then prevalent.

And Wilford had found a new target for his anger: Edward Heath. It was Heath, he believed, who bore ultimate responsibility for the operation. It was the former Prime Minister, he declared, that should be answering questions and accusations about the day. 'We were put into an arrest operation which I don't think had been thought out fully,' said Wilford. Amazingly he said that 'it smacked of "It's time we taught these people a lesson".' Which was exactly what Republicans had been saying for years and exactly the impression that Colonel Wilford had spent the last twenty-five years trying to deny. Now he confirmed it, but blamed it on a level above his own pay-grade. Not content with criticising

Heath, he also criticised General Ford for not giving him orders about what to do once he was in the Bogside. 'What was I supposed to do? Just sort of sit around there, you know, twiddle my thumbs?'

He proclaimed of his superiors, including Ford, that 'they were offered an opportunity to take over the Bogside and regain proper control of it. They decided not to take that opportunity because there had been the shooting. I think they lost their nerve, frankly.'

This was more like the paratrooper talking. It was intolerable that the British writ did not run beyond the barricades – 1 Para had smashed through the barricades and nobody had been there to take advantage of the fact and reclaim the ground for the Crown. They had done their job but everyone else had failed to perform theirs.

He was asked about the possibility that his soldiers had shot innocent people. He repeated his view that 'until someone can prove it otherwise ... my soldiers behaved in accordance with their very best standards of keeping the peace.'

And as for whether the British government should now take it upon itself to apologise for what had happened that day, Wilford was outraged at the suggestion. 'Well, I just find it extraordinary. What are they going to apologise for? Are they apologising for the government of the day? Are they apologising for the military or political machine of the day?' One thing was clear, if the government was even thinking of 'apologising on my behalf and my soldiers I would have to warn them not to do so'.

The interview with Colonel Wilford was followed by one, live, with Sir Edward Heath, who put a rather more diplomatic spin on matters.

If after that interview Wilford had any friends left in Whitehall, he was going to lose them after his next one. Compared with the next interview, his Channel 4 appearance had been a model of tact and diplomacy.

In 1999 the Saville Inquiry was preparing to start hearings. But first there were a set of legal matters to sort out. Among them was the controversial issue of whether soldiers should be given anonymity during the Inquiry. Saville had originally decided that in the interests of openness and transparency the soldiers of 1 Para and indeed all the soldiers who had been there on that day should testify under their real names. The Widgery ciphers were finally going to be dropped.

But Lord Saville was overruled in the matter. After a high- profile campaign in the press and from the top of the army, the High Court ruled that the ciphers had to stay. Senior figures in the army vociferously opposed the naming of soldiers because of fears that they could be subjected to retaliation from the IRA or other Republican splinter-groups. The Good Friday Agreement was still very recent and its lasting outcome not yet assured.

On 6 July 1999 Lord Saville was returning to the courts in an attempt to reverse the High Court's decision. The BBC's flagship morning show on Radio 4, the *Today* programme, decided to mark the occasion with a discussion about the issue. In the studio with the presenter James Naughtie was Michael McKinney, whose brother William had been shot dead on the day.

The interview with Michael McKinney went off without incident. But then down the line, just after 8 a.m., came Colonel Wilford. He was clearly bristling with anger. Firstly he was asked if he thought that the Saville process would finally lay the day to rest.

> DW: No, I don't think we shall because the idea of truth is a very ephemeral one. I've just been listening to your previous speaker. I don't really think, and I've always thought, that they have no interest at all in what we have to say. Only their witnesses are witnesses to the truth which, in effect really, is just future propaganda for the cause.

> JN: Well, Lord Saville is going to sit there, Mr McKinney has said that he, from the evidence he's seen so far, believes that Lord Saville is going to go about this task in a way which is, you know, judicially fair and which will produce a verdict. Do you not have the same confidence?

> DW: No I don't...

> JN: Why not?

> DW: I have the confidence that he will produce information but I have no confidence that it will be accepted by, if I can call them that, the other side.

As Wilford went on to say: 'I'm afraid they have all become the other side.'

Why was the issue of anonymity so important then? Now Wilford decided to really go for it, and in his ensuing exchange all the anger, marginalisation and bitterness welled up. Anger at the IRA, anger at the politicians and the army. And anger at the media.

> DW: Could I preface my remarks about anonymity by saying this: the word 'Bloody Sunday' has become a very pejorative phrase and it's now in the canon of nastiness. It was put there by the IRA, it's been kept there in the public mind by you and the other media—

> JN: Well, I'm sorry, Colonel Wilford, can I just interrupt you there? I find it slightly offensive to be bracketed with the IRA...

> DW: Well, I'm not bracketing you with the IRA...

> JN: Thank you.

The interview got worse.

> DW: I'm merely saying this is the way that this, in fact, has been kept in the public mind.

> JN: Well, for clearly obvious reasons.

> DW: And I have to ask and I really do insist on this, I have to ask: what about Bloody Wednesday, Thursday, Friday and every day of the week? What about Bloody Omagh, what about Bloody Warrenpoint, Enniskillen, Hyde Park, Bloody Aldershot and Brighton? Bloody everything the IRA ever touch?

> JN: Colonel Wilford, I think you would find it hard to argue that the IRA had had a good press in Britain. You would find it very hard to argue that the atrocity at Omagh didn't shock and horrify everyone here and hasn't been gone over endlessly...

> DW: It hasn't been gone over for twenty-seven years and Bloody Sunday has.

From this point the exchange got worse for Wilford very fast. Did he accept, he was asked, that there were plenty of people who were horrified by Bloody Sunday and were just as horrified by the actions of the IRA as Wilford himself? Then Wilford made his slip-up.

DW: I'll accept that if people have got the same attitude towards the IRA as we have then yes, of course, I accept it. But if you're suggesting that the people, in fact one of their representatives who we've just heard, I'm sorry...

JN: Sorry, we're talking about a relative of someone who was killed. He's not here representing any organisation, it's very important that I make that clear.

DW: Yes.

JN: You accept that?

DW: I accept that he's a relative, yes.

JN: Yes, exactly, okay, that's fine. I just wanted to clear that up because the phrase 'representative', he represents his dead brother and no one else.

DW: I'm sorry, we cannot accept that. He may represent his dead brother and a very, very tragic situation it is, but I do not accept that he merely represents him. He represents the Republican organisation and we are naive to the point of idiocy to believe otherwise.

JN: Well, can I, Colonel Wilford, I must interrupt you there because Mr McKinney, as you know, is sitting across from me...

DW: No, I didn't know he was sitting across from you.

JN: Well, he is, I did say he was in the studio. He was shaking his head rather vigorously and I must ask him just on this question. Colonel Wilford has said that you represent a particular strain of Republicanism. Now I just want to put that to you because you're still here.

MM: Well, that's totally untrue. I've been involved in the Bloody Sunday issue, the Bloody Sunday campaign these past seven years. I'm one of the founder members of that, myself and a number of other relatives are involved in that and we have no links with any Republican organisation at all.

JN: Right. Colonel Wilford, I mean, that's been said, do you accept it?
DW: No, of course I don't accept it. JN: Why not?

DW: Well, because they will all say that, won't they. I mean, every Republican, every, every, I regret to say, almost every Ulster Catholic will say that.

105

JN: Colonel Wilford, we have to leave it there, thank you.

Though the programme wisely decided to leave it there, not everybody else did. The interview caused a furore, particularly, understandably, in Derry. Three decades on, Wilford was tarring not just all rioters but all Derry Catholics with the IRA brush. It was not a helpful development.

National and local press picked up on the interview, many seeing Wilford's comments even all these decades on as symptomatic of the way in which the army must have viewed Catholics in the early 1970s. The anger was summed up by a local Social Democratic and Labour Party politician who described Colonel Wilford's interview as 'a case of adding grievous insult to grave injury'. A statement was issued by Wilford's erstwhile employers at the MoD saying that 'the lieutenant colonel retired from the army sixteen years ago and the views he expressed on the *Today* programme do not represent those of today's army.'

And for Wilford himself matters got worse. Shortly afterwards he was the subject of a libel suit from Michael McKinney in which the BBC were also a named party. When approached by press and asked whether Wilford would be paying his own costs in this case an MoD spokesperson pointedly remarked that this was not an army matter but rather 'concerns an action taken by one civilian against another'. If Wilford had ever enjoyed the protection of the British establishment as Republicans had for years claimed, then it was clear that they had washed their hands of any such responsibility now. When asked about the *Today* programme interview at the Saville Inquiry Wilford had to explain that his lawyers had advised him not to comment any further on the matter.

The testimony of Colonel Wilford was one of the most anticipated events of the new Saville Inquiry. Not just because of his notoriety and the disputes over his actions on the day, but because he was arguably the only senior army figure who could conceivably have been able to shed new light on the muddiest aspects of the day. It had also become clear to the press that Wilford made good copy. From his first clipped television and media appearances in the immediate aftermath of the events, all the way over three decades to his anger at a relative of one of his men's victims, Wilford was expected to put in one of the most colourful as well as potentially enlightening appearances of the whole Inquiry.

By the time he came to testify to the Inquiry for the opening days of questioning by Counsel, Colonel Wilford was almost seventy with a thick mane

106

of white hair. He had the appearance of someone trying to be helpful, courteous and indeed interested, like an interviewee who wished to impress an interviewer. And this manner broke a little and became more barbed only when the questioning became more searching.

After Wilford had answered the questions from Counsel to the Inquiry about the specific commands, orders, movements and records, the first of the families' representatives to question him decided to go for a scene-setting point before getting on to the specifics of the day. It was put to Wilford that over the course of thirty years and a number of media appearances it was the case that he thought neither he nor any of his men had done anything 'improper' on 30 January 1972. Was that right?

Wilford agreed: 'We did nothing improper.'

Could you, he was asked, have done anything better? Wilford stalled a little: 'I really have no idea.'
Another questioner tried to push him further on this point. 'Your position is this, is it not. You cannot believe that any of your soldiers were guilty of misconduct or worse.'

'That is so,' said Wilford.

'And it is upon that basis, belief but not knowledge, that you have loyally said that your soldiers behaved admirably?'

'Yes.'

As the families' representatives started to narrow in on some of the specifics, and especially as they went over his ill-judged appearances in the media over the decades, a slightly different Wilford emerged. More careful, more cautious and slightly more humble.

In the final report Lord Saville noted that during the course of his testimony Wilford had been frank about his doubts over his memory. On a number of matters he had expressed a concern over whether the picture he had in his mind was what he had seen or was derived from what someone had reported to him afterwards. Saville also noted that Wilford had 'sought to resile from or qualify much that he had said to the media decades after the event'. Which was a polite way of expressing the fact that Wilford had some considerable backtracking to do. Not so much about what he had done on the day. His biggest embarrassments in the box were not caused by that. Rather, they were caused by what he had said across the years afterwards.

For instance, he was asked about what he had said in the Channel 4 programme about feeling that once he and his soldiers had gone past the barriers and finished shooting they now 'controlled the Bogside'.

Q: You certainly thought, in 1999, that you controlled the Bogside, did you not?

A: I think it was just being cocky.

Q: There are a number of occasions during your Channel 4 interview when you say that you controlled the Bogside, and that, somewhat to your surprise, it appeared that nobody was prepared to take advantage of what you had achieved.

A: Yes. This is talking, what, twenty-five years after the event. I think the remarks that I made were – and I said this before in this room – were the result of frustration and angry – anger, perhaps a certain amount of bitterness, all those sort of things. I think many of those remarks I made were foolish, insupportable, inadvisable, and I was certainly doing what I deplore in others, becoming an armchair general.

He was not the only army man to have to admit to something similar. A lieutenant-colonel in the Royal Green Jackets, Peter Welsh, who later rose to become a major general, gave an interview twenty years after Bloody Sunday in which he described having told one of his senior officers that it would be 'mad' to deploy the Parachute Regiment in Derry. In evidence before Saville he expressed embarrassment about this. It was not the way in which anyone would have spoken to their superior officers, he conceded. Why had he said he had to a journalist? 'Twenty years later.' Yes. 'I probably had too many drinks,' he had said frankly.

In the same way, Wilford's embarrassments were palpable. The attempts he had made over the years to stick by and support his men continually came unstuck. Over the course of many years he had spoken about the day, but never on oath. In questioning before the Tribunal he had sworn to tell the truth. It became clear he had not always felt the same pressure.

During the course of the *Daily Mail*'s campaign to secure anonymity for the

Bloody Sunday soldiers, Wilford had given an interview to that newspaper saying he had seen Soldier H firing. He said that he believed that Soldier H was firing at an enemy sniper inside a building and was doing so to keep the sniper's head down. This was certainly not in line with what he had said in his statement or anywhere else.

'Yes, I got it wrong,' said Wilford slightly pathetically.

'You did not see any of that?' he was asked.

'No.'

But the words were there in the newspaper: 'I actually saw this soldier [H] firing and the truth is that he believed there was an enemy sniper in the building and he was firing to keep the gunman's head down. He was perfectly entitled to do that. It is all very well, if you are not in the firing line, to condemn such actions, but my soldiers had to make split-second decisions when they were being shot at.' So had he seen that or hadn't he? If he had got that wrong, how had he got it wrong?

A: I think I had transposed that event to the soldier that I had seen firing a shot at Kells Walk, simple as that.

Q: The soldier that you saw firing a shot at Kells Walk, you claimed that he told you he was firing at someone behind a barricade?

A: Yes, that is so.

Q: You claim that he fired one shot?

A: Yes.

Q: How could you conceivably transpose that event with the much-publicised criticism of Soldier H for firing nineteen rounds through a window of a house in Glenfada Park?

A: Because thirty years later that is what I did.

Q: And thirty years later your view of this, as a professional soldier, that a person armed with an SLR rifle is entitled to fire nine- teen rounds into a house if he thinks there is a sniper there, in order to keep his head down; is that right?

A: Yes.

Q: When you gave this account to the Daily Mail, firstly, it is wholly inaccurate; is that right, in relation to what you saw? In relation to this particular incident?

A: Yes.

Q: Wholly inaccurate?

A: But I have told you that I got it wrong.

Q: Do you not prepare for interviews with journalists where facts are supposed to be sacrosanct?

A: I never prepared anything when I was speaking to journalists, I – foolishly perhaps – spoke on my feet, as we say.

Q: You saying you saw it, you appreciate, to the reader, who was the person who purchased this newspaper, was simply saying, 'There is the commanding officer of the paratroopers who was actually there, saw and witnessed there and, therefore, that gives it authenticity'?

A: I tell you, Mr Harvey, I got it wrong, and I accept that. And I got a lot of things wrong and I accept the fact that I got them wrong.

Q: I will come to deal with that in a little while. The situation is: can you tell the difference between loyalty and blind allegiance?

A: I am afraid this is sort of semantic words which I try never to get involved with. I regard loyalty as a very, very good thing.

Q: Do you believe if it turns into blind allegiance it becomes degraded?

A: I do not think I have ever been forced into that situation of being blind to what you described as 'allegiance'.

Q: Part of loyalty as a commander is responsibility, is it not? A: Oh, yes, of course.

Q: And responsibility often means having to take action against one's subordinates?

A: Yes.

110

Q: It also means that the stamp of the commander that he puts upon his regiment is one where they know that if they misbehave or commit criminal acts, they will be censured?

A: I think my soldiers knew that very well.

Wilford had lied to the newspaper. But why? For the same reason that Colonel Wilford had said so many things over the years. Because still, after all this time and faced with all this questioning, he refused to budge from standing four-square behind his men and even saying, outside of the Tribunal, things that were untrue in order to protect them. Had Wilford said such things as deliberate lies? Or were they attempts – cack-handed attempts, but attempts all the same – over the years to approximate the truths he believed his soldiers could not express?

But he had been shown to have very obviously and knowingly lied to cover for one of his men. Even if that had happened on just one occasion, it was inevitable that some would see that as representative of a larger problem that Wilford had with the truth.

The interview with the *Daily Mail* came up again and again and it was a profound humiliation for Wilford. His own words – his own recent words – had been shown to have been a lie. He had lied to the *Daily Mail*. But here, sworn on his oath to tell the truth and mindful of the fact, he simply had to show that it was a ruse – an attempt to protect one of his men.

At the end of his testimony a suggestion was put to Wilford by one of the lawyers for the families. One of the problems he had been faced with over the years, it was suggested, along with an inability to believe that his men had done anything wrong, was that he could not accept that the people killed on that day were innocent. From his first interviews, in the hours after the shootings happened, right up to the interviews he had done with the media before the Inquiry had started, Wilford had found it impossible to imagine or concede that. It was put to him that this was a problem. 'No, it has not been a problem at all,' he replied. The interview he had given to the BBC in 1992 was cited – the one in which he said that he could not accept that the dead were innocent. Yet he refused to concede that this was a problem for him.

Q: Was it not? I want to ask you now, because this may be one of the last

111

opportunities you have: do you now accept that those who were killed – and I represent two of the ones who were killed and two who were injured – the two who were killed particularly, I am only dealing with those killed at the moment– were innocent; do you accept that now?

A: I cannot accept anything, because I do not have the evidence.

I have not been following this, this Tribunal—

Q: I appreciate you might say that. Are you aware of what your own counsel has conceded to this Tribunal?

A: No, I am not.

Q: You are not?

A: No.

Q: You are obviously not aware that what has been conceded on your behalf is that the identified civilians who were killed were not armed terrorists; did you know that?

A: No, I did not know that.

Even now Wilford tried to find a way around the unpleasant realities that were coming towards him. In the light of the statement made by his own counsel that made the concession on the innocence of the dead, Wilford was asked again if he was willing to make the same concession that his counsel had made for him. He was not:

A: Well, they have made that concession because they have got evidence; they have heard evidence; I have not.

Q: I see. Is the position that even though your counsel has conceded it, you are not prepared to?

A: Well, how can I? I have had no evidence. No one has actually shown me any evidence for this to be the case.

Q: You are not prepared to accept what he says on your behalf?

A: How can I?

Q: Because I suggest—

A: I do not know what he has accepted; I have no, I have no evidence; I have heard no evidence; no one has told me; no one has proved to me that this is so.

And so Wilford's own counsel took him through it himself in front of the whole Tribunal. Edwin Glasgow QC rose at the very end of Wilford's questioning to explain the matter to his client. The submission had been made years ago, by Glasgow, at the very start of proceedings, before even the first witness had been called. The statement said: 'That those of our clients who fired live rounds aimed and shot at and only at those whom they believed to be gunmen or nail-bombers threatening lethal violence to them or to others. However, it does not follow that those who have been identified as having been killed or wounded on 30 January 1972, were themselves gunmen or nail-bombers.' It was read to Wilford who nodded slowly. Glasgow continued: 'I think you appreciate that that, if it be a concession, that statement was made on behalf of you and those whom we represent.' Wilford nodded again, as he took it in.

He left the witness box having shed very little light on events. His appearance had been anticipated as one of the crucial moments in the search for the truth of that day. Two whole weeks had been devoted to his testimony before the Tribunal but the help Wilford could give was limited. His recall was certainly better than that of many of the soldiers he had commanded that day. But he had not been there at the crucial moments. He had been darting around the Bogside, one moment beside, another moment lost to, the young Captain Jackson. He had seen very little of what his men had done. And what he learned afterwards they had done he could not believe. In the years afterwards he had stuck by his men and their accounts of what had happened. Not – he was the first to concede in evidence – because he had seen anything much that persuaded him that they were right. Not because he had seen others doing anything wrong. But because he believed his men could do no wrong. His superiors had let him down, his superiors had betrayed him, but he would not in turn let his men down – he would not in turn betray them.

When Saville's findings were finally published Wilford, as was expected, was heavily criticised. Indeed he was the highest-up military figure to come in for criticism. In the conclusions of the final report Saville and his colleagues confirmed that Colonel Wilford should not have sent his soldiers into the Bogside. They stressed a number of reasons why.

Firstly, because in doing so he had disobeyed the orders given to him. Secondly, because he should have realised that his soldiers had no means of knowing who was a rioter and who was simply an individual taking part in a civil rights march. And thirdly, he should have realised that his soldiers were going into an area that was unknown to them but that they regarded as dangerous. In those circumstances, Saville observed, Wilford should have known that the response of the soldiers was likely to be a risk to civilians not involved in paramilitary activity.

But the report also concluded that Colonel Wilford 'did not foresee that his soldiers would act as in the event they did; and we consider that in this regard he cannot be fairly criticised'. He had 'set in train the very thing his Brigadier had enjoined him from doing', Saville concluded. The Tribunal decided that Wilford had been motivated 'to demonstrate that the way to deal with rioters in Londonderry was not to shelter behind barricades like "Aunt Sallies" while being stoned, as he perceived was what the local troops had been doing'. Wilford was condemned from his own mouth. His own recklessly free words to a journalist had come back into the final judgment given by the final report into his actions.

And another final judgment came that Wilford could not avoid – the verdict on Wilford's men. After decades of denial about what his soldiers had done and after decades of trying to protect them, in the last analysis there was nothing that Wilford could do to protect his soldiers from the verdict.

Within a day of the Saville Report being published, six anonymous ex-Paras who had served that day (none of them shooters) spoke to BBC Northern Ireland to defend Colonel Wilford. They claimed that he had only been criticised because there was a political need to criticise someone of rank in the army. Both Irish and British radio had already reported that he was dead. But he was not, nor was he in hiding. The press went in search of Wilford to hear his side of the story and it was not hard to track him down. Derek Wilford, as he was now simply known, was living with his wife where he had lived for three decades, teaching fine arts to US military families at a NATO base near to his 'ivy-covered' retirement cottage in a small village in Belgium.

A number of papers ran photos taken of Wilford in what was generally described as the 'sleepy' or 'idyllic' Belgian village. Neighbours were interviewed and expressed shock about the identity of their 'very private' neighbour. Some papers seemed deter- mined to make his location as easy to work out as possible. One Irish paper pointedly named the location of the small village he lived in, the type of car he drove, descriptions and photos of the house, the name of the street and even the name of the house. It was clear that Derek Wilford was not going to be allowed to live out the rest of his retirement in perfect peace.

And of course the press tried repeatedly to get Wilford to react to the Saville Report. But he had learned his lesson with the media. He told the *Irish Mail on Sunday* when they appeared on his doorstep and asked for comment, 'I don't want to talk about it. It's all been said.' He referred the reporter, if he wanted comment, to the MoD.

An elderly neighbour spoke of Wilford's daughter, who had been to school locally with her own daughter. 'I think she is in England now.' What few if any of the papers mentioned was Wilford's son. For another Colonel Wilford had followed on from his father, had followed him into the Parachute Regiment and had also become an officer with 1 Para. Colonel Wilford the younger fought with his regiment during the 2003 war in Iraq.

9

THE WHISTLEBLOWER?:
027

As the testimony of the soldiers who fired on the day showed, in the hours, months and years after Bloody Sunday the stories from the army about what happened remained in almost complete opposition to those of most other witnesses.

The version of events that came out of 1 Para from the evening of the event and afterwards was uniform. Every soldier who had shot said that his targets were nail-bombers and civilian gunmen. As Soldier H's testimony had shown, they stuck to these stories even when they were entirely ridiculous or contradictory.

As the years between the Widgery Inquiry and the beginning of the Saville process drew on and accounts of the day proliferated, the question was frequently thought and asked: what if one day one of the soldiers, one of the members of the Parachute Regiment, broke ranks and came clean? What if a soldier – one of those who had shot or seen their colleagues shoot – would finally reveal what the soldiers really did that day, who had shot where, and why?

The soldiers – and a very few soldiers at that – held the key to what had happened in those minutes. But from the moment the Widgery Inquiry finished, nothing more was heard from them. None of them spoke, none of them identified themselves. They sank into anonymity and stayed there. And after two and a half decades had passed there seemed little or no hope that anything would change. As long as nobody from the Parachute Regiment broke ranks the full truth of Bloody Sunday could never be known. And then everything changed. Or at least it appeared to.

It transpired that one soldier at least who had been in 1 Para on the day certainly did think differently. He was nineteen years old when he joined 1 Para in 1971. Initially a member of the Signals Platoon, on 30 January 1972 he was a radio-operator in the Anti- Tank Platoon. Immediately after events he had given an account to the Royal Military Police but he had not in the end been called to give evidence to Lord Widgery. Most crucially, he had been right alongside the soldiers who fired the most bullets that day. And it was this man who decided, for whatever reason, to break the Para line and speak out. The story of how he got there was certainly a strange one.

The man who was the radio-operator on Bloody Sunday had had a difficult time after the day. He said he had kept notes throughout his period of service, and when he left the army had 'two or three clumps of such paperwork'. These notes were, he said, written 'within hours or, at the latest, days' after the events they attempted to describe.

He had certainly been with the Paras during a crucial period. He had arrived in Belfast in the late summer of 1971. And he appeared to have seen some things that had stayed with him. He spoke about a murky episode in a Belfast backstreet in which a woman was blinded. But the important thing about this soldier's purported notes was that they were contemporary – telling of events right after they had happened. For any attempt to get to the truth these notes could be vital. The soldier was known, like all others, by a cipher. He became '027'.

Details of his life after Bloody Sunday were necessarily vague. He said that he had left the army two years later, in the spring of 1974, and had wanted to leave the whole thing behind him. 'Psychologically I was looking forwards,' he told the Saville Inquiry. But in 1975 he was in New York and there met an American called Sean Patrick McShane who was interested in Northern Ireland. He was a journalist and was meant to be writing a book about the conflict. On returning home – 'without being selective or really looking through it first' – 027 said that he sent his material to New York to this journalist, but did not part with the original of the diary he had kept. Among the papers he had sent was an account, probably written in 1975, that constituted a personal record of Bloody Sunday. Looking back he said that he was not particularly aware of the potentially sensitive nature of the documents he had sent.

They certainly included some devastating details. In the 1975 account 027 had said that Soldier H had gone into Glenfada Park firing from the hip, that he,

117

027, had seen a man fall from a bullet fired by Soldier H in this manner, and that he saw the bullet pass through the first man into a second. He also claimed that on the day Soldier F had carried modified rounds known as 'dum-dum' bullets, which would fracture on entering a person's body and cause massive internal and external injuries.

These and other parts of the story were shocking. And unknown to Soldier 027, as the twenty-fifth anniversary of Bloody Sunday came along, this document that had lain unnoticed for all these years suddenly came to light.

Shortly before Christmas 1996 an Irish journalist called Tom McGurk, who had worked on a Bloody Sunday investigation for RTE, was sent an archive of information about the day. McGurk gave a statement to Saville in which he said that he would not reveal who had sent the archive to him but confirmed that it was not 027 himself. Saville worked out that McShane had passed the documents to an Irish journalist who in turn passed it on to another person who was involved in publishing, who did nothing with them until renewed interest in Bloody Sunday led him to read them again. Realising their importance, he passed them on to McGurk.

The archive that all these people had been sitting on for years included the memoir about what had happened that day as well as what appeared to be an interview with the soldier. This material included some extraordinary claims, including that in the briefing Wilford had given the night before Bloody Sunday members of 1 Para were ordered to 'get some kills' the next day. Also, the soldier claimed that evidence had been officially manipulated and doctored by army Counsel before the Widgery Tribunal. These were astonishing and highly damaging claims for the army. But if 027 hoped to remain anonymous all these years later, he had made a number of errors along the way. Among them was the fact that the documents sent to McShane, which had ended up with McGurk, included legal documents relating to the soldier, presumably to authenticate what he said. They included a number of classified army documents and his service number. They also contained the real name of the soldier – that is, the real name of the man known as 027.

Realising from this that the documents he had been sent were authentic, McGurk started trying to track down Soldier 027. But he and his paper in Ireland were unable to trace the soldier, and claimed that they received no assistance from the British Ministry of Defence when they approached them. As a result, realising what a story they were sitting on, McGurk and his paper, the *Sunday Business Post*, ran the story of the memoir early in 1997 without having spoken to the soldier himself.

Understandably, it caused a sensation in Ireland when the story appeared. As the press and public clamour grew, spurred on by the fresh revelations, the Irish government appealed to the British government to hold a fresh investigation into the events of Bloody Sunday. Soldier 027's stab at a memoir, when it came to public view, ended up having a unique result: the Saville Inquiry. By no means the least reason for this was the simple fact that parts of the story – if not all of it – seemed so entirely authentic. At long last, it seemed, the missing piece of the Bloody Sunday jigsaw had surfaced.

In what constituted a considerable build-up of events, around the same time as the Irish newspaper got hold of 027's memoir, the soldier took steps to make his story known himself. In early 1997 an extraordinary letter arrived at a Belfast newspaper. It was about Bloody Sunday. The author said he had been a private in 1 Para on the day and it was signed 'Former Paratrooper, now living in the West Country'.

The letter included descriptions of the 'inflated expectations' the soldiers had of what they were going to encounter ahead of the march. It talked of how a few 'hot-heads' had opened fire and sparked a 'knee-jerk reaction' from others to join in. And he saw it all as stemming 'from the mindless actions of a handful of cowboys'. The person who had been there and served alongside these 'cowboys' was clearly angry. The question was whether he would go more public. But whether he realised it, by firing off this single letter 027 started a chain reaction of events that meant that decision was taken out of his hands. What he had said was of such importance that what followed was something he could not control and finally may have had much cause to regret.

Soldier 027 later claimed that he had been prompted to write his letter after watching footage on television of the twenty-fifth anniversary commemorative march and a speech by John Hume. It was, he said, 'an impulsive act with no larger project in mind'. He later told Saville that 'I feel, and always have felt, a great loyalty and respect to my former unit and most of the people with whom I served. The regiment and what it represents is greater than the individuals within it. However, part of me wanted the truth to emerge.' And so 027 made his slow progress into the public eye. At some stage he said that he had spoken to the

119

paper to which he had written the letter. They told him that Channel 4 were trying to get hold of him and left him a number. He phoned Channel 4 and agreed to take part in a programme they were making on Bloody Sunday. As long as he was not recognisable on screen 027 was happy to be interviewed.

During this time 027 claimed that he had gone 'to the north of England to hunt for' his original handwritten diary. And he claimed that he had used it as an aide memoire when doing the programme. But 027 himself said that the experience of doing the programme left him feeling betrayed. He had, he said, been unaware of the Irish paper's article on his 1975 document, but after filming the Channel 4 crew showed him the article. He felt that he had been duped and claimed that had he known about this he would never have gone ahead with the interview because he would have been 'too alarmed'. By this time, on the back of the Belfast newspaper letter, he had also agreed to do a radio interview with Radio Ulster. His ability to keep control of events was slipping every time he allowed himself to step a little further into the spotlight. But he seems to have trodden into it anyway, though each time he claimed to be willing to step back again.

Perhaps he genuinely had no idea quite what an impact his claims were going to have. But his personal life was about to change swiftly and severely. When 027 saw the final Channel 4 film he was horrified, believing that he had been exposed in too obvious a way. They had promised him that he would not be recognisable in the film, he said, and he was filmed speaking in the dark. But he claimed afterwards that anybody who had known him would have been able to tell from his voice and his profile who it was. It seemed an early sign that the people 027 appeared to fear most were not the IRA but his former comrades.

He recorded some of this in his eventual statement for Saville:

> It was a very stressful period for me. I spoke to a former Army colleague. His attitude to my appearance on television and my alarm over where this was all this leading prompted me to destroy the diary within a day or so of seeing the article in the Irish news- paper. I ripped it up and flushed it down the toilet (in the Channel 4 building). Perhaps it was inappropriate to do so but the whole episode was such an unreal and tense experience at the time. I do not have any copies of that original material.

This action itself posed a set of questions that were typical of those that would begin to be raised about 027. Why had he been in the Channel 4 building after speaking to the former army colleague, which he said was after seeing the programme? Like a lot of 027's evidence, around the edges certain parts of the testimony began to fray. Was he after publicity? Was he trying to cover some of his tracks? Or was he playing some other game entirely? Each time he spoke about almost anything the question-marks surrounding 027 got larger. Was he, as he portrayed himself, an honest former soldier just out to tell the truth? A damaging set of facts were starting to emerge that suggested that the great army whistleblower of Bloody Sunday was not everything he seemed.

Soldier 027's information was such a vital part of the impetus for a new Inquiry into Bloody Sunday that it was of course essential that the Saville Inquiry get hold of the man and gain his co-operation. Their efforts were rewarded when, in April 1998, 027 approached the Inquiry through a London lawyer.

Although 027 was, he said, willing to give evidence, he was also clearly exceptionally worried about doing so. He also, uniquely for a witness to the Inquiry, wanted to be rewarded for doing so. Clearly he had become concerned about his safety after the exposure of his story by Channel 4 and the Irish newspaper and felt that threats to his safety made it difficult for him to seek normal employment. So 027 said that he would only give evidence if he was given certain assurances and, more controversially, was paid for doing so.

It left Lord Saville in an unenviable situation. On the one hand the evidence of 027 was obviously of unparalleled importance and the Inquiry could well be deemed to lack any legitimacy if he was not persuaded to appear. On the other hand the principle that no witness should receive financial compensation for giving evidence was paramount.

Normally when a witness refused to co-operate or give evidence the Inquiry would have served a summons. But 027's whereabouts were unknown and he of course refused to reveal them. Even the lawyers representing him did not know where he was living. The Inquiry later admitted that it had issued summonses against a number of utility companies and even employed the services of a 'tracing agent' in an attempt to track 027 down. But all of these efforts failed and as a result Saville was left with few options. Finally, in an effort to ensure the Inquiry itself kept its hands clean it did so by a circuitous if transparent route: the Tribunal allowed an agreement to be reached between 027 and the Northern Ireland Office. It resulted in a written statement by 027 being handed to the

Inquiry in July 2000 and the assurance from 027 that he would give oral evidence to the Inquiry, screened from the public, in 2002. In the meantime the details of the deal done between 027 and the Northern Ireland Office came to light, and were the basis of significant concern. Soldier 027 had agreed to give his evidence on condition that the Inquiry provide him with a lump sum of £20,000 for a deposit on a house, a sum of up to £6,000 to purchase a car and a salary of £1,400 a month. It also became clear from the copies of these negotiations that were subsequently made public that at every stage 027 had attempted to get more money out of the Northern Ireland Office. His original claim that he needed the money because he only had £400 in his bank account was shown to be false. As were his claims that he had no other means of earning money. Among other things it was later to transpire that during this period he had attempted to sell the rights to a book he was working on.

In the end 027 had got what he wanted, both in terms of assurances and also in payment. But in the latter case this fact did him and his story no good at all: the deal was deemed to reflect very badly on him. If he truly hoped, as he said in his statement, that a 'positive effect' would emerge from the Inquiry and that 'the truth of what actually happened' would 'surface', then why was it a hope with a price-tag attached?

In any case, the co-operation of 027 was vital. And not merely for cosmetic or procedural reasons, but because much of what 027 claimed had not just a ring of truth but a missing ring of truth about it. And some of it even distinctly chimed with what other soldiers had said.

For instance, Colonel Wilford had talked of the Paras' disdain for 'Aunt Sally' soldiers, who just stood around as rioters threw missiles at them. So 027 recorded that 'if a crowd of hooligans were throwing missiles and acting in an aggressive manner, certain units would go through an almost ritualistic procedure of facing them with plastic visors and shields. Because of the nature of our outlook, the Paras thought of that in a derisory way.' And in the regiment from which 'Colonel Callan' was discharged for robbing a post office, 027 recalled an occasion after a riot when he reversed a 'Pig' into the window of a cake shop, and the men filled the vehicle with the cakes before driving away. 'Living in a situation where many people were preoccupied with working out ways to kill us, that sort of thing seemed fairly innocuous,' he said.

Soldier 027 even recalled being beaten up by 'Callan' (whom he calls by the cipher UNK 180) soon after arriving in Belfast. Despite acknowledging his 'positive attributes' – including his reputation as 'an excellent shot' – 027 describes 'Callan' as 'an individual who lived in a world that I cannot comprehend'. He relates a version of the story of 'Callan's' dishonourable discharge from the army, saying that for the post office robbery 'he was given five years and, during his trial, he threatened to kill the prosecuting officer.' Like a lot of 027's testimony, it was almost right, but stretched to improve it in the telling. Elsewhere he related the story of a soldier called 036 who he said was renowned in the unit for allegedly shooting a waiter in a Chinese restaurant after an argument over the bill. By the time Saville wished to question 036 he lived in a foreign jurisdiction, but when questioned there by a representative of Saville he denied knowing anything about any such incident.

Others of 027's claims also seemed to be stretched, not least the claim that dum-dum bullets were passed around the back of his 'Pig' and used by some of the Paras on Bloody Sunday. The claim had caused huge media interest in the years since 027 had first publicly made it – as had his statement that in fact far more shots were fired on the day than those recorded because some soldiers had carried private supplies of ammunition. Both these claims were dismissed by Saville as untrue after hearing substantial amounts of evidence, not least the fact that nobody killed on Bloody Sunday had wounds consistent with the use of dum-dum bullets.

But far more important than the places where 027 seemed to embroider his story were those claims that rang true. Perhaps most striking among them was his description of what happened immediately after de-bussing, in the crucial seconds when so many soldiers started, almost simultaneously, doing so much firing.

Soldier 027 said that he saw some of the soldiers in his section reaching the low wall at Kells Walk that faced the rubble barricade. He described seeing one soldier raise his rifle to his shoulder and start to fire 'without pause or hesitation' into the centre of the crowd. Others joined in within seconds, some standing, some kneeling. Soldier F was down on one knee, beyond the far end of the wall, as he was shooting. What 027 described next sounded eerily right:

> One chap … ran up beside me pushing his way between two soldiers who were firing, so that he could commence firing himself. He indicated to me that he thought what was happening was great. He was exuberant.

I stood at the wall and put my rifle to my shoulder. I looked through my sights, scanning across the crowd. I was as keen to find a target as anyone, but I just could not identify a target that appeared to justify engaging. I did not see anyone with a weapon or see or hear an explosive device. I was looking across the crowd with some concentration, aware of the firing immediately around me. I lowered my weapon and looked at the guys firing and tried to locate what they were firing at. I still failed to see what I could identify as a target and it caused me some confusion. I have a clear memory of consciously thinking, 'What are they firing at?' and feeling some inadequacy. What was I not seeing that I ought to be seeing?

Soldiers F and G – who 027 said always acted as a pair – seemed to have, he said, 'a preconceived idea of what they were going to do that day'.

Soldier 027 recalled getting the ceasefire order from Major Loden over the radios. 'Cease fire, cease fire,' he recalled him shouting. As the radio-operator, 027 said he relayed the command to the other men himself. It was a vivid memory to him. He said he recalled going around tapping men on the shoulder and telling them or otherwise shouting the order to cease firing.

But it was at this point, he said, when the firing had come to an end that four soldiers, F and G first, followed by E and H next, turned to their right and ran into Glenfada Park. Soldier 027 remembered F and G moving 'with purpose', knowing what they were doing. He followed and in a very short space he recalled a burst of firing. He admitted in his statement that the order in which things happened and what exactly he saw in Glenfada Park were not clear. He said that he had read a book about Bloody Sunday as well as participating in the Channel 4 documentary and by his own admission did not know the degree to which his current impressions of what happened were generated from his long-term memory 'coalescing with other accounts of the day'.

But he said he did remember certain details that he was confident were accurate memories. He remembered a shot man lying on a pavement or in a gutter, a crowd of civilians huddling. And he said that at no point did he see anyone who posed a threat and that on the day 'it never entered [his] head' to fire his rifle.

He said he also had a true memory, as the firing stopped, of standing and surveying the scene. 'It was absolutely timeless,' he recalled. 'It may have been ten seconds or ten minutes.' He saw men in donkey jackets and flat caps close to him picking up a body and walking away. 'I remember wondering', he said, 'if I was supposed to be shooting these people.'

One thing in particular that emerged clearly from the sometimes fuzzy details of 027's current memory was that F and G used the opportunity to 'assert themselves and influence events'. Even Soldier E, he claimed, whom he had always previously found 'a sound bloke', seemed to have just got caught up in it. Soldier 027 was in no doubt where blame lay. F and G had 'initiated' the events of the day, he said. He identified them as the 'prime movers' in the area, and said that their 'aggressive, positive actions' were what 'incited a few other loonies to join in'. Crucially, he said that shooting had started in Glenfada Park after the ceasefire order had been given. F had started the shooting at the rubble barricade and, in the same way, the shooting in Glenfada Park had started as soon as F entered the area.

Soldier 027 also claimed a memory that, though vague, was still distinct: that he had heard a conversation between Sergeant Major 202 and Colonel Wilford after firing had stopped, and that they were talking about Soldiers F and G. He said that he remembered Colonel Wilford saying that both men had 'better be packed off to the SAS' and that he believed both soldiers had indeed started SAS training as soon as they returned to England.

One other memory also seemed to confirm a suspicion about one of the mysteries of the day. Soldier 027 said that he remembered being in the 'Pig' after firing and that the soldiers were trying to work out their stories with each other. A part of this that rings true relates to Soldier H when he told the other men that he had fired twenty-two rounds. Soldier 027 said, 'There was no anger or vindictiveness directed at Soldier H. It was more a case of "What are we going to do about it?"'

He said that he had a 'vague memory' of H saying that he had been shooting at someone on the pavement, that he had kept firing at the body and that each time the body moved and so he fired again. 'We thought,' 027 said, 'as he fired a round, he hit the body and made it move and that he was so stupid he thought the body was moving of its own accord.' The problem with this memory is that there was no body of anyone who died on Bloody Sunday that had more than two bullet wounds and certainly none with the multiple wounds H would have inflicted had he pumped repeated rounds into a body.

Nevertheless, 027 said, 'The whole thing about Soldier H was characterised

125

by the fact that no one knew quite what to make of what he had been up to and he was not circumspect enough to keep quiet.' He said the story of a man popping up repeatedly from behind a car might help. H said he had shot at a window and that perhaps that could be the explanation. Even at the time, 027 said, 'we thought that story was laughable.' He went on:

> We could not take Soldier H seriously as he was smiling and talking about people popping up behind cars and shooting at windows. Soldier H thought what he said was quite clever. He was not a furtive character. He was a berk. As we were talking, the Platoon Sergeant was standing by the open doors. He heard Soldier H say that he had fired twenty-two rounds and the situation was then beyond our control. The Platoon Sergeant's response was 'Ah' and he stood there shaking his head.

In April 1999, a year before the main hearings got under way, the Inquiry met for two days of hearings on the issue of soldier anonymity. The arguments were long and complex, not least because of the contention of the lawyers on behalf of the families that certain soldiers' names were in the public domain already. It was an exceptionally delicate issue.

Certainly a number of names were publicly known, not least from the Widgery Inquiry. These included the name of Colonel Wilford and of other senior officers. It was also true that over the ensuing years certain other names had come into the public domain. One was a former soldier called David Longstaff whose name was public because in 1995 he had taken part in a television programme called *A Tour of Duty*. The Tribunal ruled that his Inquiry number, INQ 23, was not needed.

That was a relatively easy case. But there were others that were very borderline indeed. The families of course wanted all soldiers to be identified by their real names. But though this was eventually impossible, there were good reasons for certain name details to be known. For instance, the family of James Wray, shot in Glenfada Park, wanted to know all soldiers in 1 Para who had the first name 'Dave'. A civilian called Joseph Mahon who had been wounded in Glenfada Park claimed in his statement to have heard a couple of Paras shouting. One shout was 'I've got another one.' Another shout was 'We're pulling out, Dave.' In Mahon's original statement 'Dave' was redacted, but the name had to be discussed in hearings and asked of witnesses, so where relevant the name 'Dave' was allowed to come out.

126

Any time a military witness was asked about a fellow military witness they would be referred to a list of ciphers that they were given, and each time, before answering a question, they were warned not to read out the name. But it was a practice fraught with perils. Throughout the Saville Inquiry Edwin Glasgow QC acted as the counsel for most of the soldiers. He took great care during proceedings, not least with the issue of soldier anonymity, for which he had argued strongly.

But on the second day of the hearings on anonymity Glasgow himself made a slip. 'Of course we know that Byron Lewis has publicised his views and his name, but that is not what we are concerned about; he brings that on himself.'

Counsel to the Inquiry intervened. Glasgow had, he coughed, given the name of a soldier that was in fact not in the public domain. Glasgow had been using the unexpurgated version of the Irish government's dossier – which had been based on the files 027 had sent to America in 1975. In the expurgated version of this information that had been made publicly available the name had been redacted. The Tribunal was in a quandary.

Counsel to the Inquiry suggested that perhaps the name could be removed from the transcript of proceedings that was printed and made publicly available at the end of each day in hard copy and on the Inquiry's website. The MoD's lawyer said that it was his understanding that the name had not previously been made public but suggested issuing an order under the Contempt of Court Act that would make repetition of the name illegal. But, as Lord Saville noted, there was 'nothing to prevent anybody who has any of this information from taking a loudspeaker and going outside and regaling the public with it'. The MoD lawyer questioned whether the court's powers could postpone publication of the information. 'What do I do,' asked Saville, 'forbid the members of the public sitting here from telling other people what they have heard today?' Glasgow's slip had caused a problem. Eventually Saville decided that since the hearings were public the question came down to whether the name should be available 'to a small section of the public or a large section of the public'. He decided that the transcript of the proceedings should be published unredacted in the normal way. But in his May 2001 ruling on anonymity Saville redacted the name in his own account and ruled that 'the Tribunal directs that in any future proceedings soldier 027 will be referred to by that coded description only.' Even in quoting Glasgow's slip, Saville redacted himself. But the reference, unredacted, remained there for anyone who knew about it to read.

127

The reason Saville did this in 2001 was probably because by that date there were alleged to have been consequences from Glasgow's slip. The exposure had left an already paranoid man even more paranoid and this, in turn, had an impact on the Inquiry.

Before the Glasgow slip, 027 had a history of fearing for his physical safety. He claimed that a Parachute Regiment website had described him as a traitor and that suspicious incidents had occurred around him. These, he said, had culminated in a physical attack on the landlord of the place where he was staying. In exchanges via his lawyer, 027 claimed that his landlord had been mistaken for him and beaten up and had to go to hospital. Soldier 027 would not name the man or the hospital but he said that the man's attackers had warned him, 'Keep your mouth shut.' He was convinced that these were people connected with his former colleagues.

Later, one of the lawyers for the families asked Soldier F about this incident. F said he did not know anything about it and did not even recognise the real name of 027. Excerpts from 027's claims were read to F:

Q: This is information that was given before this Tribunal and confirmed in evidence about an attack made on Soldier 027 and the man who was his landlord in about 1998, January, by people who beat up his landlord and dragged him into a car and said: 'That is your one chance, give it your best shot because afterwards we are going to kill you.' They mentioned Bloody Sunday, blood money, the SAS, that friends of theirs had been killed and people who dealt with the media. Were you party to threats and attacks being made on a man who had dared to speak out against you and your mates?

A: No, I was not.

Q: There seemed to be a group of you who had been in the Anti- Tank Platoon for a number of years by January 1972. You had been in it for about four years?

A: Nearly four years, yes.

...

Q: You had a strong sense of loyalty towards each other? A: Yes, we relied on each other, yes.

Q: You relied on each other and you would, I suggest, lie for each other.

128

A: No.

Q: A soldier who speaks out about another soldier's wrong-doing becomes very unpopular in a unit like that, does he not?

A: It is possible, yes.

027 said that he would not co-operate with the Inquiry unless they provided a security package for him including the components of a witness protection programme and, eventually, a change of identity. Not helped by the Glasgow remark, there were many times when the Inquiry and indeed 027's lawyers must have wondered if he would ever turn up in the witness box at all. The volume of correspondence between 027's lawyers and the Tribunal continued to grow as the scheduled arrival of this sensitive key witness drew near. But in October 2002, Lord Saville finally got him there, in Central Hall Westminster.

He was the first member of the Parachute Regiment to give evidence. And he was also the first witness to appear entirely screened from the public and lawyers: only the Tribunal were able to see him. Central Hall was going to get used to hosting some high-security witnesses over the coming months, but even by these standards Soldier 027 was whisked in and out of the building with extraordinary care and precaution for each of his four days of testimony.

And for all the preparations and expectations it turned out that 027 was like a lot of the witnesses – some of what he had to say stood up and a considerable amount did not. By his own admission, the former soldier said that thirty years on he could now no longer be sure about the details of his memory. Nor, he admitted, could he be entirely sure of the reliability of his 1975 account. Of that document 027 said, 'I do not know now how much of that account was first-hand experience and how much of it was hearsay or anecdotal.'

Counsel for the Inquiry led questions as usual on the first days that 027 was in the box. He and then lawyers for the families took the witness through matters that arose from his statement. It soon became clear that the multiple versions of events that 027 confessed to writing over the years were not only inconsistent but inconsistent in inconsistent ways. For instance, at the time of his interview with the Royal Military Police, kept on file like everyone else's, 027 had said that on the day he had seen incoming rounds hit the road. In his later statement he said that he had a guilty conscience about claiming this. But then in 1997 when he had met with Channel 4 he had repeated the incoming rounds story.

Asked how he had come to this memory, he said that he had been reading from his contemporary notebook. In other words 027 was claiming that he was using a version of events he believed to be false as the basis for a version at the time he was claiming to tell the truth. He got into several such muddles.

His 1975 memoir mentioned that shortly after arriving in Belfast 'the initiation for my battalion was a prolonged gun battle on the first day from a sand-bagged Henry Taggart Hall across the Springfield Road to Ballymurphy. A child was killed during this incident.' One of the lawyers for the family asked 027:

Q: Was that an incident during which you were present, or was that a gun battle during which you were present as a soldier?

A: No, I was not present.

Q: How do you explain the fact that you have given this account?

A: Perhaps I was trying to put what follows into context, I do not know.
Q: Is this an invented account so far as your involvement in it is concerned?

A: I was not there at that time, so it is what I gleaned from some source or another, I do not know from where.

Q: Was your battalion there on that day, do you know?

A: No, I do not.

At another point in the memoir he appeared to be implying involvement in the shooting of a man in an incident that he in fact turned out to have had nothing to do with.

Why had he claimed to be involved in firefights he was not involved in? Was he, as was subsequently suggested, trying to put himself at the centre of incidents he was not at the centre of? Why? For credibility? To spice up material for a literary venture?

It was not unusual or surprising that details of 027's memories of 1972 and of the circumstances of his 1975 memoir had been lost beyond recall. But why was it that even crucial, major and basic details of a recent event – like the attack on him he claimed had happened only a few years earlier – were now lost to his memory? It also transpired that the police had decided on each of the three occasions when 027 felt his security had been threatened that there was no credible evidence that any of the incidents ever occurred. Soldier 027's testimony seemed to be swiftly descending into a heap of self-contradiction and confusion.

On another occasion 027 was asked about his anonymity issues. He admitted that he had started his new book about Bloody Sunday while having a struggle with the Northern Ireland Office, Tribunal and Metropolitan Police over the issue of his security. As was pointed out to him, at the very time he was demanding security protection he was writing a book that, in the portions that were shown to the Inquiry, had to be heavily redacted before being made public, to protect his identity. In other words he had been getting ready to potentially expose his identity at the very moment he was claiming such a move would put him at risk.

Even the manner in which he answered questions gave rise to suspicions. After almost every question was asked there was a long pause before the disembodied voice from behind the curtain answered. One of the lawyers for the families remarked on this to 027, pointing out that it seemed he was spending an inordinate amount of time thinking about his answers before giving them. Was he just being cautious now that he was finally testifying? Or was he thinking through the contradictions of his statements and trying to keep whichever line he had prepared to take this time?

Confusingly, there were totally unnecessary elements to some of his lies. For instance 027 tried to deny that his 1975 memoir had clearly been written for publication rather than for personal use. A lawyer read examples of his stylistic tropes. They were not consistent with diary form:

Q: 'The reason I mention these early days of training is because...', and so on. This is written in a book style, is it not?

A: (Pause)

Q: Is it not?

A: (Pause) You could say that, sir, yes.

Q: Not only could I say it; it is, is it not?

A: It is something that is written with the intention that somebody else can read it, certainly.

And it seemed that in material written for other people, at the very least 027 had 'embellished' certain things. It was pointed out to him that his memory of being alone in Glenfada Park after the bodies had been carried out was impossible on the known timescale of events. Was it a lie, an embellishment, or was it simply that, like so many witnesses, thirty years on he had collated memories of what he had seen with what he felt he had seen and produced a new version?

In any case, by the time that the lawyers for the majority of the soldiers – the legal representatives of those people 027 was incriminating so damningly – came to question him, there was certainly plenty to question him on and flaws in his story and apparent character to tear into.

He was portrayed by Glasgow as a money-grabber. Soldier 027 said repeatedly that he wanted to reveal his story because he had a great desire for the truth to come out. But, going through the documents about 027's dealings with the Northern Ireland Office, Glasgow said, 'You have driven a very, very hard bargain to be here, 027, have you not?' And it was shown that the most serious fresh accusations against the army – that a senior officer had called for 'some kills', that the Widgery evidence was rigged and that the army used dum-dum bullets – all emanated from 027, but that he now no longer remembered the major facts about any of them.

But there was, for the soldiers' lawyers, a great deal of sport at the expense of some of his other claims.

Why was it that while claiming to have been 'reluctant to participate with TV news' he had done interviews with Channel 4 and Radio Ulster, he was asked. 'I see those things as being entirely consistent,' said 027. 'Oh, consistent, are they?' said the soldiers' lawyer, before adding, 'Was yours a live performance?'

For as many parts of his testimony that had a ring of truth, a similar number were hard to even treat seriously. His claim to have flushed his notes down a lavatory at Channel 4 was a source of much amusement. As was his claim that another of his original accounts of the day was no longer in existence, for an even more surprising reason. Soldier 027 asserted that the diary he had kept at

132

the time of Bloody Sunday had in fact been stolen years later, on the Paris Metro, by a gang of transvestites. The claim led to one of the few amusing headlines to come out of the whole proceedings, with a delighted Irish paper running a near-perfect tabloid head- line: 'Transvestite gang stole my Bloody Sunday evidence.'

Glasgow, questioning 027 on behalf of a number of soldiers, drained every drop of incredulity from the situation. Having questioned 027 on the lavatory episode he observed that 'it is a sad coincidence, is it, that your only other contemporary diary suffered an almost equally invidious fate in that your literary style apparently attracted some Parisian transvestites who took it off you in the Metro?' Soldier 027 complained that the incidents were entirely unrelated. 'Completely unrelated, that your diary was taken by some transvestites in the Paris Metro?' asked Glasgow once more.

'It was a completely unrelated incident many years before,' 027 said. 'I happened to be mugged and I just related who the muggers were.'

'I trust it will lose none of its colour when it appears in translation,' Glasgow concluded.

Sir Allan Green, the legal representative of Soldier H, was harsher. 'Would it be fair', he asked as an opening question, 'to describe your 1975 memoir as a pile of badly written tosh?' Soldier 027 objected. Green read an extract from the draft of 027's latest book attempt, where he had written himself, on rereading his earlier memoir, 'I read it through and thought, God, what a pile of badly written tosh.'

Green tried to demonstrate exaggeration in 027's accounts of other incidents during his tour of duty in Northern Ireland. Regarding his most recent work Green questioned him about his claim that while a prisoner was being held in an armoured 'Pig' on a separate occasion one of the other soldiers 'from somewhere produced a set of drumsticks, pushing them up the bloke's nose'.

Q: Is it usual to find drumsticks in a Pig?

A: I believe that incident occurred, sir.

Q: Any other musical instruments there?

Though 027 himself acknowledged that his current memory of certain events was defective, it was nevertheless probably a mistake for Soldier H's lawyer to attempt to make much play with this. And on a matter more closely linked with his client H, he asked 027 why he now had no memory of some important things he had earlier said he had seen. 'If you really had seen H do what he did, you would never have forgotten, it would be seared or scored on your memory for the rest of your days,' he suggested.

By the time the soldiers' lawyers had finished with him 027's standing as a witness had certainly taken a knock down from the height of 1997 when he and his writings were first discovered. At the very end of his questioning Green quoted 027's own words back to him once again. In his latest work 027 had written, 'I retain a great respect and in some cases affection for the memory of these blokes, equally there were those I thought complete shits and fantasy merchants.'

'Would you say', Green asked 027, 'that of those two categories a person who told malicious tales about other soldiers fell into the first category?'

'I believe, sir,' 027 replied, 'if you told malicious tales about other soldiers in a premeditated way, that would be, that category would be appropriate, yes.'

Green concluded, 'You are a fantasy merchant, are you not, selling fantasies in the way that has been examined during your evidence, are you not?'

'I believe, sir,' 027 concluded, 'I was living in an environment where there is – an element of fantasy was par for the course, it was in the nature of a large number of men in an unusual situation.' Green had finished with him.

Even the legal representatives for the majority of the families whose case 027 most supported finally described him as a 'wretched witness'. It was a judgement that Saville ended up agreeing with.

His final analysis of 027 was damning. Saville showed that some of 027's notorious claims, which had kick-started this whole process, including the claim that modified rounds of ammunition had been used, were baseless. He was also highly critical of 027's allegation that he had been encouraged to change or alter his evidence before the Widgery Inquiry. Saville wrote:

In our view, what is likely to have happened is that Private 027 felt that he had to invent a reason to explain providing a statement for the Widgery Inquiry that was inconsistent with his later accounts; and chose to do so by falsely laying blame for the inconsistency on others.

At the same time, Saville wrote:

> We take the view that Private 027's evidence cannot be wholly dismissed on the basis that it is such exaggeration, fantasy and deceit as to be of no assistance. Our conclusion is that it would be wrong to ground any of our findings about Bloody Sunday on his evidence alone, but equally wrong to ignore it where there is other material that tends to support what he told us.

Saville noted the contradictions throughout 027's accounts. And he expressed serious scepticism about some of his motives.

> His explanations about his 1975 meeting and subsequent dealings with Sean Patrick McShane, the loss of his diary and the reason for his destruction of the field notebook tend to stretch the imagination. His various 1997 encounters with the media and his 1999 book tend to show him as an attention-seeker. When Private 027's allegations, partly at his own instance, became public in early 1997, he became caught up in events over which he had no control and he became reluctant to step forward.

At the same time, the criticism was tempered. For instance Saville concluded that 'we cannot say that he did not have honestly held security fears.'

The evidence of 027 was of unparalleled importance. But it was also shaky, confusing and in the end incapable of being accepted on its own merits. As Saville concluded, the evidence proved 'hard to categorise'.

The Irish journalist who had brought 027's accounts out of the past in 1997 wrote a considered piece after Saville's final verdict. In it he reflected that the soldier known as 027 was now somewhere 'beyond the shores of Britain' living with a false identity and under a witness protection scheme. 'He will not have been surprised', wrote McGurk, 'that Saville found him a "wretched witness" in the face of the attacks by the lawyers representing the military because, by the time he had arrived, hooded and furtive, behind the screens at the tribunal, he was terrified for his life. Of the hundreds who gave evidence in the end, could there have been a lonelier place than the one he occupied, terrified equally of the

135

IRA and of his former colleagues in the Para battalion?'

It is of course possible that we have not yet heard the last of Soldier 027. Perhaps he will at some point succeed in getting one of his memoirs finished and published. Or perhaps he has decided that he has had enough of having to defend drafts of books he wrote thirty years ago or three years ago. Perhaps his new life has worked out better than the old one he might finally have managed to escape. In any case, riddled with unresolved agendas, possibly real, possibly imagined, and haunted by events, possibly real, possibly imagined, 027 can at least console himself with one thing. For though his testimony was partly discredited, and though his experience in the witness box must have been painful, had he not decided to pen that letter in 1997 and – for whatever reasons – come out partially into the open, the whole process of getting to the truth might never have begun in the first place.

10

AGENTS AND
HANDLERS: INFLICTION

Among the thousands of people whose evidence was considered by Saville and the hundreds who testified, many had serious security risks. But only one person was deemed to be so much at risk that they were not even allowed to give evidence. It is not known who the person is. It is not known where the person is. Indeed at times observers wondered whether the person even exists. It is someone who at some time was an agent of British Intelligence, someone known only by one word – a codename: 'Infliction'.

The reason that even this small amount of information managed to come out was because of a single sentence of evidence. It was a sentence that suggested a line of questioning and a line of inquiry that threatened to turn the proceedings and indeed the whole story of what happened on Bloody Sunday on its head.

On Day 8 of his epic opening statement in April 2000, Christopher Clarke, Counsel to the Inquiry, arrived at the subject of Martin McGuinness, who had yet to come forward to give evidence. The Inquiry had approached him several times to submit a statement but had so far received no response. McGuinness's evidence was of interest for, as Counsel laid them out, a number of reasons. Firstly, McGuinness was believed to be the commanding officer of the Provisional IRA around the time of Bloody Sunday.

Secondly, he had been on the march and had demonstrated that he had some knowledge of what happened. And finally because, as Clarke put it, 'there are before the Inquiry certain documents in which it is claimed that Mr McGuinness was in his capacity as a member of the Provisional IRA actively involved in the events of Bloody Sunday and that he was armed with, and may have fired, a Thompson submachine gun.'

This was something to make observers sit up. The story grew more curious. It became clear that the 'certain documents' before the Inquiry were ones that could have repercussions far beyond the remit of Lord Saville.

During its initial stages the Inquiry had requested of the UK intelligence services – MI5 and MI6 – any documents relevant to the events of Bloody Sunday. The intelligence services had duly provided a number of often heavily redacted materials relating to the events. The Tribunal were permitted to see unredacted versions. None of these documents would prove as controversial as one single page of paper. In the end extra weeks of hearings were needed to try to get to the truth not so much of a single page, as of a single sentence.

The sentence was part of a document relating to the debriefing of a UK government agent. The debriefing took place in The Hague, Holland, in April 1984. It read as follows:

From: THE HAGUE To: [REDACTED]
Copy: Head Office [REDACTED] INFLICTION NOTES
Please find attached notes connected with the debriefing of INFLICTION

And then over the page simply the following:

INFLICTION: DEBRIEFING

Below are a number of separate items of intelligence, reported by INFLICTION at various times, for dissemination as you see fit.

And then, item number one under the headline 'Martin McGuinness':

'Martin McGUINNESS had admitted to INFLICTION that he had personally fired the shot (from a Thompson machine gun on "single shot") from the Rossvill [sic] flats in Bogside that had precipitated the "bloody Sunday" episode.'

That was all. The other nineteen lines of type on the page were redacted. Only this remained.

But the revelation that this document existed and the claim that it made caused shockwaves. Martin McGuinness was by then not only a Member of Parliament but the Northern Ireland Education Minister. For years he had also been a prominent voice in calls for a full Inquiry to be set up. Now it looked as if he might, in fact, have started the whole tragedy.

McGuinness himself immediately and strongly denied the allegation, telling press that the claims were 'an attempt by British military to divert attention away from the fact that the Paras killed fourteen innocent civilians on that day'. But the ramifications of the document were undeniable and its release started a process that proved central to the Inquiry's efforts to get to the truth of what happened that day.

The Inquiry now had a lengthy additional task: to attempt to ascertain the truth or otherwise of the Hague debrief document. And the best way to do that was to find the person who had first made the claim. The task for the Tribunal was to hunt for the source: to search for Infliction.

During the course of what became known as the Troubles the British intelligence services were a determining factor in the state's war against the IRA. While the security forces, army and police carried out the day-to-day tasks of trying to keep law and order on the streets, the intelligence services fought a parallel and complementary war. Part of this work was the hard task of infiltrating the IRA, not just in order to find out what they were doing and enable the other forces to operate in a more effective manner against them, but also to pull apart the IRA from the inside. It is only in recent years that the success of this operation has begun, though only begun, to come to light.

At the end of the 1990s, Sean O'Callaghan, a former commanding officer of the IRA's Southern Command and a member of Sinn Fein's ruling council, revealed that he had been an informer for the Irish Garda, and had thwarted a huge number of IRA plots along the way. He wrote a book on his experiences, *The Informer*. Around the same time a number of British agents within the IRA also began to emerge. In 1997 Martin McGartland, who had been Agent 'Carol', published *Fifty Dead Men Walking*. By the time that the Saville Inquiry came to look into the matter of Infliction the trickle of informers appeared to have become a stream and then a flood. While the Saville hearings were going on there was the dramatic outing of the British agent known as 'Stakeknife'. The revelations about, and the identifying of, Freddie Scappaticci were particularly devastating to the IRA. 'Stakeknife' had been the deputy head of the IRA's 'nutting squad', an internal IRA organisation whose job included discovering and murdering supposed informers. That one of the heads of the IRA's unit searching for informers was himself an informer was a particularly bitter pill for the IRA, who liked to think that they ran their organisation not only effectively but autonomously.

In 2005 one of Gerry Adams's closest aides and Sinn Fein's most senior figures, Denis Donaldson, turned out to be an MI5 agent, and in 2008 it came as little surprise to discover that even Gerry Adams's driver – who was also on Adams's security team – had been an informer for MI5.

These informers, agents and double agents infiltrated the IRA to an extraordinary extent and rendered it, by the end, operationally all but incapable. With notable exceptions, most IRA bomb plots became known to – and were able to be thwarted by – the British authorities before the IRA had a chance to carry them out. And the network was wide as well as deep. Informers informed on informers to verify information. And in some cases, as is now becoming clear, certain informers appear to have been allowed to kill if it allowed them to retain or deepen their cover within the organisation. The network was not simple, is still not fully understood and remains the source of considerable controversy.

Given all of this, the revelation in 2000 that there was still another agent – yet to be discovered – who had been close to the leaders of the IRA was newsworthy in itself. As of course was the agent's only known allegation. But the steps that were taken both by the Security Service and eventually, and necessarily, by Lord Saville himself to protect the witness exceeded anything that had previously been heard of and suggested that the story of Infliction was a very deep and significant one indeed.

For two years after the single page of Infliction's Hague debrief was made public the question was whether or not the agent would make an appearance in front of the Tribunal. Many witnesses – noticeably the majority of military witnesses – had been given the right to testify behind pseudonyms or ciphers to give them the reassurance of anonymity. Other witnesses had been granted the right to testify from behind a screen. Some would testify from a foreign location. But Infliction, it soon became clear, was in a different league altogether. For this source the rules were different. During May 2002 there was a day of submissions during the course of which Counsel to the Inquiry explained that the Minister of State and the Tribunal had examined a 'bundle' of material relating to Infliction and said that 'so far as the practicalities are concerned, I think it is appropriate to observe that whatever decision the Tribunal reaches will produce an unsatisfactory result because, at any rate from the Inquiry's point of view, the only wholly satisfactory result would be for the Inquiry to call "Infliction" to give evidence before it.'

At which point Lord Saville intervened to make an important announcement. It had been decided, he said, that 'to call or indeed to make any attempt to call the individual known as "Infliction", who is overseas, would be in breach of the rights of that individual under Article 2 of the Convention on Human Rights. Accordingly', he said, 'we shall proceed upon the basis that "Infliction" will not be called to give evidence at this Inquiry.'

The legal representative of the Secretary of State explained this by saying that 'the risk of disclosure posed by the questioning envisaged here in relation to these witnesses would be so great that if this were a criminal trial ... the prosecution would have to be dropped and that is how serious the risk to "Infliction" is assessed to be.'

It all suggested the unparalleled fragility of Infliction's identity and the obviously vital importance of stopping any opportunity that anyone might have to work out who the agent was. If the extraordinary efforts carried out to protect the identity of other witnesses were still not enough to protect Infliction, then it was clear that the risk to the agent must be very considerable indeed. If he was in a foreign jurisdiction then why could he not speak from there? Others did. What was it about Infliction that made him different? Part of the answer came through by watching the lengths to which the Inquiry had to go even to secure hearings on the reliability of Infliction as a source.

The evidence could not simply be forgotten or discarded from consideration and so it had to be assessed in some other way. With serious implications for delay the Inquiry would now have to approach the Infliction evidence by an extremely circuitous route – taking the next best option by interviewing security agents who had knowledge of Infliction in order to try to ascertain his reliability as a source. A range of serving and former agents of the intelligence services were duly called to give written and finally oral evidence to Saville. This was arrived at only after further lengthy days of submissions by all the interested parties, not least the MoD and Security Service themselves. The process was not simple.

It soon became clear that even acquaintance with details relating to Infliction led to a level of precaution that was outstanding even for the British Security

Service. Two cases in point were those of 'Officer A' and 'former Officer B' – two of the witnesses called to testify on the reliability of Infliction. Both were Security Service witnesses. Both were obviously given anonymity and allowed to testify from behind a screen. With these provisions in place they were allowed to give written and oral evidence to the Inquiry. But they were deemed to be a particular risk by the Security Service because both of them were believed to have 'some knowledge' of Infliction's current whereabouts and it was possible that in the course of questioning a detail leading to Infliction could accidentally come out.

In order for Officers A and B not to be able to accidentally disclose any of those details the Security Service applied for the oral evidence of the Officers to be given under a so-called 'time-delay procedure'. This meant that anyone who wanted to ask questions of the witnesses must give a list of those questions to Counsel to the Inquiry, who then, alone, would be allowed to put approved questions to the witness. He would do so in a closed session in which the only other people present would be the Tribunal judges, legal representatives of the Security Service and current active members of the Security Service. And as if that was not already secretive enough, the Service requested that at the end of this process they should be given time to examine the transcript, redact anything they did not think should be further disseminated and all of this should be done on a schedule that would allow them time for judicial review if they and the Tribunal at any stage disagreed.

In the end Saville refused this application from the Security Service but he did rule that:

> No questions may be asked of a witness which might lead to the identification or whereabouts of Infliction. It is no doubt possible that something may be said inadvertently which bears on these matters... Of course the risks disclosure may bring will vary from person to person. However any questions asked of these witnesses will be controlled by the Tribunal to avoid any risk of inadvertent disclosure. As part of that control counsel for the Security Service may intervene to express concern at any question asked and indeed before any answer is made to a question.

And so began the strange and circuitous process of hearings from witnesses testifying about the reliability of a witness who was not allowed to testify.

The hurdles and obstacles had been considerable, but on 6 May 2003 observers of the Inquiry came in to find the witness stand screened. Behind the screen was an agent who could be heard but not seen. He was a senior intelligence figure to be known only by the rather disappointing name 'Julian'.

But the morning that Julian's two days of testimony began, and before the agent was even sworn, a lawyer acting for Martin McGuinness stood up and addressed the Tribunal. He objected to the hearing and attempted to make an application on behalf of his client, but, as Saville pointed out, there was a process for such objections and he was too late in making his. The lawyer protested that 'it does not need me to explain the importance of the sequence that is now to take place to Mr McGuinness in terms of his common law right to protect his good name and reputation and his right under the Convention Order, Article 10.'

But Saville refused the request. McGuinness's lawyer was told to put such matters in writing in the normal way. So Julian began to testify and so began one of the most extraordinary fortnights of evidence ever heard before a British judge.

None of the witnesses over the next two weeks were known by their names. There were senior agent-handlers who referred to simply by the names 'Julian', 'James' and 'David'. There was also an increasingly prominent former agent known by the pseudonym 'Martin Ingram'. Accompanying their evidence were officers of the Security Service known as Officers A, B, C and so on. To make it all the more confusing, the people to whom they were referring were known only by another set of ciphers. For instance, before the main hearings on the reliability of Infliction the Inquiry had to hear evidence on the reliability of another informer, now dead, who was known as 'Observer B'. There was also 'Observer C' and so on.

For the intelligence-witness period of the Inquiry all witnesses testified from behind a curtain, able to be seen only by the members of the Tribunal. Some were not even there in person. The former director of intelligence, known only by the name David, was eighty- four years old by the time he gave testimony. He was in a foreign jurisdiction somewhere and testified by video link. The monitor on which his face was seen could be viewed only by the Tribunal and lawyers. The screen itself was behind a curtain. Sitting beside the television with the former director of intelligence's face on it was a representative of the Inquiry ready to pull the plug on the television if anybody attempted to make a leap for it and pull back the curtain. As a result, for day after day, disembodied voices of agents sometimes speaking from a foreign country, talking in a different technical language from any of the other witnesses and with their own unique frames of reference, punctured the silence of Central Hall Westminster.

The caution appeared to be appropriate. For among those testifying were some of the most senior agents in the British services. In each case it was almost certainly the first and only occasion on which they would speak in public about what they and their colleagues did – and do.

By 1972 the first intelligence witness – Julian – had been in the Security Service for five and a half years and had worked as an agent-runner in Northern Ireland. Along with someone called James (also deceased after giving a statement to Saville) he ran the agent known as Observer B. James had been forced to give a number of updates to his original statement to the Inquiry as new questions arose and new evidence came to light. And though much was redacted in the published version, an idea of how the British services ran their agents began to emerge. For instance, talking about an agent known as Observer C, Julian said:

> Observer C was described as reliable i.e. his reporting had been substantiated by other intelligence or borne out by events. On one occasion, his reporting was judged of sufficient merit to be shown to the Home Secretary and the Prime Minister. In the weeks prior to Bloody Sunday, he produced a series of reports about attitudes among the Republican community in Londonderry to the army and to the IRA; plans for civil unrest and the IRA's activities locally. While he was not a member of the IRA and therefore did not have direct access to its decision-making, Observer C was a very accurate observer of events around him and was a member of community groups such as the Londonderry Tenants Association. He was thus well placed to report on reactions to British government policy in Northern Ireland and on plans for protest marches, demonstrations, etc.

Apart from Infliction the most significant intelligence evidence was from Observer B, and like Infliction this was partly because his evidence seemed to fly against almost all other evidence given about what happened that day. This person's extraordinary evidence had been released to Saville several years earlier. Observer B had even made a statement to the Inquiry but had died before being called to give evidence. And so, like Infliction, the hearings had to attempt to discover his reliability. His evidence was important because it appeared to show the IRA to have been very much less innocent than it had tried to present itself.

Observer B said in his statement that on 25 January 1972, five days before the civil rights march, he and somebody referred to only as 'X' had seen IRA Auxiliaries (IRA affiliates who were not full members) parading and drilling in Derry. He claimed that while he was in the area of the Rossville Flats the IRA Auxiliaries were drilling in Glenfada Park. He said that he saw the men march across Rossville Street and go into the flats. Observer B saw another source whose name was redacted and replaced only with the letter 'X' and stated:

> I saw X. I said to him, 'What's going on?' He replied, 'You've noticed them?' I said, 'I've noticed them – I've seen them practicing – what do you think they are up to?' [Redacted] X replied, 'They are practising for Sunday. They were here yesterday at the same time.'

Observer B went on:

Observer B claimed that he saw similar drilling by the IRA on 27 January.

On the day after Bloody Sunday he reported speaking to two men who had been in the city on the day itself and who said that, after a few minutes of shooting, they had seen men running from the Rossville Flats to a car by Free Derry Corner. One of the witnesses, 'A', said they saw two men 'open the boot of the car and throw in two Thompson submachine guns, a rifle and pistol before getting into the car and driving off '. The other witness, 'B', said that the back of the car was 'full' of Thompson submachine guns.

Observer B met up with Julian and related this to him on the Wednesday after Bloody Sunday. He also revealed one other fact, which was that one of his sources, 'X', claimed that when the shooting was starting up on the day he saw the IRA Auxiliaries firing from the balconies of the Rossville Flats.

> He did not see how many guns were used but said that there were a wide variety of firearms used and that not all of the Auxiliaries had a weapon. He said that 'it was pandemonium – absolute bedlam'. He said that the Paratroopers had made it to the Flats faster than that section of the crowd that had been rioting had anticipated. This had caused panic among the rioters and their response was to run. He said that the Auxiliaries also panicked when the Paras reached the Flats

and they [four lines of text redacted] stashed their weapons in small rooms off the landings where water mains were housed. X said that the first shot he heard was the thud of a Thompson and was convinced that the IRA had fired first that day.

I told [redacted] X to keep quiet about what he had told me. He said, 'Why? – it was their fault – the Army are being blamed.' I told him that if he carried on saying that that he would get himself into trouble but he was adamant. I got the impression that he had told a number of people what he had told me.

Observer B says that he saw X only once or twice again after this conversation. There is then a long-redacted section and B's statement ends. Contemporary debriefing notes revealed that Observer B's account of events at the time claimed that the guns were not only in the cars at Free Derry Corner, but had been distributed just behind the Rossville Flats.

The first thing that was needed to assess the reliability of Observer B's evidence was to see if the contemporary intelligence documents from Observer B in 1972 had made the same points as he had in his statement thirty years later. The internal Security Service reports signed by James and Julian in 1972 came back out of the files and corroborated that this was indeed what Observer B had told them at the time. These memos included summaries of debriefings sent to the Director of Intelligence for Northern Ireland in London. The reports from Observer B in the days immediately after Bloody Sunday included the details of the guns in the cars but interestingly not any details of the alleged 'drilling' in Glenfada Park in the days before Bloody Sunday. During questioning, his former handler, Julian, conceded that it was a 'possibility' that Observer B had, looking back, confused this occasion with another. But on the matter of the guns in the cars and other points, Observer B's evidence was consistent across the decades.

During his evidence Julian revealed that he and James had taken over responsibility for Observer B from an army source in July 1971. He said that in his experience Observer B was 'a very valuable agent', adding, 'He didn't have anything to gain by lying to us. I believe his motivation to have been a desire for peace. He was a brave man,' Julian went on, describing the work he undertook as 'very dangerous'.

But some of the less ideological motivations of informers also came to light. It transpired that Observer B had refused a salary and accepted only expenses until the August after Bloody Sunday, but that from August 1972 he was given a salary of £50 a month. That same August he was given an unannounced one-off bonus of £500. Most importantly Julian was able to confirm that the intelligence services' own files on Observer B in the year of Bloody Sunday and the year following rated him as 'a reliable agent ... whose reports are essentially detailed'. This last point, Julian pointed out, was important. 'The more detail an agent gives the easier it is to check his reliability.' On a number of occasions they found his intelligence corroborated by other sources. Julian also recorded that the files show that by February 1973 Observer B was very tired and being seen 'too frequently for his own good' by his handler – seven times in one month in one case. In 1974 his file recorded that he was assessed to have given 'four years valuable service under very hazardous conditions'. Those responsible for him from 1972 to 1974 rated him extremely highly, and although it transpired that Observer C was the main agent in Derry, Observer B, according to Julian, visited the city regularly and was certainly an important source whom the handlers, looking back, and the paperwork from the time show to be a reliable and important informer.

It became clear that before the march had taken place the intelligence agencies received substantial amounts of information suggesting that the IRA were going to use it as an opportunity to draw the army into a gun battle. The intelligence services released the contemporary Joint Intelligence Committee papers. Among other things these reported that the recent disturbances in Derry had been inspired by the IRA and that the IRA were thought to be planning to 'organise disturbances in Londonderry designed to draw the security forces into the Bogside and there attack them'. There was a specific briefing that the march on 30 January 'might well develop into rioting and even a shooting war'. The Inquiry had already heard from INQ 2241, the former senior military intelligence officer in Northern Ireland, who had said in his statement that 'it was one of the IRA's Province-wide Standard Operating Procedures [SOPs] to use disturbances as cover for its activities. The real surprise would have been if they had not followed these SOPs.'

Much of the questioning on this was answered by the 84-year-old man known as David. While questioning David, Barry MacDonald, the lawyer for the majority of the families, became angry.

> Q: Can I ask you first of all, without saying where you are, why you were not prepared to come to London to give evidence to this Inquiry?
>
> A: The reason for that is that I now find it extremely difficult to concentrate for any length of time and I am fairly shattered when I have had to do so and it takes time to recover. [These exchanges were happening on 13 May.]

Q: Can I ask when you last travelled to London?

A: When did I last travel to London, um, I know, yes, it was on, on the 11th when I signed the document.

Q: The 11 April. Is that the 11 April this year?

A: No, sorry, I signed it here, sorry, I have got it wrong, yes.

Q: Sorry, are you saying this on the basis of your own recollection or are you saying this on the basis of prompts that you are receiving in that room? I ask you that because you seem to be looking around a lot.

LORD SAVILLE: I think, be assured on that point, Mr MacDonald, we have Mr Tate [the representative of the Inquiry] in the room.

MR MacDONALD: It appears that there are other people in the room, maybe I have misunderstood this, but it looks as if there are other people in the room apart from Mr Tate; is that right?

MR TATE: Lord Saville, in addition to myself there is David's son, the technician and a gentleman from the Security Service who is helping me hand documents over to David.

LORD SAVILLE: I would assume, Mr Tate, that you were ensuring there was no communication between the last of those you mentioned and the witness.

MR TATE: Indeed.

MR MacDONALD: It is just, David, I can see you looking for reassurance, perhaps, from other people in the room and I was going to ask you whether there was a member of the Security Service in the room with you and that appears to be the case; do you understand? Can you hear me?

A: Yes, but as has just been explained, there is a member of the Security Service.

Everybody was aware that the evidence was secretive by nature, but developments like this threw even some of the lawyers. During David's evidence at least one of the relatives of the dead, Eileen Doherty, the widow of Patrick Doherty, who was shot dead behind the Rossville Flats, walked out in protest. She told press that the proceedings were 'supposed to be open and transparent but had descended into farce' and said she would not return until David had

148

finished giving evidence.

Amid all this spookery there came two brief, though not brief enough, comic interludes.

The first involved the intervention of a former army intelligence officer known by the name 'Martin Ingram'. By 2000 Ingram's name had been appearing in the press for a while and when the matter of Infliction arose he stepped forward to the Inquiry to tell them that from his experience in the army's Force Research Unit in the 1980s it was his belief that the document about Infliction might not be authentic. In his statement he suggested that Infliction might not even exist though by the time he came to testify he had changed his mind on this and decided he did.

Martin Ingram was unusual for a witness in that he was verbose, almost chatty, in the box. He clearly enjoyed the opportunity to speak and get asked questions as an expert. The problem was that he had very little to say about Infliction because he had never come across the agent or his information during his time working in army intelligence. Nor would he have done. It swiftly became apparent that the purpose of the appearance seemed to be vanity. But it had its moments. At one point Ingram had the probably unique claim of using his time as a witness at the Bloody Sunday Inquiry to tell an old joke. Questioned by Edwin Glasgow, representative for the majority of soldiers, he was asked a set of questions on the nature of agent-running. Ingram was clearly enjoying himself and decided to stretch his legs:

> A: Now the local IO [Intelligence Officer] has no real need for any knowledge of any source information. If that information is going to be exploited, which it obviously was during that period, then if the IO needed to be told, he would be told. He is treated very similar to a mushroom; he is kept in the dark and fed on shit, until you need to use him.

'I am sure that is very entertaining,' Glasgow replied, 'and will feature well in somebody's book.'

If anybody was left wondering, after Martin Ingram's testimony, what type of people can go into the intelligence business, two other people who stepped forward at the same time to share their concerns over Infliction helped clear the matter up. For in the same period that Ingram gave his evidence there were appearances by the man who was then probably Britain's best-known ex-spook.

And he brought his equally ex-spook girlfriend.

David Shayler came to public attention in 1997. He had joined MI5 six years earlier. When he left his employment he alleged in national newspapers that his former employers had been involved in several plots including an attempt to assassinate the Libyan leader, Colonel Gaddafi, and had also spied on people who were now members of Britain's Labour cabinet. The revelations were a sensation in the British press and led to attempts to arrest Shayler, who, amid ferocious publicity, fled to France to escape the jurisdiction of the British courts. From there he made various high- profile appearances on the British media and became a celebrity. After three years in France – where he was joined by his girlfriend Annie Machon, who had also been in the services – he gave up and returned home to Britain where he was charged with a number of offences including breaking the Official Secrets Act. He was tried, found guilty and sentenced to six months in prison. Along the way Shayler continued to keep press interest in his case alive by feeding titbits of remaining stories from his time in the Service.

By 2003 he was out of prison but he had one more burst of publicity. Machon and Shayler had read about the Infliction– McGuinness allegation when it emerged, and of their own volition approached the Saville Inquiry claiming that they had vital information for the Inquiry about the agent. In 2001 Shayler wrote about the matter for a Sunday newspaper. All this was happening while Shayler was fighting for the case against him to be dropped and his name cleared. Publicity remained high as he let it be known that in his and his girlfriend's opinions, Infliction was known within the service to be a 'bullshitter'. In 2002 they signed statements to this effect and in May 2003, amid a rare burst of press interest, Machon and Shayler entered Central Hall Westminster to greet journalists on the front steps before giving evidence to the Tribunal. No witnesses were on the stand for a shorter space of time. It took just an hour for the Inquiry to question both.

Shayler claimed that he came across the codename Infliction while going through a file relating to someone else in 1993. He had been in the Service two years and when he asked a colleague about the source he had seen referenced, the source told him, 'This guy's a bullshitter.' But it transpired in evidence that Shayler had never seen the file on Infliction, never saw any documents about the reliability of Infliction and never had any idea of Infliction's identity. He had also said that he thought Infliction was not a Security Service agent because such agents do not have single-word codenames, but two- word 'nicknames' or code numbers.

Annie Machon meanwhile claimed that entirely separately from her boyfriend, and when taking up a new post, she was reassessing old files and came across one that referred to the reliability of Infliction as a source. She claimed that the file had the words 'the reliability of this agent is being assessed' at the top. She asked her predecessor in her post what this meant and she said that he responded 'to the effect that he thought everyone' in the section 'knew he [Infliction] was a "bullshitter"'.

Unfortunately for the running of the Tribunal these satellite claims about the reliability of Infliction now themselves had to be followed up by hearings on the reliability of Shayler and Machon. Unfortunately for both of them and their subsequent media careers it became obvious that this was a far easier matter.

Machon's predecessor in the post, Officer N, gave a statement in which he said that he had never had any such conversation with his successor. Furthermore he said that he understood that Infliction had been long resettled by the time that Machon had entered the service in 1991, and that there would have been no reassessment of the files of the type described by Machon. They were reviewed for things that might have been missed in the past and for 'exploitable leads' but not for a reassessment of reliability as Machon claimed. And, contra Machon, if in fact his past information was being gone through again, it would demonstrate that Infliction had been a reliable source. If he had been a 'bullshitter', his files would not still be being combed over for any missed or now relevant evidence. Officer N added:

> I am not, nor have ever knowingly been, aware of Infliction's identity. The identity of an agent was and is kept on a strict need to know basis. If an officer unintentionally discovered the identity of an agent, the officer should by rights confess to the agent-running officer and be entered on a list.

> I do not recall having formed any particular view of the reliability or accuracy of Infliction's reporting.

He also denied that he or anyone he had ever worked with had ever described Infliction as 'a bullshitter'.

Meanwhile Shayler's former line manager, by then a member of the Security

Service for twenty-one years and now in 'senior management', had, by his own admission, heard of Infliction but had also never seen the Infliction files. And he denied that he had any knowledge of Infliction's reliability. 'I was not his handler, nor did I have regular access to his reporting.' He said that he had never discussed Infliction with either Shayler or Machon.

The man who had been Infliction's handler, Officer A, was forced to give another statement reacting to Shayler and Machon's comments. As he pointed out, Shayler and Machon had joined the Service 'long after Infliction had ceased to provide intelligence to the Service and long after 1984', the date of the Hague debrief. He also stressed how wrong Shayler was to think that Infliction was not a Security Service agent. He said, 'I understand that investigation of Service papers has shown that Mr Shayler is not recorded as having had access to any of the Infliction files. Nor was he ever posted to the Irish agent-running section.'

Though they both tried to string their claimed information out in the box, Shayler and Machon made unimpressive witnesses. By their own admission, they were talking about an agent who had not only been dealt with above their pay-grade but had finished dealings with the Service long before their time. The canteen gossip that Shayler related was not borne out by any of the former colleagues who had to testify in reaction to their claims. Their day of evidence turned out to be a forgettable one, memorable principally for the number of times very proper and highly paid lawyers were forced to use variants of the word 'bullshit'.

Both Shayler and Machon have, in the years since testifying to Saville, eked out careers as conspiracy theorists, in particular relating to the attacks of 11 September 2001. Shayler is the main source for a claim that the planes that flew into the Twin Towers in New York were actually missiles camouflaged by holograms. In 2007 Machon and Shayler were part of an unsuccessful attempt to sue President Bush in the Irish courts for alleged complicity in the attacks. In subsequent speeches Shayler has approvingly cited the fake *Protocols of the Elders of Zion*. In 2007 he declared in an interview with the *Daily Mail* that he was the Messiah and was recently revealed to be living as a transvestite alter ego called Delores Kane. Machon and he have since separated. In 2009 Shayler was evicted from a squat in Surrey. He was quoted by the press saying that he was not bothered by the eviction, because he was 'the son of God'.

Though it transpired that Machon and Shayler could not shed much light on the reliability of Infliction there were others who could.

152

One of the principal witnesses to testify to the reliability or otherwise of Infliction was Officer A. By the time he came to make his statement to the Inquiry he had been in the Security Service for twenty-five years and currently held 'a senior management position'. In 1984 he had been involved with running and handling agents. One of the agents he had handled was Infliction. And he was the author of the now famous memo about Martin McGuinness.

Officer A said they had a relatively short professional relationship. He handled Infliction for only six to seven months. But during that time he saw him a lot. He described Infliction – at the time that he was handling him – as being 'an established agent' but confirmed that he had not been an agent in 1972.

> With hindsight I can say that Infliction was a reliable agent. I say with hindsight because it is not always possible to judge immediately the accuracy of the information supplied, and it is often years before corroboration of it comes to light. Sometimes information never gets confirmed in this way. In 1984 Infliction was providing information which was potentially of great value, but much of it could not be verified at the time. This lack of ability to verify the information meant that some recipients of the information viewed Infliction's reporting with scepticism. Also, there were, as with most agents, some things he (Infliction) did not or would not tell me. Looking back at Infliction's information, there has been corroboration for much of what he told us, but not everything.

And relating to the particular, explosive, statement given to him by Infliction he said that he wrote his report shortly after the conversation, and confirmed that the redacted lines on the same page of debrief had nothing to do with Bloody Sunday, and that the information about McGuinness related to a conversation Infliction had had with McGuinness 'some time previously. I understood that this conversation had taken place fairly soon after Bloody Sunday...

Infliction was relating to me the terms of a conversation he had personally had with Martin McGuinness.'

Made public along with Officer A's evidence were a number of other documents, some heavily redacted, that provided crucial extra details about Infliction. One telegraph from Northern Ireland to Government Intelligence and Security Officers, dated 17 May 1984, describes Infliction as 'a former prominent member of the Provisional IRA'. A desk comment adds that 'at the time of Bloody Sunday McGuinness was a senior member, if not Officer

153

Commanding (OC), of Londonderry PIRA. Although we have no collateral for the above report there is intelligence that McGuinness was actively involved in PIRA attacks in the city shortly after Bloody Sunday.'

An internal document from later in the year fleshed this out further, saying that the former prominent member of the PIRA says that 'although not widely known, it was McGuinness himself who fired the first shot on Bloody Sunday which in turn led to the killing of thirteen civilians by British troops. According to the former prominent member McGuinness, who is a devout Catholic and has problems equating Marxism with Catholicism, has considerable guilt feelings about his own involvement in that incident.'

Finally one further released document states that 'this seems to be on McGuinness's conscience.' This suspicion arose from the fact that McGuinness 'has spoken to Infliction about it several times'. This comes from a document from November 1984 that is a transcript of a tape. It relates a conversation between Officer B (B) and Infliction (I). It says:

> B says I has already told him about the fact that McGuinness has this conflict because of 'his' Catholicism. McGuinness seems to be Mr Nice Guy, although really 'he' was a pretty hard terrorist.
>
> I says that McGuinness found himself in a certain position. 'He' found himself as OC in Derry [sentence redacted] One thing that bothers McGuinness about the Bloody Sunday thing was that 'he' fired the first shot, and no one knows this. This seems to be on McGuinness's conscience – 'he' has spoken to I about it several times. B comments that I has said no one knows about this: I knows for one. How many people know?
>
> I doesn't know.
>
> B asks why McGuinness told I.
>
> [Sentence redacted] McGuinness has a lot of ups and downs. B asks if McGuinness would be alarmed to discover that 'we' knew 'that' (that McGuinness fired the first shot on Bloody Sunday). I pauses before saying that it would be a big destabilising point with 'him'. But how and why would you make it known? And when would be the best time? He asks, 'Do you do something on him to say that there's evidence?'
>
> B wonders if Adams knows.
>
> I doesn't know, but reminds B that the fact that the Brits murdered thirteen

people on Bloody Sunday, which they did, is one of the main planks of IRA mythical martyrdom. What no one else knows is that it was pushed by Martin McGuinness who in 'his' own mind feels he is as much to blame as the British.

B says this is why he is asking whether 'he' would be concerned to know that 'we' know.

Intriguingly, according to Officer A's statement, this conversation is not only in document form.

Apparently it is from a tape recording 'found' in the Service archives. So a tape recording exists somewhere in the Security Service's archives of Infliction speaking. Why was this not able to be released? Presumably, again, because even the sound or tone of the voice could drastically narrow down the possibilities of who Infliction is.

When Officer A testified on Day 326, Counsel to the Inquiry questioned him carefully on the central issue, on which he above all other people could be able to shed light.

Q: Looking at the information Mr McGuinness is said to have provided to Infliction and the account that Infliction gave to you, did Infliction at any time tell you why he had provided you with this information about Mr McGuinness?

A: Sorry, did Infliction tell me why he had provided – no, he did not say, no. Not specifically about, you know – he did not say, 'I am telling you this because...', no.

Q: As far as you are aware, did Infliction have any reason to lie when giving you this information?

A: Well, I have thought about this a great deal, particularly since I was asked to make a statement about it. I cannot – I cannot think of any credible reason why Infliction should have lied about this particular issue. He was not asking for, nor did he ask for, any additional payment for this piece of information; he did not dislike or resent Mr McGuinness, as far as I know, and certainly never said that he did, so I cannot think of any critical reason why he should have lied about this piece of information.
...
Q: You have told us that Infliction provided you, on other occasions, with information about Mr McGuinness and you have also said that it was sometimes impossible for information to be verified. Did Infliction ever give you any other

155

information about Mr McGuinness that could be cross-checked?

A: Yes, he provided us with many reports about Mr McGuinness, many of which could be verified, some of which we could not. I do not recall any reports that he provided about Mr McGuinness proving to be wrong.

Q: Did Infliction ever tell you how he came to know Mr McGuinness?

A: Not specifically, but he knew him quite well and was friendly with him.

Q: Was that something that he told you, that Infliction told you?

A: Yes.

Q: He told you that he was friendly with Mr McGuinness. Did that friendship seem consistent with what you knew yourself of Infliction's activities and role?

A: Yes, it was entirely consistent.

Q: Did you have any intelligence from any source other than Infliction about the relationship between Infliction and Mr McGuinness?

A: Yes, we had some information which corroborated the fact that they knew each other and had known each other for some time and appeared to get on well.

Q: Did you have any information that was inconsistent with what Infliction told you about his relationship with Mr McGuinness?

A: No.

Q: You have said that Infliction did not appear to harbour any resentment against Mr McGuinness, in fact he no longer had access to the organisation. Did he ever express any resentment, for any reason, against Mr McGuinness?

A: Not that I can recall, not to me.

Q: Did you ever discover from any source any evidence of bad feeling between Infliction and Mr McGuinness?

A: No.

Q: Do you know from any source of any incident that might have caused Infliction to bear any sort of grudge against Mr McGuinness?

A: No, I cannot think of any such instance.

Two questions then had – and have – to be addressed; though neither could, as it turned out, be answered by the Inquiry. Firstly: was Infliction's claim true? And if it was true: who is Infliction?

If Infliction was telling the truth then it is something that McGuinness has obviously spent decades trying to hide and there are two consequent possibilities. Either McGuinness told numerous people – perhaps a great many – that he had fired the first shot on Bloody Sunday, or he told only one person. It would seem an unlikely secret to impart to a large number of people or even more than a couple. And so if Infliction is telling the truth and if, as is likely, McGuinness did not spread this secret around widely then it leads to an obvious but important point. If McGuinness only told one person or if he told people only very selectively then it follows that McGuinness must know who Infliction is.

It is possible that the pool of candidates is very small. And this leads to the question of why even now Infliction's right to life was threatened – why even a heavily redacted statement or an appearance to testify even under the tightest restrictions was impossible.

It is possible that the reason is that Infliction would have been immediately identifiable to McGuinness once even one word was uttered. One possibility is that Infliction is a woman, and that obviously even from the first word uttered from behind a screen this would make the number of former close confidants of McGuinness involved at a high level in the IRA immediately identifiable.

The second possible explanation is that Infliction is someone who is still close to McGuinness and/or other senior Republicans. It remains a possibility that Infliction is still, or is once again, high up in the Republican movement and either is once again working for the intelligence services or stopped some years ago but is currently in a sufficiently important position that his usefulness would be jeopardised once he/she was identified as Infliction. Perhaps the agent was a priest to whom McGuinness confessed and who broke the secrets of the confessional while reporting as a British agent. Perhaps this would have become clear the moment he gave evidence. It would certainly explain why McGuinness had mentioned the wrestling with his conscience to the agent.

Which itself leads to the few remaining possibilities. These include the possibility that something else entirely is happening here. And though we are in the smoke-and-mirrors game of the intelligence services it is worth pointing them out.

It is possible that there is not a word of truth in the claim. Which means that there are a number of explanations. One is that the Security Service put out – that is, deliberately forged – the allegedly contemporaneous documents in order to implicate McGuinness in the tragedy of the day. The motivations for doing that could be various. One could be an effort to, in however small a way, try to let the army off the hook for their actions on the day. Or perhaps they did it for some other motive that nevertheless in the end still aimed to lay the blame on, or simply smear, McGuinness.

Alternatively there is an entirely different game being played here that we know nothing about and can guess little about. Broadly speaking these possibilities fall into a couple of forms. First, it is possible that the whole episode is a colossal double, triple or quadruple bluff. Conceivably, as McGuinness climbed higher and higher into the firmament of the British establishment, he had to be able to show that, although part of the new establishment in his ministerial and deputy-first-ministerial roles, he was nevertheless not 'of ' the establishment. In other words it is possible that a situation like this has been planted –unconvincing, but perhaps enough to give out the signal that he might still have enemies – and the Service is deliberately trying to show hardline Republicans and others that McGuinness, far from being a sell-out, is opposed even now by powerful forces within the security establishment. That is a powerful narrative and one that plays directly to certain egos and well-entrenched beliefs.

The other possibility is perhaps the most complicated of all. But it bears consideration.

For many years now it has been said that there is one more very senior informer still to be exposed at the very heart of the Northern Ireland IRA progress from guns to government. As high-level informers have been outed one by one, this rumour and suspicion has nevertheless remained.

If one man has enjoyed a particularly easy ride by the standards and company of his time, that man is Martin McGuinness. Perhaps McGuinness does indeed know who Infliction is. Perhaps he knows the identity of the person who told the

Security Service that he felt guilt over Bloody Sunday. Perhaps McGuinness knows – because McGuinness is Infliction.

11

THE PRIME MINISTER:
EDWARD HEATH

At the time of Bloody Sunday Edward Heath was the Prime Minister of Great Britain. By the time he came to testify to Lord Saville he had a reputation as one of the most bitter and curmudgeonly men in Britain. When he appeared at the Saville Inquiry in January 2003 it became clear that he was not as pleasant as he was reputed to be.

Heath had remained in office until 1974 when he lost the year's second general election to the Labour Party and Harold Wilson returned to office. In the aftermath of the election defeat Heath of course suffered another defeat, one he appears to have taken far more personally, as he was replaced as head of the Conservative Party by a woman whom he had promoted into the cabinet and first made a force in British politics: Margaret Thatcher.

The succeeding years were not kind to Heath. Furious at his party's treatment of him and bitter at his successor, he refused any cabinet posts and spent the next twenty-six years on the back benches of the Commons, finally serving for more than half a century as an MP.

Late in 1997, as the possibility of a new Inquiry into events and an official apology from the new Labour government was being considered, Sir Edward Heath gave a rare interview on the subject to Channel 4. He appeared live from their Salisbury studio, following the simmering interview given by Colonel Wilford in which the colonel had tried to lay some of the blame on the former Prime Minister. But as he was to repeatedly state, Heath believed that he had done everything that he could do. He had invited the Lord Chief Justice to preside over an Inquiry and was proud of the fact that Lord Widgery's swiftness had meant that he had been able to hand over the completed report to the House of Commons in two and a half months. He described the report as 'very balanced' and expressed himself 'saddened by some of the things which the colonel has just been saying'. Lord Widgery, he said, 'didn't blame his forces' but said that 'they carried out their orders' and 'were not blameworthy'.

Asked if he would recommend a new Inquiry he said that he could not comment because that was a matter for 'the Prime Minister of the day'. But if there were a new Inquiry would he be prepared to give evidence? 'I have no evidence to give,' he said. 'All the evidence I can give is everything which was handed to the Widgery Inquiry.'

And he denied that politicians like himself should take any responsibility for what happened. 'I can't accept this view at all,' said Heath, 'and I was astonished to hear the colonel saying it. It's the first time I've heard anybody in the army say they wanted to pass it off to the politicians. And when I was commanding a regiment I certainly didn't take that view.'

As far as Heath was concerned his actions, and the actions of his government in 1972, had not merely been correct, they had been exemplary. He was right, he said, to declare the marches illegal. And he was right, in his statement to the House of Commons immediately after the events, to express the fact that government 'deeply regrets' the casualties. 'You can't go further than that,' he claimed.

The interviewer flattered him with his legacy in Europe. But, thus softened, he was asked if Ireland was a 'dark chapter' for him.

> No, because Northern Ireland was in a state of war and what we succeeded in doing was to have a conference which brought about the unity of Northern Ireland by establishing a coalition government. This was in November–December 1973. And that operated with all three parties and it went on until May of the following year. By this time Mr Wilson had taken over, and unfortunately he didn't give it the support which it needed... But we were the only people – we still are the only people – who have reached a governmental solution to the problems in Northern Ireland.

And thus he summed up his position. No regrets over the way in which he had handled things. Regrets over the loss of life, but a certainty that everything that could be done had been done in the right and proper way.

161

And there Heath's position might have stayed, had not two events occurred. The first was the setting up of the Saville Inquiry shortly after the Channel 4 interview. It was obvious from the outset that Heath would prove one of the Inquiry's most senior and important witnesses. The second event was that as the Inquiry got under way, new evidence of Edward Heath's involvement emerged. The former Prime Minister was the most senior figure in the political landscape of 1972 and the most senior scalp that Republicans could hope to get from the Inquiry. Some of what came out seemed to suggest that the darkest conspiracy theories of the Republican movement might have some basis in fact after all.

Sir Edward Heath signed his first statement to the Inquiry in 2000 and, as more evidence came to light, a second in January 2003 just days before his lengthy testimony got under way. By that stage there were some serious charges that he had to rebut.

In his statement to Lord Saville, Heath gave the commonsense reason why a top-to-bottom government conspiracy could hardly have been planned. What happened on Bloody Sunday was very much against the interests of the British government of the time.

As Heath said, 'The tragic deaths in Londonderry on 30 January 1972 outraged the Catholic community, increased support for the IRA and destroyed the prospect of a political initiative. It is there- fore absurd to suggest that Her Majesty's Government intended or was prepared to risk the events which occurred.'

Of another of the 'smoking guns', the Ford memorandum about shooting ringleaders, he was equally dismissive. His government's aim in January 1972 was, he repeatedly said, a 'general wish that the temperature should be kept as low as possible' in Northern Ireland and that the government wished for a 'quiet performance' at the march. And he said that he had been completely unaware of the confidential memo from General Ford to General Tuzo until it had been recently declassified. In any case, again, it made no sense, he said, because it went directly against his government's principal aim and policy of using 'minimum force'.

And as for the allegedly damning quote by Lord Hailsham (the former Quintin Hogg) about shooting the King's enemies, Heath dismissed the comments as an 'outburst'. 'I think it must have been at some gathering at which he jumped up,' he said. 'He exploded in a very Quintin-like way and said we must realise we could take this action – in fact, we were under an obligation to take this action.' But he was dismissive. 'People just said, well, that was Quintin and we got on with it. Certainly as a government, of which I was Prime Minister, we took no notice at all.'

He was backed up by the statement of the then Chief of the General Staff, Lord Carver, who gave a statement to Saville in 1999 but died in 2001 before being able to give evidence. In his statement to the Inquiry Carver had said that 'there was never any question of shooting the ringleaders of a riot in Northern Ireland. It would have been totally inappropriate; we did not want to create martyrs.' But there was one other accusation against Heath that had arisen during the course of the Inquiry. That was the accusation that he had 'fixed' the Widgery Inquiry from the outset. Heath completely rejected the accusation. He described Lord Widgery as a man whose 'integrity was beyond doubt and question'. The quote about 'fighting a propaganda war' as well as a military war in Northern Ireland was not meant to influence him. It was, he said, a legitimate point to make to him because he foresaw that the Inquiry would attract substantial media attention and that Lord Widgery would find himself in the middle of it.

Those were the explanations that Heath had for his actions. But they were certainly not enough to satisfy the legal representatives of the families. They, the families and their supporters had waited many years to get to the man who was at the head of the government at the time and who, it was hoped, could still be shown to have been at the centre of a plot.

Going in on this basis – that Heath was guilty until proven innocent – was probably one of the worst tactical mistakes made by any of the lawyers during the course of the Inquiry. Indeed, it backfired terribly. Now with a hearing aid, dressed in a dark suit, and with one eyebrow almost permanently cocked in the direction of his questioner, Heath responded to the interrogative approach very grudgingly, revealing almost nothing.

If he was rarely treated with the respect that he felt was due, nevertheless he did not expect to be treated like this. The clashes with Michael Lavery QC on behalf of most of the families proved some of the most entertaining as well as contentious of the Inquiry. Heath may have been old, but he was far from tamed, and Lavery wound him up from the outset. Lavery put it to Heath that he had wanted direct rule to succeed because the alternative was 'deemed to be contrary to British interests'. 'Not at all,' said Heath.

Q: Was that one of the reasons?

A: I have given you the answer.

Q: Are you saying to the Tribunal that it was the only reason and that British interests were not taken into account at all?

A: I have nothing further to add. I have made it quite plain what my view is.

Lavery tried to go at it again, repeating what he presumed the situation to be. Heath's reply was straightforward.

A: Completely wrong.

There was no better luck when Lavery tried again. 'That is not for me to answer,' Heath told him. Lavery claimed otherwise. Heath got gruffer.

A: I have given you my answer. Q: You have not, Sir Edward.

A: Yes, I have. I have nothing more to say.

Q: In other words, you are refusing to answer the question; is that right?

A: Not at all. I have answered it.

Q: If you say you have nothing further to say, then why do you not answer my question? It is a simple question, Sir Edward.

A: You have had my answer and I ask the Chairman to deal with it.

Not for the first or last time Lord Saville was forced to intervene. Every time the lawyers got more pressing Heath clammed up further. He was clearly as unhappy with the manner of questioning as the lawyers were with the manner of answering. At a number of stages Lavery was forced to appeal to Saville. 'I have been trying to elicit an answer from [him] for the last five minutes and he still has not answered it,' Lavery complained more than once.

'You can keep on pressing, but you will not get an answer,' Heath told Lavery when he tried to come back again.

All of this was the prelude to perhaps the most difficult exchange between Heath and his interrogator. Lavery was trying to ask Heath about his involvement in the issue of Northern Ireland. Quoting Heath's statement to the Inquiry, he read Heath the portion in which he had described how his own 'principal preoccupation in January 1972 was the UK's entry into the European Economic Community'.

Q: That is what you said there; that is true, is it?

A: The statement?

Q: Your statement, yes.

A: Yes.

Q: At a time when people in the United Kingdom were being killed and murdered on if not a daily basis, at least a weekly basis, the principal preoccupation of their Prime Minister was Europe; is that right? ...

A: That is what I have stated.

Q: How do you think the people in that part of the United Kingdom, who are being killed and murdered, what do you think they might make of that?

A: The fact was that there were two very senior ministers who I appointed when I became Prime Minister to cover the two spheres involved and they looked after military matters and development and the other one looked after home affairs and he was responsible, in those days, for Northern Ireland and they had the responsibility, they were very senior and they carried it out very well.

Q: 'I would generally only become involved if they wished to refer important matters to me.' Could you give the Tribunal an example, in the context of people being killed and murdered, what is important and what is not important?

A: Those problems of law and order are problems which both of them could deal with perfectly adequately. If they had any bigger one, they would come to me.

Q: Like what?

A: I am not going to give you examples. It was for them to decide what they want to bring to me.

165

Q: Can you think of any examples?

A: I am not going to give examples.

Q: Why not?

A: Because there is no reason to do so.

Q: Then you go on to say: 'GEN 47 meetings were generally short and discussions brief.'

A: That is quite right.

Q: Here again – let us see if we can see the sort of thing that you discuss in your brief discussion: 'Only seven people killed this week. Let us get on to the next item on the agenda,' would that be the form these meetings would take?

A: No, that is putting the whole thing in an obscene way, that bears no relationship to what we did and the reasons we did it and I strongly object to your offensive language and attitude.

Lavery, none too sincerely, apologised if he was causing the former Prime Minister any offence, but went on to compound the matter.

Q: Do you consider that you were fulfilling your duty to your people, who were being killed and murdered, by saying 'Well, although I am Prime Minister and I have been elected, I am not going to have anything personally to do with you, I have some very good chaps and you can trust them'? That is what I am putting to you, sir.

A: Yes, and you are quite wrong. You wish to be offensive and you are succeeding.

Lavery's tactic for questioning Heath turned out to be woefully misguided. The more he grandstanded for his clients in taking on the former Prime Minister of the British state, the more the witness clammed up and, as a result, failed to assist on any of the lines of questioning he was trying to develop. Again and again Heath replied with 'That is what I have stated' and 'That is a silly question.' When one of Lavery's questions seemed to imply that Heath might not have been fully briefed about what was happening, the man's ego was obviously pricked, prompting him to huffily reply, 'I was fully informed the whole time.' The result of the questioning was that Heath refused to agree to even the simplest propositions put to him by Lavery. At the end of his second afternoon of questioning, which had lasted only a couple of hours, the members of the Tribunal as well as the questioning lawyers looked worn out.

It didn't get any better when Heath returned. Lavery's questions to the former Prime Minister were wide in range. 'Why did the Catholics and the Irish government apparently resent and find unpalatable military action, do you know?' was one of his questions. Saville was forced to intervene. 'Which particular time are we talking about, which particular military action are we talking about?' he asked. 'I find the question – I do not know about Sir Edward – so broad as to be virtually meaningless. We all know from the material we have gathered together for this Inquiry that at one stage at least the Catholics and quite probably the Irish government tended to welcome military activity. Things then changed. You really have to make your question much more focused before I understand it, let alone Sir Edward.'

Few lawyers were so chastened by the judge throughout the Inquiry. 'I thought I was relatively clear,' complained the lawyer. 'Can you focus your question?' asked Saville politely. 'I thought I had,' replied the lawyer. When he eventually asked a more focused question Saville thanked him for it. 'I do not accept that my question was not focused,' he complained again. 'With great respect, Mr Lavery, it was, I am afraid.'

It got worse. Lavery tried to question Heath on General Ford's memorandum.

Q: Tell me this: if you had seen it at the time, would you have accepted General Ford's suggestion?

A: That is an entirely hypothetical question.

Q: It is not.

A: We are here to deal with realities.

Q: I am asking you, Sir Edward, to look at the document, read it and say, if that had come to your notice in 1971 or 1972, would you have said to General Ford, 'That is fine' or would you have said, 'No, I do not agree'?

A: I have told you.

Q: You have not answered my question, what would you have said?

A: Because I do not accept your question.

Q: Why will you not answer my question?

A: Because it is an imaginary question, it is not—

Q: It is not an imaginary question.

A: It does not deal with the facts of life.

Q: It is a fact of life, Sir Edward.

A: It is not, because we knew nothing about it; we never saw the document and there is therefore no question as to what we would or would not have done.

Q: As I have said, a lot of people claim not to have seen it. The question for you, Sir Edward, is: if you had seen the document what would you have said?

A: You are just wasting everybody's time.

Q: Is your reluctance to answer that question because the answer would be: well, yes, I would have thought it might have been a good idea?

A: This is all imaginary.

Q: Would you have thought it was a good idea?

A: I am not going to answer that question.

Q: Why?

A: Because it is an imaginary question. For heaven's sake, you are just wasting time.

Eventually Heath said that of course he did not think it a good idea to shoot selected ringleaders in a riot. Again Lavery pushed him as to why not. 'I am sorry, you are incapable of answering [sic] sensible questions,' Heath scolded him confusedly.

Lavery was trying to draw Heath into admitting that he had considered a policy of allowing troops to shoot outside the terms of the Yellow Card.

Stressing his general point that British government policy was to keep the temperature in Northern Ireland 'as low as possible', Heath went off into a long explanation of the movement towards the short-lived three-party-government deal agreed at Sunningdale in 1973. This was clearly the achievement that Heath was most proud of in his involvement in Northern Ireland and it became increasingly clear that he wished the achievement to be brought out more and himself acknowledged and congratulated for it. Finishing off this panegyric for his own achievement he told Lavery, 'Those are the fruits of the action we took and that is what matters and we are proud of it and so are the people of that country, despite all the muck which you produce from time to time, whenever you can get a hearing.' Lavery was goaded:

> Q: I reject those allegations. I am not going to engage in a slanging match with you, Sir Edward, I am simply trying to ask questions and I am simply trying to elicit your answer to it. The question we started with: what was the problem with shooting selected ringleaders? I suggested the problem with it is that it would be murder; do you agree with that or not?
>
> A: There was no problem because we did not want to shoot ringleaders.
>
> Q: If you had done—
>
> A: Oh, heavens.
>
> Q: What is your problem, Sir Edward?
>
> A: It is your problem, not mine.
>
> Q: Would you like to listen to my question?

Again Lord Saville was forced to intervene. He explained to Lavery that Heath did not seem disposed to answer hypothetical questions. Lavery tried again by asking straightforwardly why General Ford had not been 'drummed out' of the British army for the suggestion. Heath was straightforward in return.

> A: I am not responsible for discipline in the British army.

Lavery tried again:

> Q: If it had been brought to your attention, would you have ensured that he was drummed out of the British army?

169

A: Hypothetical. If you cannot think of anything better to ask, then you had better stop.

It was a display of astonishing high-handedness, not to mention rudeness, but Lavery tried again. Was it really possible that as Prime Minister he could simply wash his hands of such a matter? Heath simply ignored him. There was silence.

Saville intervened again: 'Mr Lavery, I am not finding these questions very helpful.' He tried to sum up what he thought Lavery's point was. But now Saville too was confused and when he tried to clarify the question he thought the lawyer was trying to make, the lawyer denied that it was the point at all. Eventually Saville explained to Lavery again that his questions were too general and hypothetical and that these questions really were not helping. In response Lavery tried to question the whole questioning process of the Tribunal.

MR LAVERY: This is an inquisitorial Tribunal and one does not have to put suggestions about anything to anyone.

LORD SAVILLE: No, you do not, Mr Lavery. It is indeed an inquisitorial Tribunal. The Tribunal is in charge of the questioning because it is the Tribunal's duty to try and discover what happened on Bloody Sunday, and you may have gathered by now that neither I nor my colleagues are particularly helped by these questions and I would be grateful to an answer to my question to you: are you making a suggestion of the nature outlined to Sir Edward?

MR LAVERY: I am not making it at present. What I am endeavouring to do – and I am sorry if I am not making it clear to the Tribunal – I am trying to ascertain what Sir Edward's attitude was to Northern Ireland and, more importantly, what signals his attitude was sending to the people who were actually responsible for day-to-day activities in Northern Ireland.

LORD SAVILLE: Then the suggestion you are making in that regard is that Sir Edward was sending a signal, by some means, to those in charge of security in Northern Ireland that they could act outside the limits of the Yellow Card.

MR LAVERY: In a sense, it is either wilful blindness or indifference.

LORD SAVILLE: Which is almost precisely the suggestion I put to you about one minute ago, which you said you were not putting at present. This is why we are not at the moment being helped, Mr Lavery. I will repeat: are you suggesting to Sir Edward that he either acquiesced in or actively promoted the use by the

Security Service in Northern Ireland of lethal force outside the limits of the Yellow Card? What is the answer; are you making that suggestion or not?

MR LAVERY: Not in those terms.

LORD SAVILLE: Can you please formulate the terms of the suggestion you are making to Sir Edward?

MR LAVERY: With respect, sir, I do not have to make any suggestion.

LORD SAVILLE: In that case, Mr Lavery, you are not helping us and I will have to ask you to sit down.

Eventually Lord Saville began to act not only as an intermediary but as an interpreter between Mr Lavery and Sir Edward Heath. Finally it brought Lavery on to more solid ground.

Q: Did you bring anybody after Widgery to account for their failure to keep within the terms of the Yellow Card?

A: Well, the Widgery Report gave his judgment and this was accepted by the government, by our government, it was accepted by the opposition in the House of Commons, by the Liberal Party in the House of Commons; we accepted his conclusions and action has been taken upon them.

Q: I am asking you, Sir Edward: was anybody brought to account after Widgery for failure to keep within the limits of the Yellow Card?

A: Well, these things are still continuing, of which this is a part.

Q: If in fact you took no action when you realised that there were breaches of the Yellow Card, is it not a fair inference to make from that that before Bloody Sunday you would have been indifferent as to whether the Yellow Card was breached or not?

A: Entirely fallacious statement, I really do not know what you are talking about.

Lavery tried to draw him on whether the Prime Minister is or is not responsible for taking action if the armed forces behave in a certain way. Heath denied that these were Prime Ministerial responsibilities, insisting that the military deal with military matters.

171

Q: Is that a true statement, Sir Edward, of the British constitutional position?

A: Absolutely.

Lavery was incredulous, which simply made Heath ruder.

A: I am sorry, but you have no experience of these things and you do not understand them. But it is the military forces themselves who are responsible for those actions.

Each time he was pushed he made the same point. 'The forces have their own discipline' and they know 'perfectly well' how to go about such matters. The question still remained open though, and essentially unasked, as to why it was that after Bloody Sunday even soldiers who had been found by Lord Widgery to have breached the rules of the Yellow Card had not found themselves the subject of any discipline.

Amid such heat very little light was able to emerge and Heath and Lavery were rattling each other very much. Heath referred to the views of Lavery. 'May I make one thing absolutely clear, Sir Edward,' he returned, 'that my personal views, whatever they are, are of absolutely no interest to this Tribunal ... do you understand that? I am asking you questions as an advocate and I am trying to elicit answers. Do you understand that – that my views do not matter? Do not worry about them in the slightest, Sir Edward.' But Sir Edward kept going.

A: Whose views are you expressing?

Q: I am not expressing any views, I am asking questions.

A: Then it is time we got some fresh questions.

Q: Is that all you want to say, then, about the relationship between, the constitutional relationship between, your government and your army?

A: Well, if you want to study that I will send you the books.

Q: How helpful do you think that answer is, Sir Edward?

When Lavery stalled after a long point put to Heath he was told by the witness:

A: Carry on with your questions.

Q: I take it you are agreeing with what I am saying?

A: No.

Q: What are you disagreeing with? You do not have to contradict everything I am putting to you, Sir Edward; do you know that?

Saville returned once again to acting as Lavery's interpreter. He explained:

LORD SAVILLE: The proposition is that because, I think you are suggesting, no action was taken against those who used these methods of trying to obtain information, that establishes the government of the day was content that people should be shot outside the limits of the Yellow Card?

MR LAVERY: That is a grossly unfair oversimplification, sir.

LORD SAVILLE: Perhaps you could put it in your words, Mr Lavery.

MR LAVERY: I have been trying to put it my way for the last five minutes or so.

Lavery questioned Heath for a total of five days of sessions and exchanges. They were a demonstration of how the Inquiry had managed to roll on and the bill mount up for so many years. For all of these days during which questions were repeatedly asked that elicited few new answers, Lavery was watched by the serried ranks of his fellow lawyers, all totting up their bills as they listened to him polishing his questions.

By their fifth and final day of exchanges Heath was almost refusing to answer Lavery unless his questions were insisted upon – as they were – by Lord Saville. Finally, and in summary, Lavery asked Heath, 'Have you ever asked yourself from time to time and indeed on many occasions, could I have done something differently? Could I have avoided this?' Eventually the answer came, with the question reput in two parts by Lord Saville. Heath said simply, 'I think we did everything possible.'

Other family lawyers tried their best to get to Heath, but they fared no better. Occasionally, but only occasionally, irritation led to something like introspection. At one point Heath said to one of the lawyers:

I just ask one thing of you: some thirty years after all this occurred, and politics, which has taken up sixty-five years of my life, could we not please deal with the present situation and how to deal with it, rather than spend our time looking at the past?

He was asked if he accepted any responsibility for the deaths. He paused before answering clearly: 'No.' And why did he not accept any responsibility? 'Because I had no responsibility for it.' While expressing 'intense regret' and saying that 'I fully appreciate the pain and grief caused' to the parents and relatives of the dead, his response had to be limited because 'it was not my responsibility at the time.'

Some of the questioning of Heath went along these very general lines and was limited by Saville for precisely that reason. On other occasions the questioning of Heath was specific. At one point the lawyer for the family of Patrick Doherty asked Heath about the soldier who had shot his clients' relative.

Heath was probably the first person to read the report he had commissioned from Lord Widgery. And that report had substantial criticisms of the actions of individual soldiers. The Doherty lawyer read the section relating to the shooting of Patrick Doherty. Widgery had written: 'The probability is that he [Doherty] was shot by Soldier F, who spoke of hearing pistol shots and seeing a crouching man firing a pistol from the position where Mr Doherty's body was found. Soldier F said that he had fired as the man turned away which would account for the entry wound in his buttock. Doherty's reaction to the paraffin test was negative.' In the light of all the evidence he had seen, Lord Widgery had concluded that Doherty was not carrying a weapon and that if Soldier F had fired at him in the belief that Doherty had a gun then he was 'mistaken'. The lawyer read this to Heath and then asked:

> Q: I want to ask you, Sir Edward, on behalf of the Doherty family, why Soldier F was never prosecuted for murder.

> A: I cannot answer that question for you because I am not responsible – I was not responsible—

Questioned as to who was responsible Heath seemed unsure. After thirty years, he said, he would have to enquire as to whose role it would have been to chase up such a matter. 'As Prime Minister I did not have to do it and there are other people who have the responsibility for taking the legal decisions, and that was all done.'

> Q: Well, do you or do you not know why nobody was prosecuted for the murder of Mr Doherty?

> A: I do not know.

A lawyer for the families also put to him what their submission would be: that Prime Minister Heath had appreciated that there was a risk to civilians on the day but that he gave his approval for the operation anyway and that he had misled the public on this matter in 1972. It brought perhaps the most substantial reply Heath gave. It was also characteristic, filled with a desire to preserve his own reputation as well as an overriding and ever-present bitterness and hostility:

> I told the British public the truth and in your case you have failed to do that and, in particular, you and your friends who have said that on that particular period we were deliberately – we had deliberately organised bloodshed and then failed to do anything about it and it had all been built up – you do not have anything to back your accusations; you have no evidence because there is not any and it was after this that the whole world saw that when we had this tragedy nobody could have been quicker than myself in taking the action to remedy it; within forty-eight hours we had got this high-powered commission; we had got Parliament; we had told the public exactly what we were doing and I must say that the High Court judge who took it over was very independent; he worked very, very hard and in six weeks the report was there and it was accepted, and they have always repudiated what you have been saying because there is not a scrap of truth in it.

Again and again the questions tried to corner Heath. But he could not be cornered. Not simply because he played like with like, returning bombast with bombast, but because his reactions to events were often just bafflingly different from those expected by most of his questioners. Social mores and behaviour had certainly changed over the years, but Heath's had not.

He was asked about the transcript of a telephone conversation he had immediately after the event with the Irish Taoiseach. In that transcript the Taoiseach, Jack Lynch, talks of the 'unfortunate news about Derry this afternoon'. Heath is recorded saying, 'It is very bad news, yes.' Why, though, a families' lawyer asked, had he not expressed 'shock' and 'horror'. There was, it was put to him, an absence of 'the human response'. 'It is a human point,' it was put to him. 'I do not accept that at all,' he replied. It had never been claimed in his career that Heath was a very emotional man or even that he was particularly easy to understand. But these attempts in the witness box to get through the steel he had built up around himself were always destined to fail.

Towards the end he was asked about the Prime Ministerial successor who had set up the Inquiry to which he was currently testifying. Was he invited to have a meeting with Tony Blair before the announcement of the current Inquiry, he was asked. 'He very politely sent me a note just saying that he was going to announce the Inquiry. When he announced it in Parliament I stood up and thanked him for letting me have advance information.' But no meeting. 'No meeting, no.'

At the very end of his testimony Heath's lawyer protested to the Tribunal about the questioning of his client. Allegations and submissions had been made, David Mackie QC complained, in the place of questions. And 'not one single witness available to the Tribunal' was able to give support to the claims. Very serious accusations had been made of his client, he said. They were claims that, he pointed out, were not only very serious, but were 'flatly contradicted' by the central documents available to the Inquiry, comprised 'grabbing soundbites', were 'flatly contradicted by an elementary knowledge of how government works' and were 'flatly contradicted by the fact that our client had the clearest possible personal and governmental interests and motives to avoid this terrible catastrophe'.

At the end of eight days of questioning Heath was asked if he had anything at all that he himself would like to add. If any apologies or admissions of error were expected then such expectations were disappointed. Heath's final answer was as bureaucratic as could be. 'It was dealt with by a public Inquiry,' he said. 'Lord Widgery dealt with everything he received from the evidence. It was debated in the House of Commons and the House of Lords and accepted by both. He made some suggestions in his conclusions, and the government undertook to pursue them.'

That was it. A procedural issue. As he had said repeatedly, everything that could be done had been done. As Prime Minister he had followed everything by the book, he had been swift and decisive in setting up an Inquiry and so his part in the whole business was done.

Sir Edward Heath had spent a long time in the box. At eighty-six years of age he had testified for eight afternoons, which covered two full weeks of the Inquiry's hearings.

The final report from Lord Saville found that there was no evidence at all to support the allegation made in submissions on behalf of the families that there had been an intention at the top of the British government, either 'intended', 'planned' or 'foreseen'. Saville 'found no evidence to substantiate these allegations'. The final report also found 'no evidence' to support the suggestion that the authorities 'advocated the use of unwarranted lethal force or were indifferent to its use on the occasion of the march' and found, again, 'no evidence' of toleration or encouragement of unjustified lethal force.

Heath was exonerated from any blame by the final report. Neither he nor his government could have known about or imagined, let alone ordered, what had happened that day. Saville had finally shown that whatever else Heath was he was not someone who ordered massacres of British citizens. But what Heath's own response to the report would have been was never to be known. He died in July 2005 at the age of eighty-nine, two and a half years after testifying and five years before Lord Saville's final report was published.

12

THE TERRORIST: MARTIN MCGUINNESS

At the time of Bloody Sunday Martin McGuinness was on the run from the police and security forces. But he was also on the march. The only proper job the 21-year-old had ever had was in a butcher's shop in Derry. Yet when he appeared before the Saville Inquiry at the Guildhall in Derry he was the Deputy First Minister of Northern Ireland. No single individual involved in the day had enjoyed such a rise, from marcher to minister.

But his appearance before the Tribunal had certainly not always been assured. In December 2000 an application was made by McGuinness's long-term solicitor, Barra McGrory, for McGuinness to be given full interested-party status at the Inquiry. At that stage Lord Saville had reason to be terse.

The Inquiry had contacted McGuinness by letter in April 1999. Having no reply they sent a reminder in May and another two in July. They had written to him again in December and again in April of the following year, 2000, by which point McGuinness had told various journalists that he intended to give evidence. But he still had not contacted the Inquiry or replied to any of the letters. In December 2000 it was left to his representative, McGrory, to apologise on behalf of his client. The only explanation he could offer was that until oral hearings had got under way his client had, he said, been unaware of the 'full gravity of his personal situation in respect of these proceedings'. His lawyer now claimed that his client must hold back from making any statement until 'at least two or three lawyers' had gone through all the material relating to him.

Saville disputed this. The Attorney General's undertaking meant that no criminal proceedings could follow from information given openly to the Inquiry. 'Perhaps I am speaking for myself,' Saville said, 'my colleagues will tell me if they disagree, I simply cannot understand why Mr McGuinness cannot at this stage set out his recollection of and relating to the events of that day.'

McGrory said that his client was an 'extraordinary witness', firstly because of the nature of the accusations being made against him, secondly because 'he is a person, like it or not, of public importance in this jurisdiction.' McGrory listed the facts – that his client was a senior Sinn Fein representative, a negotiator of the Good Friday Agreement, Minister for Education in the Northern Ireland Administration and a Member of Parliament. 'That makes his position publicly', McGrory claimed, 'quite exceptional to the position of perhaps any other witness in these proceedings.'

That at least was to prove true. But Saville rejected the request. McGuinness would not be awarded full interested-party status at the Tribunal until he was willing to provide, like anybody else who was there on the day, a statement of his recollections of Bloody Sunday. Why, Saville repeatedly asked, did McGuinness need lawyers to go through all the evidence other people had given? How would this help him record, in a straightforward manner, his own memories of the day?

Over the ensuing years an answer began to emerge. McGuinness needed to know what other people were going to say in order to work out very carefully what he was going to say. The Tribunal might expect some truth from him, but it was certainly not going to get the whole truth.

In 2001 when the witness hearings got properly under way the Good Friday Agreement was in its third year. Dissident Republican groups were still – as they had shown with the 1998 Omagh bombing – able to wreak the most appalling death and terror in the province. But the Provisional IRA had started the process of decommissioning its weapons and in clear and tangible ways the Troubles were starting to recede into history. The city of Derry had become, partly thanks to the business brought to it by the Saville Inquiry, quite a prosperous place. It was possible to get through the whole of dinner in the City Hotel without a bored local youth even calling in a bomb warning.

But if the peace was tangible it was also fragile. Devolution had already been suspended a number of times as the various parties in the North failed to agree on key aspects of the process. And just because the Good Friday Agreement had been voted upon and passed, it did not mean that every aspect of Northern

Ireland's cycle of retributive violence was over. At the start of 1999 the former IRA activist who had turned into one of the IRA's biggest critics, Eamon Collins, was murdered in Armagh. His funeral procession passed paint brushed slogans on walls threatening him for being an 'RUC tout'. Some things were still punishable.

In this situation it was understandable that some people still felt a degree of caution when it came to criticising the IRA. But the extent of that caution – indeed fear – appeared to have been greatly underestimated by the Saville Inquiry.

It was clear from the outset that there were certain things that people were genuinely reluctant to speak about. Anything relating to civilian gunmen who fired on the day was one. But there were others. Chief among them – indeed the matter that people seemed most reluctant to speak about – was anything to do with Martin McGuinness. This was not just a matter of members of the public fearing what they should or should not say about him. It included members of his own family.

One of the first witnesses to testify before the Saville Inquiry in the Guildhall in Derry in December 2000 was someone who gave her statement to the Inquiry under the name of 'Ann Harkin'. During oral evidence she was referred to by what appeared to be her married name, Ann McGuinness. What the Tribunal was not aware of, and not made aware of until after she had given evidence, was that Ann Harkin was a former Sinn Fein councillor and the sister-in-law of Martin McGuinness. She had not mentioned a word about this.

In February 2001 another person close to McGuinness gave oral evidence: Mitchel McLaughlin, a member of the Northern Ireland Assembly and the then chairman of Sinn Fein. In evidence McLaughlin confirmed that he had been a friend of McGuinness's for thirty to thirty-five years and that they had been friends at the time of Bloody Sunday. But he said that he could not help with the naming of people associated with the IRA and denied that he had ever spoken with his old friend about Bloody Sunday. Stretching credulity he also said that he did not know whether Martin McGuinness had ever been in the IRA. He was questioned about this by Christopher Clarke:

Q: You have never asked?

A: No.

180

Q: Although you have known him for many years?

A: Indeed.

Q: And you work with him daily?

A: Indeed.

Q: And you ask this Tribunal to believe that you do not know to this day whether Mr McGuinness is or ever has been a member of the IRA?

A: I have already said, and I will repeat for your benefit: it was my practice throughout my political career not to invite myself or not to interest myself in issues that were outside my field of activity. I was involved in Sinn Fein and I simply did not want to know that information because it was dangerous information.

Q: Can I have a clear answer to my question: you do not know to this day whether Mr McGuinness is, or ever has been, a member of the Provisional IRA; is that your evidence?

A: That is my evidence and I have made it clear: I never once, and I would not ask any individual if they were members of the IRA. Indeed anyone who would confirm that to me, I would regard as being in some way suspect or unreliable.

Q: Your answer to me about Mr McGuinness is a truthful answer, is it?

A: Absolutely.

But it was clear that McLaughlin's answer was far from truthful. Nor was he any more truthful when asked about another matter relating to McGuinness. A former Sinn Fein councillor had already testified to the Inquiry, he was told, and the name under which she had given her statement to the Inquiry was 'Ann Harkin'. Was McLaughlin aware of any family connection between the person who now turned out to be Ann McGuinness and McLaughlin's Sinn Fein colleague Martin McGuinness? Despite having known both Ann and Martin McGuinness for more than thirty years McLaughlin repeatedly answered, 'No'. It seemed that nothing connected to McGuinness, even something or someone connected by marriage, could be mentioned even by a senior Sinn Fein figure like McLaughlin.

181

In April 2001 another McGuinness relative turned up and denied any knowledge of anything relating to McGuinness. In January 1972 Joe McColgan had been the boyfriend of McGuinness's sister. He married her the following year, becoming Martin McGuinness's brother-in-law. In 1990 he was imprisoned in America for four years after being convicted of attempting to import an anti-aircraft surface-to-air rocket-launcher called the 'Stinger' from America into Ireland. But during questioning by Counsel to the Inquiry not only did McColgan refuse to discuss his US conviction and deny that he had ever been a member of the IRA, he testified that although he had known his soon-to-be-brother-in-law on Bloody Sunday, he had not been aware that Martin McGuinness had been a member of the IRA.

It was clear that a conspiracy of silence had either informally or formally been created around McGuinness. He had himself by this stage called publicly for everybody with information about Bloody Sunday to follow his lead and co-operate with the Inquiry. Either people were wary whether or not to trust McGuinness's message or, as seemed more likely, they had been told one thing in public and something very different in private. The reaction of everybody, from McGuinness's closest allies and family to other citizens, suggested that there was not so much a conspiracy of silence as a conspiracy of fear.

Eugene Lafferty testified before Saville in January 2001. Eugene's brother Eamon Lafferty had been an IRA man who had been shot dead in Derry in August 1971. The following year Martin McGuinness had slipped past army cordons to address a commemorative rally for him. But Eugene Laffery refused to answer any questions about Martin McGuinness or confirm anything to do with the IRA when he testified. Another man, James Ferry, alleged to be connected to the IRA, had known Martin McGuinness in 1972, yet claimed to the Inquiry in December 2001 that he was 'totally unaware' of any position that McGuinness had in the IRA and remained resolutely unwilling to help the Inquiry on matters relating to the IRA.

A very small number of civilians mentioned that they had seen McGuinness in a variety of places on the day. A couple even remembered speaking to him. One, Noel Breslin, was moving away from the CS gas, going south down Chamberlain Street and into the High Street, when he said he saw him. 'My family knew his family, and my wife and I had nursed him as a boy,' he recorded. 'We just had a friendly chat, there was no mention of anything political. I never knew Martin to be involved with anything to do with the IRA,' he added.

But another civilian's testimony seemed to slip through. Eamonn Deane remembered meeting a group of men 'whom we knew to be Republicans' at the gable end opposite Blucher Street. 'There were around five or six men in this group,' he wrote in his statement, 'one of whom was Martin McGuinness. We were perhaps one of the first groups of people who had come away from the area where the shooting was taking place. We could still hear shooting at this time and Martin McGuinness asked me what was going on. I told him that the Brits had come into the Bogside and were shooting people. I recall Martin McGuinness's reaction was one of shock and disbelief.'

The description of McGuinness being a well-known 'Republican' was interesting. In her evidence, that other local girl, Bernadette Devlin, was just one of those who had claimed that she 'did not know Martin McGuinness in January 1972, either by name or in person.'

During questioning, Eamonn Deane was asked how he knew who McGuinness was:

> Q: Were you telling the Tribunal that you happened to know because you were a personal friend and neighbour of his affiliations and activities, or were you saying it was general knowledge and you believed that most people knew?
>
> A: The latter, that it was general knowledge and most people knew.
>
> Q: Is that something of which you were confident or something that you can only hazard a guess at?
>
> A: I would be pretty confident.

Meanwhile, the journalist Nell McCafferty said that before firing began she was one of the crowd milling around opposite the Bogside Inn, near Free Derry Corner, when she saw two teenagers appear out of a stairwell with two rifles. She said that a few of them told the pair to put their rifles away. Shortly after the two had gone back into the stairwell she remembered Martin McGuinness arriving in the area, 'having been fetched by one of the women'. This certainly didn't fit with McGuinness's version of where he had been. But he explained in his testimony that this was an example of the way in which 'people can make very genuine mistakes, including very experienced journalists.'

183

Martin McGuinness's reputation over the course of thirty years certainly suggested he was someone whom people were right to be fearful of. His career as a terrorist was distinguished by a number of factors. The first was that he had risen very high very young. The second was that he had stayed at the very top of the Republican movement for an unparalleled period of time. The third was that he had a reputation for ruthlessness that surpassed even most of those within his own movement.

He had never spent a long spell behind bars, nor ever had any specific killings attributed to him in court. He had a reputation for having a quasi-charmed existence. He also, like his colleague Gerry Adams, had a career-long capability to speak with two tongues. As a Sinn Fein spokesman he talked of negotiations with the IRA, as though the heads of the two organisations were entirely different people, as though the negotiation could not happen with the same people just staying in a room. He spoke approvingly of armed resistance while suggesting he was unarmed himself. But always at the back of the McGuinness persona was the strongest element of threat.

Interviewed on television by the BBC in the 1980s he was asked about the status of informers. He said, 'If Republican activists who know what the repercussions are for going over to the other side in fact go over to the other side, then they, more than anyone else, are totally and absolutely aware of what the penalty for doing that is.' The interviewer asks, 'Death?' As though it were the most obvious and natural answer of all, McGuinness serenely replies, 'Death, certainly.'

He may never have been convicted in the courts, but among the army and others who saw what was happening at a stage before the courts, McGuinness's reputation was unequalled. An interesting example came up at the Saville Inquiry – the harrowing story of a young private in the Royal Scots Regiment known to the Inquiry as INQ 2245, who only two weeks before Bloody Sunday met, and believed he had only just escaped being murdered by, Martin McGuinness.

The young private had a girlfriend who lived in the Creggan area of the city. In January 1972 he got into a taxi that took him in the wrong direction and headed to the Rossville Flats. It turned out to be a kidnapping operation by the Official IRA. The soldier was taken to another location in the Creggan Heights

184

where he was questioned, beaten for information and put through a number of mock-executions. He eventually admitted he was a soldier. After further interrogation he was told that he had been sentenced to death. But the Officials became persuaded that they could turn the soldier to work for them from inside the army. After agreeing to a plan of action, they left the building after dark. The soldier recalled:

> I could see a couple of cars. As I stepped outside, I could hear one of the Officials shouting, 'Fuck, McGuinness is here with his men across the road.'

The Officials rushed the soldier back inside. The soldier said, 'I couldn't believe it, as although I knew that the Officials were bad, the Provos were even worse. I asked one of them whether they were going to give me over to the Provos and he replied, "No, we are definitely not going to give you to the Provos."' The Official IRA's quartermaster, Reg Tester, escorted him out. As they got into the car the soldier remembered seeing McGuinness. 'I knew what he looked like and I recognised him instantly... He was at the time an infamous figure among the army and there were photos all around barracks of him.'

As the Officials moved off the soldier looked out of the car and could still see the Provos. As the car with the armed Officials sped off, one of them said to the soldier, 'You're a lucky boy.' The dispute between the two wings of the IRA had surpassed their common hatred.

This incident was the source of some later dispute. Towards the end of events on Bloody Sunday the Inquiry was told that an unarmed Official walking towards the Bogside Inn was attacked by three to four Provos shouting, 'You're the bastard that let the soldier go.'

For the Provos, letting the soldier go would not have been an option. For the months before Bloody Sunday, during which Derry had seen an upsurge in the murder of soldiers, RUC officers and others by IRA snipers, and over the period afterwards during which McGuinness remained involved with the IRA, the amount of blood McGuinness has on his hands is unknown. And it seems likely that it will remain that way. In 1994 when the Major government were in negotiations with Sinn Fein/IRA, the police had a special investigation under way named Operation Taurus. This investigation found at least three witnesses to implicate McGuinness in directing terrorism, with traceable links to specific murders. But the Major government's ceasefire efforts were under way. Sinn Fein insisted that they could not come to the negotiating table without

McGuinness. McGuinness would not come to the table while there were prosecutions about to be launched against him. And so prosecutors in the case were told from the top of government that the prosecutions should be halted.

This much is known about McGuinness before and after Bloody Sunday. But what of his actions on the day? Had he just been on the march? Had he carried a gun? Did he direct operations against the army? And had he, indeed, fired that first fatal shot?

General Sir Michael Rose had been a captain in the Coldstream Guards in Derry on the day. In his statement to Saville, signed in April 2000, he stated that the first gunfire he heard on the day was 'a burst of firing from a Thompson machine gun'. He explained that 'it makes a very distinctive sound and I was used to hearing it in Londonderry. There were about five or six shots. It was certainly not a high velocity weapon, nor a weapon that the army had, or used.' When asked during questioning whether there was any doubt in his mind about the type of firing he heard he said, 'Absolutely none at all. I was familiar by then with the sound of the Thompson machine-gun fire in Londonderry, extremely familiar with it.'

Did Martin McGuinness have a gun that day? And if so, what was he doing with it?

Almost two years after finally signing what turned out to be the first of his three statements, Martin McGuinness went into the witness box in Derry's Guildhall. The Inquiry had recently relocated there from London to hear the last witnesses.

Over the course of almost four years the Inquiry had heard evidence first from the citizens of the city, then, in London, the evidence of the military and now, finally, it was back in the building where it had started, in order to hear from another set of witnesses speaking from behind ciphers: the IRA. But the first of them to speak did not need a cipher and did not need any introduction to the public. The morning that McGuinness's testimony began, the press and public galleries were packed full. The press room overflowed with journalists from every news outlet waiting to watch a historic moment: a British minister who was going to speak on oath about his terrorist past.

It was obvious from the outset that the process was not going to be an easy one. McGuinness arrived looking confident and in charge. His still boyish face exuded a calm benevolence towards proceedings, the impression that he was here to be any help he could be.

The questioning as usual began from Counsel to the Inquiry. It started as it would go on. McGuinness refused to answer the very first question put to him. Christopher Clarke began by asking him about the opening paragraphs of his statement to the Inquiry in which he said that on Bloody Sunday he was the second-in- command of the IRA in Derry. Clarke asked him about a technicality of his statement:

Q: I am right in thinking, am I not, that when you use the expression 'the Irish Republican Army' in this and your other two statements, what you were meaning is what others call the Provisionals?

A: That is correct, yes.

Q: Is it right that you had originally been a member of what came to be known as the Officials, that is to say the IRA before the split?

A: Well, I do not see what relationship that has to the events of Bloody Sunday. I was a member of the Irish Republican Army on Bloody Sunday.

Q: Is the position you are not prepared to answer the question as to whether you had previously been a member of the Officials?

A: My position is that on Bloody Sunday I was a member of the Irish Republican Army.

Q: That is not an answer to the question, whether you had previously been a member of the Officials

A: My position is that I do not believe that that question has any relevance whatsoever to this Tribunal.

Q: So you decline to answer it?

A: Yes.

Clarke continued, resignedly. But the rest of the questioning went on in a similar vein. McGuinness was asked how long he had been in the IRA before Bloody Sunday. 'For some months' was his cagey reply. He refused to confirm any date.

He was asked about the titles that were used in his statement. And it became clear that despite their grandiosity (McGuinness, for instance, referred to himself as the 'Adjutant' of the Derry Command on Bloody Sunday) he wished to show that the whole business was a lot less sophisticated than it sounded. 'I think you have to remember', he volunteered, 'that at that time all of us were very young; we were not like a conventional army; we were not well-organised; we were making it up as we went along and, of course, we accorded ourselves these grand titles, which bore very little relationship to the reality of life.' And he confirmed that at the time of Bloody Sunday he 'would have been considered on the run' from the British army and the RUC.

McGuinness was clearly wary of his answers, not nervous or stalling, but certain about what questions he would answer and the way in which he intended to answer them. Like every other witnesses to the Inquiry, McGuinness's testimony was covered by the Attorney General's promise that there would be immunity from prosecution for anything said in the box. McGuinness was aware of his legal rights, but he was also from the outset reluctant to answer any questions that touched on his activities before or after the day. Asked if it was correct that he had become the OC of the Derry brigade a short while after Bloody Sunday, he refused to comment. Asked why, he said that he could not see its relevance to Bloody Sunday. Counsel patiently explained that the Tribunal had heard evidence that on the day itself he had been acting OC and was poised to take the unit over.

'Could I ask where that information comes from?' McGuinness asked. 'Amongst others, Mr Ward,' Counsel told him politely. Which led into one of McGuinness's speeches. This one against Patrick Ward.

> Mr Ward, in my opinion, is a fantasist. Mr Ward is a liar. Mr Ward is an informer. Mr Ward is totally dependent on those elements within the British military establishment who have used him down the years and his evidence to the Tribunal is a tissue of lies. I did not know Mr Ward. I never met Mr Ward and I think that those who attended the Tribunal in London when he gave his evidence can obviously make up their own minds as to whether or not they were dealing with someone who was telling the truth; in my view, he was not.

McGuinness then showed why he was going to be able to spend the next two days running some rings around the lawyers questioning him. For years people had written about McGuinness and if they were anything but sympathetic to him

188

had to do so without any help from the man himself. In 2001 the journalists Liam Clarke and Kathryn Johnston had published their biography of McGuinness. They had been refused an interview by their subject, who also tried to ensure that nobody else spoke to them either. But those people who did, including the former IRA informer Patrick Ward, became the subjects of intense ridicule from McGuinness. And in his criticisms of their book, of their sources, and indeed in his criticisms of some of the questions put to him, he was at a very distinct advantage to everyone else.

The questioning was about him, his life and his career. Nobody knew more about this than he did. Inevitably, in reporting on a man who had been as obstructive as he could be, mistakes would be made, and at every opportunity McGuinness saw such slips as an opportunity. Whenever even a tiny or tangential error not related to the subject in hand had occurred, McGuinness saw the moment to pounce and turn on his accusers. For instance, Patrick Ward had told Clarke and Johnston that McGuinness attended Derry's St Joseph's School. But, McGuinness said, as though everything hung on this, he himself had actually gone to another local school called the Brow of the Hill. How, therefore, could Ward possibly be trusted on his allegations that McGuinness had been involved in paramilitary activity on Bloody Sunday?

Clarke and Johnston had also said at the opening of their book when they were trying to find out about McGuinness's boyhood and family background that he was a nephew of the Bishop of Nottingham. This turned out not to be true, and was an embarrassing small mistake that could have easily been rectified in a future edition. But for McGuinness it was more than this. He repeatedly stressed the importance of this allegation. It was not simply an error, but a lie, a demonstration that nothing else in the book or anything from any of the book's sources could possibly be true or believable. In McGuinness's hands the Bishop of Nottingham became the tip of a terrible iceberg of lies.

The authors of the Bishop-of-Nottingham lie had suggested in their book that McGuinness had been acting OC of the Derry brigade of the Provisional IRA on the day. In his opening statement Christopher Clarke himself had said that it was 'widely reputed' that McGuinness had been the OC of the Provos at the time of Bloody Sunday. McGuinness made hay with this, gleeful in his riposte, magnifying this into a seismic matter that everybody was talking about.

'People only came back to reality whenever I made my statement that I was

189

not OC,' he declaimed, 'so I think that we should deal with the reality of the situation. I was not the OC; I was not the acting OC; I was not someone sitting and waiting to take over from the OC, as this particular fantasist [Ward] has suggested.'

It was not really that much of a difference whether McGuinness was acting OC or soon to become OC, but in his hands these sorts of details became epic in their significance and allowed him to score point after point. He was asked:

Q: Could you, in the interests of accuracy, tell us when you did become the OC of the Derry battalion of the Provisional IRA?

This set McGuinness off in what was to become a regular speech about the Tribunal itself and what it should and should not be focusing on. He answered:

A: Well, I thought that I was coming to this Tribunal to discuss the events of Bloody Sunday and what happened on Bloody Sunday and in the lead-up to Bloody Sunday. You are now attempting to take me into an area, an area where a lot of Republicans would like to take the British government into, would like to take the British military into, and examine before the world their conduct over the course of many decades, and I think if we are going to get into that ball game then we are in the ballpark of this debate around what is called the – whether or not there needs to be a forum for truth and reconciliation, such as the one which was held in South Africa, and I am of the view that in such a debate we as Republicans should contribute; I certainly would wish to contribute, but I think others have to contribute as well and you know, I, for example, would like to ask the Tribunal if, if questions such as the questions that are being put to me were actually put to people who were in the military of the British government, of the British army; were they asked about what they had done after Bloody Sunday? If they were not, why not, and why am I being made an exception?

Q: Mr McGuinness, I do assure you that I for my part am only asking you these questions, and the Tribunal will correct me if I am wrong, because it appears to me that they have a relevance to the events of Bloody Sunday, do you follow? I am not engaged in a wide-ranging examination of what you may have done for the following twenty years, I am solely interested in material that may assist the Tribunal in relation to what happened on Bloody Sunday, do you follow?

A: Could you explain to me how news reportage some months after Bloody Sunday can contribute to bringing out the truth of what happened on that day?

Q: Because it may assist the Tribunal to find the answer to what I would have thought was a very simple question, which you could very easily answer and for some reason will not, which is: when did you become Officer Commanding of the Derry battalion of the Provisional IRA?

A: The reason I will not answer it is because it is not relevant to Bloody Sunday and because that question opens up a whole other debate with huge significance for the peace process and for the discovery of truth which, of course, many people on all sides are seeking about the events of the last thirty years and I think I would be very foolish to go down that road with you at this Tribunal. I am certainly willing to participate in a discussion and a debate with others as to what is the best mechanism to bring about the discovery of truth for many people who have suffered as a result of the events of the last thirty years, but I am not going to allow anybody, any journalist, any Tribunal to hold me up as an exception to many others who will not be subjected to this type of examination.

This rattled Clarke, as it was soon to concern Saville. Clarke asked McGuinness:

Q: Do I understand that you regard yourself as the person who should determine what is and what is not relevant to the events of Bloody Sunday, so far as your evidence is concerned?

A: No, I think that I have come here to give my testimony about the events of Bloody Sunday, about the lead-up to Bloody Sunday and to give us as much of the information that is in my head about this terrible event that brought so much suffering to the citizens of this city. To ask me questions, then, about what happened in the aftermath of Bloody Sunday – I mean, we are not even talking here about the next day, we are not even talking about the next week, we are talking about some weeks and months after Bloody Sunday. So, with respect, I do not see what relevance that has to the discovery of truth about what happened on Bloody Sunday.

Q: Is the position this, Mr McGuinness: that if I ask you a question that the Tribunal thinks is relevant to the events of Bloody Sunday and you do not, you are not going to answer it?

A: No, I am going to be as forthright as I possibly can be, because I wish to help the Tribunal; I wish to help the families discover the truth of what happened on Bloody Sunday. But I, with respect, do not see what relevance questions in the aftermath of Bloody Sunday about what I was or was not doing, what relevance that has to the events of that day or the lead-up to that day.

Q: I have explained to you what appears to me to be the relevance.

191

After each round McGuinness seemed to draw more and more strength. As the fatal question did not come, as the fatal slip-up did not occur, he seemed more and more certain that he was just fine where he was.

And he excelled in the language of euphemism that he and others engaged in 'armed struggle' had used for years. A good example arrived early on. He said that on the day before the march he had met the OC and was instructed to order all volunteers not to engage with the army during the march. But what was the position to be after the march, he was asked.

'In the aftermath of the dispersal of the march that people would have went and had their tea, watched the news and would have resumed the struggle against the British occupying forces. So it certainly was my view that in the aftermath of the parade passing over peacefully that, in the aftermath of teatime, things would revert back to the original position.'

'What does that mean?' he was asked again. He tried to slip the question. The question came again:

Q: Let us not mince words: is what you are saying that after tea volunteers would be free to shoot at the British forces?

A: Well, my assessment of the situation was that after tea the march would have been over, people would have been off the streets and the patrolling of the area would have recommenced generally. In fact, the night before the march I myself was involved patrolling with an active service unit in the Creggan, Brandywell area and, of course, you know, if the British military, at any time during the course of a liberated situation, had have entered, then IRA volunteers would have taken them on militarily.

Q: You use these euphemisms; taking them on militarily means shooting them, does it not?

A: Absolutely, yes.

Another example of his euphemistic skill was the moment during questioning when he referred to the 'symbolic firing of shots' by the IRA at army observation posts on the city walls after the main events. 'Symbolic shots' were as able to kill as any other, but they entered a special category in McGuinness's lexicon.

192

As the morning drew on it became clear that though McGuinness was willing to give stock answers to a number of questions, he was willing to answer fully only a very limited number. Anything to do with members of the IRA, their activities before or after the day or locations where IRA members had met he refused to answer point- blank. But this attitude began to annoy the Tribunal.

Eventually he pushed the usually serene peer too far. Lord Saville called a very rare halt to proceedings. Questioning had been going on for barely more than an hour when McGuinness was asked about the location of the arms dumps where IRA men could collect weapons. He described simply 'a building in the Bogside'. The Tribunal had heard other evidence on this. It was a building at the gasworks, just 200 yards from the Bogside Inn. Was this not right? McGuinness would simply say that 'It was in that vicinity.' Clarke said:

Q: We can be coy about this, but is it in fact a building at the gasworks?

A: I have not identified where it was.

Q: I know you have not—

A: And I am not prepared to identify where it was.

Q: The reason I ask is that when Mr McGlinchey came to give evidence he said that later in the day he attempted to find a gun at the gas yard in one of the buildings just near one of the gas-containers; is that in fact where the dump was?

A: I am not prepared to say.

Q: Why not?

A: (Laughing)

Q: Why does it matter now?

A: Well, because I do not think it has any real relevance.

Lord Saville intervened.

LORD SAVILLE: Mr McGuinness, it is the Chairman speaking: you have refused to tell us whether you were in the Officials; you refused to tell us when you became OC; you are not telling us whether Mr Keenan was in fact the explosives officer; you are not prepared to tell us the address of the house in the Bogside where you gave instructions that the volunteers were not to engage the army on Bloody Sunday; you are not prepared to identify where the arms dump was; I fail to understand why you are not answering those questions, in view of the fact that at the beginning of your statement you express your anxiety that this Tribunal should seek to establish the full truth about the circumstances of Bloody Sunday. What we shall do now is to rise for a few moments and I would ask you to consider answering these questions, because if you do not, two things will happen: firstly, you are depriving us of the opportunity of discovering the full facts and matters relating to the events of Bloody Sunday and, secondly, of course, it will be suggested in due course that the reason you are not answering these questions is that you have something to hide.

The Tribunal rose.

Twenty minutes later it returned with one of Martin McGuinness's lawyers trying to explain that the 'problem' his client had in answering questions relating to matters before and after the day was that he was concerned that they would jeopardise his immunity from prosecution. Saville reminded him that the Attorney General's undertaking was that any information deemed by the Tribunal to be relevant to its search for the truth would be protected, and that the matters that had been put to McGuinness and that he had refused to answer were indeed deemed relevant by the Tribunal.

But McGuinness was having none of it. Asked afresh by Clarke about the location of the arms dump he refused to answer. He had a new reason and in front of his home crowd he revelled in giving it. 'There is', he said, 'a Republican code of honour.' He went on. 'On many occasions over the course of the last three decades I have been in interrogation centre after interrogation centre, sometimes for a week at a time, and I have never ever, on any occasion, given the name of a single person who was associated with me or with the IRA.' He had, he said 'a duty' to others that he would not break. Lord Saville himself tried to get an answer by asking Counsel's question again. But again McGuinness refused to answer. Finally Saville rebuked him, saying, 'I am bound to say I understand your answer as being that you feel that your duty of honour overrides the desire of the families for the Tribunal to discover the whole truth about the events of Bloody Sunday.'

But as for other questions he had refused to answer, he had taken advice and McGuinness said he could confirm that he had joined the Official IRA at the end of 1970 but had left 'swiftly' and joined the Provisionals. He also said that he could confirm that he had become the OC of the Derry IRA 'within two weeks' of Bloody Sunday.

There is one photo that exists of McGuinness on that day, on the march. It fixes him at a particular time, relatively early on. But about what he did and where he was after that photo was taken there was, it emerged, considerable doubt.

As with most witnesses, some of the details in his statement were clearer than others. He said, for instance, that in order not to be needlessly arrested he remembered that he did not join in with the rioting and stoning of the army that had begun at the army barricade. His statement also included the kinds of confusion that were common to all witnesses. McGuinness claimed that at a point he saw a wounded woman, who he later learned was Peggy Deery, being carried away. This, he said, happened before he heard any shooting. He admitted that this strange order of events had 'always mystified' him. But what mystified everyone else was what happened next.

As questioning continued it became clear that a strange gap existed in his story. The essence of it was this: McGuinness said that he moved from the top of Chamberlain Street to Joseph Place. He must have begun this trip at about 3.40. The army came into the Bogside at almost exactly 4.10. The problem, as Counsel put it to him, was that 'there appears to be something like a half-hour gap between the stoning starting and the army coming in and the firing.' There was a half-hour gap but McGuinness's account of his movements 'only deals with, at best, something like ten minutes of that period'. It was a question McGuinness could not answer, and a time-period he could not explain.

He said that when he became aware of the shooting going on he moved from Joseph Place to the Free Derry wall and then to Abbey Park. Asked if he saw anything happening in Rossville Street he explained that owing to poor eyesight he couldn't even see any of the army vehicles moving. Neither, due to his eyesight, was he able to see very much else.

Asked about the fact that other civilians had testified to seeing him in parts of the Bogside that were inconsistent with his current testimony he commented that they 'may have made genuine mistakes given the traumatic events and confusion of the day'.

195

Soon McGuinness was back into speech-making. He was on his home-turf and gave his audience a set of bravura speeches about the iniquities of the British intelligence services, the British army and much else besides. On one occasion Clarke was reduced to asking simply, 'I wonder if you could confine yourself to answering questions.' But McGuinness decided what he wanted to say. For instance he insisted that there was 'no situation whatsoever on the streets of Derry on Bloody Sunday where the Irish Republican Army [Provisionals], and I cannot speak for others, but similarly I think that their position in all this was remarkably similar to ours, would have even contemplated opening fire on the British army in the middle of a civil rights demonstration'.

Lingering over all of this was the question not only of whether McGuinness was telling the truth, but whether he was allowing others to tell the truth as well. At one point it was put to him that some evidence indicated that a number of IRA members, including one of those whom McGuinness refused to name, who had been OC on the day, had been warned off giving evidence to Lord Saville 'by, amongst others, your brother William and Raymond McCartney', the latter a particularly well-known IRA man.[2] One newspaper described visits 'from IRA men of such reputation that as one man put it: "It is the next best thing to sending round the grim reaper."' Had people been warned off giving evidence? Counsel asked McGuinness. He rejected the idea. What about other people? Had anybody warned witnesses off? 'Not to my knowledge,' said McGuinness.

There were grounds to believe that, until Patrick Ward's evidence had come up, word had gone around that McGuinness alone would give evidence for the Provisional IRA, but that after Ward came forward others were allowed to come forward to challenge his evidence. Again, McGuinness said that he had no knowledge of any such thing. In any case, he reminded people, the IRA was a different thing from him. 'If you are asking me: did I go to the IRA to seek their blessing to come forward to this Tribunal; no, I did not,' he said.

What about his own attendance at the Inquiry, he was asked. Why had it been the case that on four separate occasions during 1999 he had not replied to communications from the Inquiry asking for his assistance? 'I recognised', he said, 'that that would have serious implications for me. It would have been a huge decision to take. I decided that I had to give it careful – very careful

---

[2] In 1977 McCartney was convicted of the murders of RUC detective Patrick McNulty and businessman Jeffrey Agate. He became the OC of the IRA in the Maze prison and took part in the 'dirty protest'.

consideration.'

But there remained the allegations of a number of people who had very different stories about what McGuinness had been doing on the day. Of Patrick Ward McGuinness was contemptuous. He described Ward's version of events as 'a bucketful of lies'. 'Who are we dealing with here? We are dealing with someone who is an informer, a British agent of some description; someone in the pay of the British military; someone who has a vested interest in providing testimony to this Tribunal which in some way can provide the plausible explanation that the soldiers want to try and fit in with their story.'

Another source for Liam Clarke's book was cited at him, a man given the pseudonym 'Peter Doherty'.
'Who is Peter Doherty?' asked McGuinness of Counsel. 'I do not know,' Counsel replied.
'No and neither do I, so how do I defend myself?' McGuinness shot back.

But both these men and anybody else who had said anything against McGuinness were not, in his view, merely people who might be antagonistic towards Martin McGuinness. They were also – he stated time and again – sinister figures who were 'hostile to the peace process'. A process of which McGuinness was making himself the embodiment.

But the question of these anonymous witnesses was an interesting one. After all, there were reasons why some local people might have wanted to remain anonymous if they had anything negative to say about McGuinness's actions on the day. Counsel came straight out with it. 'Would these people be safe if they came forward?' he asked. McGuinness went off on a speech. Counsel interrupted:

> Q: Would they be safe if they came forward, is my question, which you have not yet answered.
>
> A: Safe from who? Q: Safe from attack.
>
> A: From who? Who do you think I represent?

It was a threatening moment, a flash-glimpse of the man before the politician.

When presented with another anonymous source from Liam Clarke's book he exploded with indignation at being faced with these allegations again. Saville had to intervene. The allegations were being put to him so that he could respond to them, it was explained. Then McGuinness revealed what the source of his irritation at this was – public relations. 'There is a tremendous concern within the city of Derry and among the relatives that the journalists have shown up for what they hope to be a sensational appearance at the Bloody Sunday Tribunal by Martin McGuinness, who has to refute these countless allegations from unnamed, faceless people,' he said. 'I follow that, Mr McGuinness,' said a patient Lord Saville, 'but this is one day for us out of 390.'

The next day, Day 391, was McGuinness's second and final day. But it was his most bravura performance. Patrick Ward's legal representative got to him first. McGuinness was feeling, it was clear, at the very top of his game. Ward's representative asked him if he was reading prepared statements out. He said he had made some comments from notes. 'Do you have any other prepared documents you intend to read during questioning?' Ward's representative asked him, sarcastically. 'Not at this moment, no,' McGuinness replied coolly, adding with a smirk, 'I may have later, depending on how this morning goes.'

Again and again the QC asked for an answer. 'Is the answer to my question "Yes"?' 'No, the answer to your question, you will have to wait for,' McGuinness replied authoritatively. Bullying McGuinness in the conventional legal manner got no rise out of him. He seemed unflappable. And he began to have fun. Patrick Ward's representative showed him a picture of the cover of a book called *Derry Through the Lens* by a local photographer, Willy Carson. The picture was of a cocked revolver.

> Q: Can you look at the writing that appears on 163 about this particular document: 'Cover designed by Martin McGuinness'?
>
> A: Yes.
>
> Q: Do you find this humorous?
>
> A: In fact I do.
>
> Q: Is it true?
>
> A: It is totally untrue.
>
> Q: It is totally untrue?

A: Yes, unless it is some other Martin McGuinness. Are you asking me – or are you asking the public to believe that someone who was regarded as an eminent photographer for the Derry Journal and other outlets went so far as to describe the cover of a book that he published as being designed by Martin McGuinness?

Q: Well, it must be another Martin McGuinness then?

A malicious smile played around McGuinness's lips. Ward's solicitor had slipped up and he made his move. 'Well, I just think – I think you need to get your act together here,' McGuinness told him. There was uproarious laughter from his supporters in the public gallery. 'You are the one who has been getting an act together, Mr McGuinness,' the QC tried to come back. But McGuinness was on top of him. 'This is rubbish here, folks,' he explained plainly, 'absolute nonsense.'

The London lawyer was on McGuinness's home-patch. McGuinness was talking about himself in front of a public gallery filled with supporters and voters. For the lawyer the experience became more and more crushing. A little later while being questioned on the different youth wings of the IRA – the 'Fianna' – McGuinness started asking questions of the lawyer.

A: What Fianna are you speaking about?

Q: In Derry?

A: There were two Fiannas.

Q: Yes, were.

A: What Fianna are you speaking about?

Q: One did the military stuff and one did the gardens and cars?

A: No, one was loyal to the Official IRA and one was loyal to the Provisional IRA, I am very surprised you have not done your homework.

Again, McGuinness's friends in the gallery welcomed his comments with raucous laughter. For a moment, as Patrick Ward's lawyer started to get flustered, Saville looked as if he was sympathising with McGuinness. 'I am trying to ascertain where Mr Jennings is trying to take us,' McGuinness said at one point. 'Let us hear his next question,' said Saville, 'and we may be able to glean it from that.'

But when it began to look as though McGuinness was using the room for pure slapstick, Saville shut him down. Ward's QC put up a document on the screen which was almost completely redacted. 'Can we have, please, document INT1.380. This is an intelligence—' McGuinness interrupted him: 'It does not look very intelligent to me.' There were gales of laughter from the public galleries. Saville finally intervened. 'I will have to ask people to be quiet,' he said. 'This is a serious proceeding and we do want to proceed in an atmosphere of quiet and as far as possible, calmness.'

The fact that only a line was visible must, as McGuinness picked up, have looked to the public gallery like the state trying to hold information back. In fact the redactions were to protect the identities and addresses of suspected members of the IRA.

But McGuinness was here to score PR points in front of his home-crowd and could not be held back. He questioned the source of the intelligence document. Was it the RUC? Was it Special Branch? 'Are we ignoring the fact that the British government—' he began. Saville interrupted him. But McGuinness was flying. 'What I see before me is "Martin McGuinness, 5 Elmwood Street, Derry", although they have an unfortunate title before that,' he said, referring to the fact that the document said 'Londonderry'.

But as to other names, including Gerry 'Mad Dog' Doherty, he refused to identify whether anyone else was in the IRA. He reiterated his reasons, and, consummate politician that he had become, said, 'I think the families, who are the most important people here in this building today, understand the reasons why I, as an Irish Republican, cannot do that.'

He was asked whether Gerry O'Hara, now Councillor Gerry O'Hara, had ever held the rank of training officer in the Provisional IRA. McGuinness refused to help, even when it was pointed out that O'Hara himself had now given a statement to the Inquiry saying that he had been the head of the Fianna at the time of Bloody Sunday. McGuinness would not even go along with this. 'I have not spoken to Gerry O'Hara about any of this,' he claimed, 'for the simple reason that a lot of my time is spent outside the city of Derry. We have been involved in very intense negotiations in the peace process over the course of recent weeks and months.'

McGuinness had clearly become exceptionally wily over the years, noticing traps laid for him before most people would see them coming. The final question from Patrick Ward's representative was a case in point. He picked it up and played it where he wanted to play it.

Q: I want to ask you this general proposition which I suggest is particularly relevant to the events of Bloody Sunday: do you accept that the killing of the innocent should attract dishonour?

A: On who, the British?

Q: On the people involved.

A: Who were the people involved, on the Parachute Regiment?

Q: Yes.

A: Why would you not say that?

Q: Do you accept that?

A: Why did you not say that?

Q: I have just said it: do you not accept it?

A: I absolutely accept that what happened on Bloody Sunday was a massacre carried out by the British Parachute Regiment against innocent civil rights protesters.

There was not very much more to do but sit down, and the lawyer did.

The final showdown McGuinness had in the box was with the lawyers representing the soldiers. The representative of many of them, Edwin Glasgow, started by being ingratiating, almost obsequious, in his seeking of McGuinness's help. He got going when he asked McGuinness why he had not accepted the Tribunal's initial invitations to join in giving evidence.

Q: Why on earth did you not meet the Tribunal's lawyers and tell them that as soon as this Inquiry which you had campaigned so hard to set up was sitting?

A: Well, the Inquiry that I campaigned to have set up was an inter— independent, international, public Inquiry into Bloody Sunday.

Q: Forgive me being rude, but I will if I may stop you whenever I think it will save time: looking to your right, would you accept that this is an international, independent and distinguished Tribunal?

A: I accept that it is a distinguished Tribunal, but I do not accept that it is independent.

He went off into a speech on the nature of the Widgery Inquiry and the offence it had caused to the city. Lord Saville pleasantly summed up McGuinness's attitude, saying that it was clear that he was saying that for the initial stages of the Inquiry he had been uncertain that the Tribunal could truly be independent. McGuinness concurred, but continued his oration:

I am one of these people who travels in hope in relation to the peace process, because one of the important things that has happened over the course of the last ten years is that a British Prime Minister came on the scene who decided to do things differently from any other British Prime Minister in history. I am not just talking about the setting up of the Tribunal; I am talking about the peace process and about the way in which we have managed to politically and militarily transform the situation in Northern Ireland over the last ten years.

I also travel in hope in relation to this Tribunal, because it certainly appears to me, you know, Lord Widgery came in here and spent a few days, weeks talking to people and went away and wrote a whitewash. You people are different, you have been here a considerable amount of time. This is a huge chunk out of your lives. I think that you have learnt how important this is to the relatives and to the people of this city, that there is a running sore, that that needs to be mended, and, I think, are conscious of the huge responsibility that you have to try and bring all of this to completion, and to do that against the backdrop of a very important peace process. So whilst I have expressed my reservations about the independence of the Tribunal, that does not necessarily mean that I do not have confidence that this Tribunal can get to the truth and finally clear up what has been a running sore for the people of this city.

The reason I am here is because I want to contribute. If I thought it was going nowhere whatsoever, that it was all a waste of time, then I probably would have continued with my reluctance to come forward as I did at the very beginning. But let me reassure you that my reservations about the setting up of this Inquiry and some time after were shared by the vast majority of citizens of this city. I cannot speak for the relatives, they can speak for themselves, but I think we all travel in

202

hope that we can get a proper outcome to this, that the truth will be known and that the relatives and the rest of the citizens of this city can get on with their lives.

Glasgow continued with his curiously meek line of questioning. The reason he had had the 'temerity', he said, to ask the question was because he was confused. He could not, he admitted, understand why McGuinness had said that he needed three lawyers to go through all the evidence presented to the Inquiry before he was willing to give evidence himself. Why the multiple lawyers employed in going over the evidence for years if all he ever needed to give was 'the simple, truthful explanation' that he had given over the last two days?

McGuinness again explained that this was to do with the peace process, the importance of 'moving forward' and the 'massive impact' that his earlier intervention could have had on 'rejectionist forces within the Unionist community'.

Glasgow was suggesting this for a reason though. One of the *Sunday Times* team, John Barry, had said in evidence to the Inquiry that his feelings in 1972 were that after interviewing McGuinness he did not think the IRA 'party line' fitted the 'totality of the firing'. Had McGuinness now, Glasgow wished to know, as in 1972, waited to find out what the press knew before speaking to them and only then giving them his side of the story? Had he waited until he had heard what everyone else had to say and only then decided what evidence to give? McGuinness denied the accusation.

Then what was the reason, Glasgow went on, that members of the public, other than Patrick Ward and others whom McGuinness had dismissed, had not come forward with information about the Provisional IRA's activities on the day? McGuinness had only the day before referred to the 'huge significance' of the fact that nobody had come forward with evidence against the Provisionals. Was this not because the IRA carried out and was capable of the most 'horrific punishments of people who crossed it and did anything that it disapproved of?' Glasgow quoted the Derry author Eamonn McCann at McGuinness. McCann had said in testimony that 'it should be kept in mind that the IRA is a secret organisation, and that it has, on many occasions, killed people who have revealed its secrets.' McGuinness agreed that this was 'an historic fact'.

Only the weekend before McGuinness was giving evidence the body of Jean McConville had finally been buried after being stumbled upon by members of the public out walking. In 1972 she was a 37-year-old widow. That December she was 'disappeared' by the IRA, taken by them in front of her children, shot in the head and her body dumped in a secret though, as it turned out, not deep enough hole in the sand. Implausibly accused by some of being an informer, she was most likely suspected because she had once been seen showing kindness to an injured British soldier. In 2005 Martin McGuinness's Sinn Fein colleague Mitchel McLaughlin said on the television that the murder of McConville was 'not a crime' and in 2010 it emerged that former IRA commander Brendan Hughes had recorded that the killing had been ordered by McGuinness's Sinn Fein colleague Gerry Adams.

Was not the murder of Jean McConville, Glasgow asked, for even showing sympathy for a wounded soldier evidence of what the IRA did with dissenters? At that stage McGuinness clearly still felt confident on this point. 'Neither you or I know anything about the details of the case which you have just put to me,' he said.

Soon he was back on more confident comedic form. Glasgow asked for some help over the matter of the IRA's handbook, the 'Green Book'. What is it, asked Glasgow. 'I think it means the book is green,' replied McGuinness. There was uproarious laughter from the public gallery.

Relating to the rumour that the convicted IRA killer Raymond McCartney and McGuinness's brother had gone around the city in the preceding years stopping people testifying, McGuinness was asked whether Raymond McCartney was known to him and whether he was somebody 'of whom people in this city would have reason to be very afraid'. There was laughter from the gallery once again. Raymond McCartney was in the gallery. 'I do not think people in this city have any reason whatsoever to be afraid of Raymond McCartney,' McGuinness replied confidently, stressing that Raymond McCartney was a Sinn Fein candidate in the forthcoming Assembly elections. 'He comes from a highly respected Republican family in this city. He is a man that I admire tremendously.'

McGuinness's presentation of the IRA as just harmless old boys included himself. On one of his rants against his biographer Liam Clarke, he mentioned that he had seen Clarke the day before in the Guildhall Square. He was watching the questioning of his subject next door in the press room. 'I am not sure if he is here today,' said McGuinness, 'he probably is, so it does not strike me that he fears for his life at all. Why should he?' A few days earlier McGuinness's own lawyer had questioned Liam Clarke and during the course of questioning had asked, in a line of questioning Saville swiftly stopped, if Clarke carried a personal firearm. Barra McGrory sought to show that since Clarke had been advised in the past by the RUC that he was a target for assassination by the IRA he could not be trusted in his evidence. Here over the course of a few days McGuinness and his lawyer played a good double game: on the one hand trying to shame Clarke's alleged lack of objectivity by highlighting his fears of an IRA plot and on the other ridiculing the idea that any such threat to him could exist.

When questioned on the IRA's Green Book he claimed that this was the first time he had ever seen or read the IRA's book for volunteers. Glasgow tried to remain helpful.

> Q: It may well be, sir, you had already left the IRA by the time this document in, the form that we have it, came into existence. When did you leave the IRA?
>
> A: Here we go again, on another trawl through the Martin McGuinness fixation.
>
> Q: No, it is not at all, sir, not at all. May I just explain to you, because you have been very concerned, understandably, to be treated in the same way as the soldiers, and it is precisely the same question, word for word, as was asked, I think, of some seven or eight soldiers.

Eventually he stated – the only time McGuinness had ever had to do so on oath – 'I left the IRA in the early part of the 1970s.'

Asked why he had not co-operated with the Inquiry by getting in touch and encouraging his former comrades to testify, even just picking up the phone and calling them, he replied, 'To pick the telephone up would be a particularly stupid thing to do, I thought you would have known that.'

On one of the main issues – whether the IRA's weapons had been hidden away in arms dumps on the day or whether they had been available to members – McGuinness had a strange hole in his testimony. The claim was that if they were in a dump then young 'hot-heads' from the IRA would not be able to disobey the orders allegedly given not to fire on the day. But what about McGuinness? Why did his weapons have to be hidden away in a dump, Glasgow asked him. 'I mean, in no sense were you a hot-head or anybody who would behave irresponsibly, why on earth did you not at least hang on to your own weapon?'

205

'Because I did not need a weapon,' he said.

One final question was put to McGuinness by one of the soldiers' lawyers. Mr Elias QC asked about one of the soldiers he represented. This soldier, numbered 227 by the Inquiry, had been in the 22nd Light Air Defence Regiment and had been positioned on the city walls on Bloody Sunday. He also testified at Widgery. One of the things that he had sworn both then and now was that he was able to hear and identify the first shots fired that day and that the first firing he heard was, as General Rose had also sworn, the sound of a Thompson machine gun. It had come from the Bogside and was undoubtedly the first firing he heard that day. Soldier 227 had been fired at by a Thompson in Derry before Bloody Sunday and said that he knew the sound well.

Elias asked McGuinness about this. Was Soldier 227 lying about this, he was asked. 'Probably, yes,' McGuinness replied. Elias explained just one other thing to McGuinness, which was that Soldier 227 was a very important witness for another reason. He was the soldier who, from the same position, had seen and testified that he had seen a soldier kneeling at the corner of Glenfada Park and shooting Barney McGuigan. Was 227 lying about that incident as well, McGuinness was asked. He had no answer.

At the end of the final day Lord Saville explained to McGuinness that Counsel for the Inquiry had asked the witness to identify people who were vital in helping the Tribunal arrive at the truth of what happened that day and that, as the chairman, he was now forced to direct the witness to answer the questions that had been put to him and that he refused to answer. Again, and for the final time, McGuinness reiterated that the code of honour of people who were members of the IRA in 1972 could not be betrayed and that he could therefore not comply. 'I rather thought you would say something along those lines,' said Saville and concluded by saying that the Tribunal would now have to consider what steps to take against him.

As McGuinness left the box a final round of applause for him rang out from the public gallery.

Outside in the square the show continued. McGuinness came out and gave an address to the press. Damien Donaghey, who had been wounded on the day, and Gerry Duddy, brother of Jack Duddy, who had been killed, paraded in front of the press with a banner saying, 'It is a Bloody Sunday Inquiry, not an inquiry on Martin McGuinness.'

McGuinness was flanked by a number of colleagues, including Raymond McCartney. Behind the press gaggle a gang of McGuinness's supporters pressed up close. As their hero spoke about what he had just achieved and the threat Lord Saville had just made they cheered him on. He spoke derisively of the idea that after all these hearings the only person who might go to prison would be him. As he finished with a final self-congratulatory speech his supporters surrounding the press clapped and cheered him on even louder. Eventually Martin McGuinness turned, and flanked by his ageing but still threatening friends, he took his leave of the Guildhall and the media that had surrounded him.

13

THE SOLDIER: 'F'

After firing at the rubble barricade from Kells Walk on 30 January 1972 four soldiers moved as a brick, or a pack, into Glenfada Park. They were Soldiers E, F, G and H. The shooting that went on in the sector into which they moved led to the largest number of casualties of any area. If the Saville Inquiry was to get to the truth it had to find out what had happened there.

But there was one unalterable problem from the outset. By the time that Lord Saville began his investigations, only two of the men from that brick of four were still alive: Soldiers F and H. Soldiers E and G were dead. How they had died, when or where were not known, although it was believed that at least one died while in Britain's special forces.

And so the two surviving members of that brick were all that the Tribunal had to rely on. Soldier H had shown in his testimony that he intended to stick to his unbelievable version of events. But what of F? What would he turn out to say? And would he be the soldier to snap?

For the testimony of Soldier F the extended families of the people he was known or believed to have killed travelled over from Derry to Westminster specially to see and hear him. There was considerable excitement and tension in the room before he entered. As he came in the noise died down and, just as with any of the other hundreds of witnesses, Lord Saville introduced himself and invited the witness to keep close to the microphone as he had, literally, a thousand times before. And then the questioning began. Short, stocky and in late middle age, Soldier F was, like all the other soldiers, the subject of considerable efforts to maintain his anonymity. But the families knew his name. They had known it for years. And he was warned at the outset that although the rest of his name would be protected, regarding his first name he did not have anonymity. That name was deemed to be in the public domain – because members of the

208

public had heard it being shouted thirty years earlier in Glenfada Park.

Soldier F was first taken over the new statement that he had, like every other witness, provided to the new Inquiry. Even by the standards of some other statements provided to the Inquiry by soldiers, Soldier F's statement, running to only eight pages, was extraordinarily devoid of content. He revealed that he had first gone on a tour of duty to Northern Ireland in 1969. In 1970 he had gone back on a two-year tour of duty. His first visit to Derry was 30 January 1972.

But about that day, Bloody Sunday, Soldier F could, it appeared, remember nothing. He could remember his colleagues. He could remember seeing a low wall and a rubble barricade. He could remember patrolling the city the day after Bloody Sunday. And he could remember giving evidence to Lord Widgery wearing his best uniform and dark glasses. He could remember that he and the other soldiers had felt 'fed up with the fact that a Tribunal took place'.

But what he could not remember was anything that he had done on the day. Midway through his statement he said simply that 'I remember firing my weapon but I do not know when, where or why I fired it.'

That was it. Or it would have been had not Soldier F been forced to attend, apparently even more unwillingly than his appearance before Lord Widgery, the Inquiry of Lord Saville.

The questioning was begun by Counsel to the Inquiry, Christopher Clarke.

Q: Had you fired live rounds in an operation before Bloody Sunday?

A: Yes.

Q: How many times?

A: A few times.

Q: What do you mean by that, do you mean two or three?

A: I think it was two or three, I am not sure, it was about three.

Q: According to your evidence to Lord Widgery, you fired thirteen rounds on Bloody Sunday. Had you ever fired as many as those before in an operation?

A: No.

Q: How many rounds approximately had you fired on previous operations?

A: I cannot remember, but possibly four or five, I am only assuming that number.

Q: Did you ever fire as many as thirteen rounds in an operation after Bloody Sunday?

A: I cannot answer that question.

Q: You cannot answer that question?

A: No.

Q: Why not—

LORD SAVILLE: You could limit it to Northern Ireland.

MR CLARKE: Okay, in Northern Ireland?

A: No.

He was asked if he had ever killed anyone before Bloody Sunday. He said, 'No.' Or after Bloody Sunday, in Northern Ireland? Again, he said, 'No.'

Q: This must, therefore, must it not, have been a pretty dramatic day?

A: It was, yes.

Q: And are you being truthful when you say that you remember practically nothing whatever about it?

A: That is correct.

Again and again questions specific and general about the day were asked of F, and again and again he answered either 'No' or 'I cannot remember'. In reply the measured Mr Clarke tried to press on. Occasionally he added a slightly incredulous statement like 'You cannot even remember that?'

Though he couldn't remember why he had fired his gun that day, Soldier F could remember, and recorded in his statement, hearing an exchange over the radio between the OC, Major Loden, and Colonel Wilford. He said, 'I heard Major Loden inform Colonel Wilford by radio that we were "taking fire", "receiving fire" or "under fire" … The response from the colonel came a few seconds later. I could hear it over the radio set. He said, "Go, go, go!"'

Questioned about this incident by Counsel, Soldier F was asked whether he had been on the same radio net as the colonel on the day. In an unusually lengthy answer he replied that he could remember that 'I was close to the radio, I did not have a radio.'

Soldier F obviously wanted to get out as soon as possible and was making the experience as swift as he could. But this was the easy, procedural, part. What he could not escape was what was going to happen next – questioning not on his memory but on the well-documented details of the people he had killed that day. The first of his victims was the first of the people to fall at the rubble barricade, Michael Kelly. It was over the killing of this man the net had first tightened around Soldier F. Not in this courtroom, but within hours of the shot being fired, in the early hours of the morning, back in 1972.

At 2.40 in the morning of 31 January 1972 Soldier F had given his first statement to the Royal Military Police. There, like all the other soldiers, and with the aid of a map, he first pointed out to the RMP the positions of the gunmen and bombers whom he claimed to have shot at. None of the shots suggested that he had fired near the rubble barricade where Kelly had fallen, shot side-on in the abdomen. Unfortunately for Soldier F this bullet, which had gone through the victim's bowel and main artery, had come to a stop inside the body. The small 7.62mm calibre bullet was wedged in the sacrum, the triangular bone at the base of the spine. And while Soldier F was speaking to the RMP, in the mortuary of the local hospital the bullet that he had fired was being dug out of Michael Kelly's dead body.

The second statement given by Soldier F in 1972 was given on 19 February. It was part of the proceedings for the upcoming Widgery Inquiry. And there, almost three weeks after the shootings, Soldier F for the first time had said: 'I have now read my previous statements and looked at maps and photographs of the area, and realise that I have mistaken the sequence of events. After we first left our vehicles in the Rossville Flats area, I did not, as said earlier, fire at a window in the Rossville Flats. I fired these shots later. I did however fire; I aimed round at a man I saw behind the barricade about 40 yards from me who was about to throw a bomb.'

Appearing before Lord Saville, Soldier F was asked why he had originally forgotten about firing at, and killing, an alleged bomber at the rubble barricade at the start of his firing. An answer was suggested by Counsel as to why he had omitted any reference to firing there and in another 'very controversial area', the south side of the Rossville Flats.

> Q: Is the reason why there is no mention of either of those firings because the firing that took place from the Kells Walk wall to the barricade and from Glenfada Park to below the Rossville Flats was known by you to be unjustifiable and you wished to hide the part that you had played in it?
>
> A: No.

The reason that F was prompted to recover this memory a few weeks after Bloody Sunday seems in fact extremely clear. He 'remembered' that he had shot in that direction because he became aware either before or during his interview with Colonel Overbury that the rifles that had been fired on Bloody Sunday were being sent by the army to the Department of Industrial and Forensic Science (DIFS) in Belfast. Twenty-nine self-loading rifles were sent off to Belfast to try to help trace individual bullets to individual soldiers' rifles. F would have known that his bullets could be traced to his gun. And sure enough, when the tests returned in relation to the bullet that had been dug out of the body of Michael Kelly, the Principal Scientific Officer declared himself 'satisfied that the bullet was fired in rifle No A 32515 referred to as JLS/6'. That is, the gun belonging to Soldier F.

After firing at the rubble barricade Soldier F ran into Glenfada Park with Soldiers E, G and H. In this sector of shooting seven people were killed or wounded. A total of twenty-nine rounds were fired in Glenfada Park. Counsel to the Inquiry asked F:

> Q: Did you learn from the other members of your platoon after the events of the day were over, what shots they had fired?
>
> A: No.
>
> Q: Or approximately how many?
>
> A: No.

Q: What about G, who was your mate and friend; did you learn from him what he had fired?

A: No.

Q: You never discussed it?

A: No.

Q: Is that really so?

A: As far as I remember, yes.

He was questioned about the fatalities in Glenfada Park:

Q: The Tribunal has also heard evidence that the soldiers who came in were not firing in a disciplined way, but randomly, either firing from the hip or with a rifle held at chest height or with a barrel fanning from right to left. Is that what happened?

A: No.

Q: As I told you, the person who is next door to the fence in this photograph is Joe Mahon. He was shot by a bullet that penetrated his abdomen, above the right side of his pelvis, as he was making his way along the wooden fencing that we can see, according to his account, banging on the fencing to see if anybody would open a door to him, by a soldier who was firing from the north-east. Was that soldier you?

A: No.

Q: Do you know which soldier it was?

A: I do not.

Q: As we can see, William McKinney fell close to him in the gutter, shot by a bullet that entered the right side of his back and another that entered his left arm. Could that have been you?

A: No.

Q: Do you know who it was?

A: I do not.

Q: James Wray, the one in the far right-hand corner of the photograph in the south-west, was shot twice in the back. Did you shoot him?

A: I did not.

Q: Do you know who did?

A: No.

Q: Joe Mahon, who looked as if he was dead and feigned death, was, as I have said, not [dead]. His evidence to this Tribunal was that he saw James Wray shot twice at point-blank range whilst Wray was on the ground, shot by a soldier, probably the first who had come into the square, who had blond hair. Did you see that happen?

A: I did not.

Q: Mahon identified the soldier as being Soldier G. Is that what Soldier G did?

A: I do not know what Soldier G did.

Q: What, you have no idea what he did?

A: That is correct.

Q: You never asked him and were never told?

A: That is correct.

Under analysis Soldier F's version of events looked even more implausible than it had on first viewing. It was pointed out to him that the targets F and his colleagues claimed to have fired at and the 'nail-bombers and gunmen' whom they claimed to have killed didn't even correlate with the dead found in the area. Adding up those killed in Abbey Park, the neighbouring Glenfada Park and the area behind the Rossville Flats, there were seven targets accounted for. But in these areas alone there had in fact been a total of thirteen victims.

And in relation to the two men killed behind the Rossville Flats, McGuigan and Doherty, and the two men wounded in the same location, there had not even been any explanation offered as to why these men had been shot. No explanation had been given to Lord Widgery and none had been given in the intervening thirty years as to why these people had been killed or wounded.

Q: Can you offer any explanation as to how that situation arises?

A: No, I cannot.

Q: It must follow, must it not, if, as appears overwhelmingly likely, these two were killed and the other two were wounded by shots fired by soldiers, that there has been a cover-up of their deaths and woundings?

A: (Pause)

Q: Is that not so?

A: Not as I am aware of, no.

The evidence given to the Inquiry by 027 was given to him. Was it true that he had been, along with G, the prime mover in the Glenfada Park area in which so many casualties had occurred? Had he and G indeed been 'self-sufficient and a law unto themselves'? Had they, as 027 had claimed, 'probably enjoyed all of this'?

As some observers noticed, F's answers to questions being put to him by all of the lawyers before him were classic counter-interrogation tactics: continuous denial and claims of a lack of knowledge. In F's case the main advantage he had, as he clearly knew, was that he could claim that thirty years on it was impossible to remember anything – because not only the details but everything about the day could only be solved if his memory yielded up its contents. Yet nobody could force him to do this. All he had to do was to sit through the questions and answer each one while saying that he had no memory of whether things had happened or not.

What Soldier F did not grasp, had not appreciated or simply had no way around was that his memory was not in fact needed to determine his guilt. Because plenty of other people there on the day, both army and civilian, had seen him do things and certainly did have memories. The picture they built up showed plenty of reasons for F to feign forgetfulness.

For instance, there was the evidence of Father O'Keeffe, a local priest and

215

university lecturer in Derry. O'Keeffe had been in the barracks at Fort George, taken there with a crowd of other civilians charged with rioting after the shooting had finished.

In his evidence O'Keeffe remembered the real name of Soldier F, a name which, as he recorded in a supplementary statement, he had never forgotten. Partly, he said, because he remembered thinking that the name was an Irish Catholic name. He described F's physical appearance accurately, and also recalled a number of incidents involving him at Fort George. Father O'Keeffe had not known that the young man he had seen shot earlier in the afternoon, Michael Kelly, was the first victim of the man now stalking the room he was in at Fort George.

While waiting there to be charged O'Keeffe witnessed two soldiers, one with 'scary eyes' and an 'almost psychotic look' and the other 'smaller, about 5'7" or 5'8" with a thin face and a regional accent, maybe Scottish. He was called [ ].' As usual in the Inquiry when a real name was mentioned, the cipher – in this case F – had been placed in the statement in the place of the actual name. The other man described by O'Keeffe was almost certainly G. The latter, he said, he remembered as 'even having the sadistic edge on Lance Corporal F'. O'Keeffe recorded in testimony how these two soldiers had 'roamed' among the arrestees, stamping on people's feet, kneeing them in the groin and engaging in other acts of 'idle brutality'. They appeared to be in charge, he said. One soldier came into the room and ordered heaters to be brought in. F and his colleague made two young men stand with 'their faces very close to the heaters for a long time'. Father O'Keeffe recalled F saying to one of these young men as he got increasingly upset, 'Do you want a drink?' The young man said 'Yes' and F promptly spat in his mouth. At another point he recalled F kicking someone in the room and a uniformed RUC officer reprimanding him and telling him that unless F stopped abusing people in police custody he would charge him with assault.

When it came to O'Keeffe's turn to be charged he recalled an army officer coming into the room.

"'Who is charging those men as stone-throwers? Lance Corporal F – you saw those men throwing stones?" F replied, "Yes, sir." The English officer said, "Well, charge them then." At that point, F came up to me and said, "You were throwing stones, were you not?" I said, "No, I am a Roman Catholic priest and a lecturer in philosophy and I do not throw stones." F stepped back, paused for a

216

moment and then kicked me very hard in the groin.' F then posed for an arrest photograph with Father O'Keeffe.[3]

Questioned about this thirty years later, Soldier F could of course recall none of this. He was asked how it had come about that charges of stone-throwing had been levelled by him at a priest who had thrown no stones. He had no answer for that.

But if F thought that with a day of denials and forgetfulness he had escaped the problem he was mistaken. And there were far more serious charges to come. The second and final day of his testimony was going to be a lot harder than his first, for he was finally going to face the legal representatives of his victims. His cover, and indeed something of his identity, was about to be if not blown then exposed. As usual, at the end of his first day, Saville requested that the witness ensure that he did not talk with anyone else about the evidence he was giving until he had finished giving it.

First up the next morning at 9.30 was Seamus Treacy, who represented a number of the families. He made it clear from the outset what he wanted to achieve. He began by telling Soldier F to keep close to the microphone because a large number of people had come to hear his evidence, and it was important that they heard everything. He then asked F how long he had been in the Parachute Regiment. He had been in it for some time before Bloody Sunday and, it turned out, he had been in the army for another twenty-two years afterwards. 'Twenty-two years?' the lawyer asked. Yes. So until 1994. No, until 1988, F said.

And what about his rank? He had been a lance corporal on Bloody Sunday, Had his career progressed 'fairly smoothly'? 'It all depends what you mean,' said F. 'Well, you did not remain a lance corporal, did you?' he was asked. No, he had been promoted from time to time. And what rank had he arrived at by the time he left the army? F said that he had left the army with the rank of warrant officer, Class 2, a fairly senior position among the lower rankings in the British army. Though it certainly did not demonstrate a glittering progress over a decade and a half in the army, Treacy put it to him that whatever he had done on Bloody Sunday clearly had not counted against him in his career. F denied that he had been promoted because of what happened, and the lawyer corrected him. He was not saying that he had been promoted because of Bloody Sunday, rather that

---

[3] That photograph is available on the new Inquiry's website, appendix four of O'Keeffe's supplementary statement, labelled H21.126.

whatever he had done on Bloody Sunday had not counted against him. Soldier F confirmed that. Then came what was, for the British army, the most scandalous part:

Q: You were never disciplined or reprimanded for anything that you did on Bloody Sunday?

A: No.

Q: Not even after the Widgery Report came out, in which Lord Widgery indicated that those who had fired in Glenfada Park, he described it as 'bordering on the reckless'?

A: No.

Q: No one ever came to you and drew that report to your attention and questioned you about that?

A: That is correct.

Q: It is clear, therefore, is it, that you yourself never felt that you had done anything other than your duty on Bloody Sunday?

A: That is correct.

Q: And you had done, on Bloody Sunday, what had been expected of you?

A: I was doing my job as a soldier, yes.

Q: And you behaved loyally and you were rewarded for what happened, in the sense that your career progressed normally and you were promoted through the ranks in the course of time?

A: Due to my career in the service, yes.

Q: As far as you were concerned and obviously as far as your chain of command was concerned, they never expressed any disapproval to you, at any stage, in relation to your activities on Bloody Sunday?

A: That is correct.

Next up was Ms McDermott, representing the family of Patrick Doherty, shot behind the Rossville Flats as he was crawling away. McDermott showed

Soldier F a photograph of Doherty's dead body.

> Q: He is the person you shot dead over by Joseph Place. He was a working man, aged thirty-one; he had a good job; he was a family man and he left a widow, aged twenty-nine, and six children, who were aged between eleven years and seven months old, and all of them are here today, along with grandchildren of course he never saw, who never saw him, because that is the human reality of what happened on this day; is that not right?
>
> A: If you say so.
>
> Q: Do you not know that?
>
> A: Well, on reference what you have just told me?
>
> Q: He was an unarmed, an innocent man and the Doherty family would like to know how it came about that you shot him dead. They are entitled to know that; do you agree?
>
> A: They are.

But he did not seem incredibly eager to help. He was asked:

> Q: Why have you come here, Soldier F?
>
> A: I was asked to come here to assist the Inquiry.
>
> Q: Have you come because if you do not come you realise you could end up going to prison?
>
> A: Yes.
>
> Q: And that is the real reason?
>
> A: No, I am here – the real reason I am here is to assist the Inquiry and tell the truth.
>
> Q: That is another lie, is it not?
>
> A: I do not think so, no.

But nobody watching F saying this could have believed him.

He was next asked about the fatal shot he had fired at Doherty – one of the shots he had originally 'forgotten about' back in 1972. Doherty had been shot in the buttock. The bullet had travelled through his crawling body, destroying the body – the colon, the diaphragm, the left lung – as it made its way through, and exited from the left side of his chest. And there, shot, he had lain, crying out in pain and calling for somebody to come and be with him because he did not want to die alone. A young woman who had seen this, who was there, called Donna Harkin, described it as follows: 'It was a coward that shot Mr Doherty, not even shooting him in the back, they shot him as he was crawling away, trying to save himself.'

F was asked about this by Doherty's family's lawyer.

Q: You were then and certainly in all the years that you spent in the Army since, you are very experienced at shooting?

A: I had experience in many things.

Q: Is shooting one of them?

A: That is one of the—

Q: Sorry?

A: That is one of the points, yes.

Q: That was a cowardly shot, was it not?

A: I do not agree with that.

Q: You cannot remember anything about it?

A: I am just referring to your question.

Q: Do you know anything about hunting?

A: Hunting?

Q: Hunting animals?

A: Something about them, yes.

Q: Do you ever engage in that yourself?

220

A: What, now?

Q: At any time?

A: I used to, yes.

Q: It is a well-known hunting shot, is it not, the shot that you used to shoot Mr Doherty dead?

A: Which shot are you referring to?

Q: A Texas heart shot; have you ever heard of that?

A: No, I have not heard of that one, no.

Q: The sort of shot that you take if you can get no other kind of shot?

A: Normally—

Q: A cheap shot?

A: Normally on a hunting shot you shoot to kill the animal to cause less pain and less damage, to put the animal out of its misery, you do not just shoot anywhere.

Q: That is the way you shot Mr Doherty, was it not, as if you were hunting him down like an animal?

A: That is not correct.

Finally the Doherty family's lawyer put it plainly to F.

Q: I want to suggest to you on behalf of the Doherty family that you murdered Mr Doherty and that as you sit there, you have got away with murder and that you have no intention of alleviating the suffering that they have endured over all these years by even attempting to explain to them your role and what went on.

A: That is not correct.

Q: Do you have anything to say to that?

A: I am just saying I fired at a person who had a pistol and as I mention in my statement.

221

Q: Do you have anything to say to them?

A: I am very, very sorry for what happened on that day, but I am here to help the Inquiry and to assist and tell the truth as much as I can.

Q: What are you sorry about?

A: The circumstances that happened that day, there was obviously innocent people killed, there was also gunmen and bombers killed. So for their grief, for their personal grief, I cannot do anything about that.

If F thought that would do he was soon to be shown very wrong. After being taken through the circumstances of the killing of Patrick Doherty Soldier F was taken over his shooting in the head of Barney McGuigan. Again, he said he had no memory of firing the shot that killed McGuigan. But as the legal representative of the McGuigan family pointed out, he did not need Soldier F's memory to recreate what he did that day. He had remembered shooting in that sector only when he had realised that bullets would be traced to him. And so he made up a story about that area too, to explain his shooting. He had invented a story about a man with a pistol whom he had fired at. And if he thought he had got away with it, then it was because he had no knowledge of the fact that up on the walls, out of his immediate sight, had been another soldier, another member of the British army, who had seen what he had done and had testified to it. It was put to Soldier F that he had killed Barney McGuigan by shooting him in the head. He acknowledged that he had shot a man, that the man must be the person who had been shown to him, but stuck to the utterly impossible position that the man he had shot had a pistol. Barney McGuigan did not have a pistol. At most he held a handkerchief. And he had been shot in cold blood.

Then finally, after all the drama of the questioning by the McGuigan family's legal representative, during which the man's widow had had to leave the room and now came back, the questioning of Soldier F was still not over. It was now the turn of Lord Gifford, representing the family of James Wray, shot in Glenfada Park. And shot again as he lay on the ground, dead or dying. He was one of three young men shot in a row as they fled across the opposite end of the park. Lord Gifford offered a possibility for Soldier F.

Q: If it were true that you could not remember, then one reason why you cannot remember may be that what you did was so inexcusable and wicked that you have blanked it out of your memory.

222

A: That is not correct.

Q: You do not know that, do you, F; you do not know that, do you?

A: That is not correct.

Q: How do you know whether or not you were one of the three who shot unarmed civilians, because you do not remember?

A: I can only refer to my statements.

Q: Which may be true and which may be a lie; is that not right?

A: I can just refer to my statements.

Q: Which may be true and may be a lie; you do not know which, do you?

A: That is not for me to comment on.

Q: I think it is. Because if you had been that shooter, firing in that way you would have to have lied about it to save your skin, would you not?

A: I did not.

And amid all this there suddenly came a most unexpected revelation. Lord Gifford said to Soldier F: 'Your name is Dave – it is in the public domain and your counsel has accepted it – is Dave, is it not?' It was as simple as that. The name of Soldier F was in the public domain. And it had been released for a reason. Because unknown to Soldier F, one of those who had been shot in Glenfada Park, who had been wounded but not killed, was Joe Mahon. He was lying on the ground behind the dead body of William McKinney. As Mahon lay there he had heard one of the Paras shout to another, 'I've got another one,' and then, 'We're pulling out, Dave.'

Soldier F's anonymity was slipping. But his cover, his alibi, his story were slipping faster.

At the very end of that day, having been confronted for the first time by the families of the people he had killed thirty years before and having been confronted, as he was, by the mountain of evidence which pinpointed his actions as closely, on occasion, as though he had been caught on film, Soldier F had the charges put to him by Counsel to the Inquiry.

223

It was put to him that the Tribunal could conclude that he had shot William McKinney in Glenfada Park.

It was put to him that the ballistic evidence showed that he had shot dead Michael Kelly.

It was put to him that he had shot Barney McGuigan. It was put to him that he had shot Patrick Doherty.

Spelling it out clearly, F was told by Counsel to the Inquiry:

> Q: What is alleged in relation to each of those four people is that you shot them without justification, that is to say, that you murdered them; do you follow?
>
> A: I follow, it is not correct, but I follow, yes.
>
> Q: And you say that it is not correct, because?
>
> A: Because, as I refer to my statements, the people I shot were either petrol bombers or a person who had a weapon.
>
> Q: I also put to you that you may have wounded Joe Mahon, the boy whose body is on the ground behind William McKinney's in Glenfada Park. The suggestion is also that you may have wounded the two others who were wounded below the Rossville Flats; do you follow?
>
> A: Yes.
>
> Q: Is there anything that you can say about that or would wish to say about that?
>
> A: No.

It was put to him that the evidence he had given to the Royal Military Police hours after the events, the evidence he had given three weeks later and the evidence he had given to the current Tribunal were all false, 'both as to what you have said and as to what you have not revealed'.

> Q: And that, in the case of the evidence that you gave to Lord Widgery and to this Tribunal, evidence being given upon oath, is evidence that constitutes perjury; do you follow?
>
> A: I do.

Q: The suggestion is that the reason why that evidence is false is because you have needed to conceal unlawful activities on your part and on the part of your colleagues; do you follow?

A: I do.

Finally, for one last time, one last effort was made to see whether Soldier F would crack; whether even now, with the protection of anonymity, the assurance that no prosecution would follow if he told the truth, and many of his former comrades dead, he could finally solve, definitely, the mysteries of the day. Counsel asked him:

Q: Is there anything more that you wish the Tribunal to take into account or to hear from you in relation to those matters?

A: No, I have nothing further to add.

He was asked if he also understood that he was accused of being guilty of brutality and mistreatment of prisoners at Fort George. He said he did.

And he was asked if he understood that he could be accused of having identified people as rioters who had not in fact been rioting. He said, 'Yes.'

Finally he was asked:

Q: Is there anything more that you would like to say to the Tribunal in relation to that or, indeed, any other matter –

A: No.

Q: – about which you have been asked to give evidence? A: No.

MR CLARKE: Thank you.

On the day itself, a civilian named Joseph Doherty had seen Soldier F firing, down on one knee at the bottom corner of Glenfada Park, separated for a moment from his mate G. Doherty saw F shoot Barney McGuigan through the back of the head. After seeing this Joseph Doherty said, 'I can recall that the other soldier came back up to him and called him back. Both turned around and went out of my sight.'

This time on his own, his friend G dead, his story in tatters, but still belligerently sticking to it, Soldier F made what would probably be his last appearance in front of a roomful of people who knew who he was and what he had done. Turning, he got out of his chair and once again went out of sight.

14

THE IRA

Members of 1 Para had gone into the Bogside that day and gunned down innocent citizens of Derry. Nothing could absolve them from blame for that. But there were still questions.

Why had so many members of a highly trained brigade started shooting nearly simultaneously, in different sectors? All of the dead were unarmed, save Gerald Donaghey, who was carrying nail- bombs, but even Donaghey had not been in the act of throwing a nail-bomb when he was shot. Members of 1 Para said that they had aimed and fired at nail-bombers and gunmen. Yet if they had they had missed them. Were there none there? Or were there gunmen, but fewer than the soldiers subsequently decided to say there were? And if those gunmen were there, did they cause the firing or was their firing in the end unconnected to the army shooting that day?

Over the course of thirty years Irish Republican legend had it that on Bloody Sunday the army had gunned down civilians in cold blood and without provocation. The events were such a recruiting sergeant for the IRA that any change in this story could have been hugely damaging to them. The Provisional IRA's own Green Book from after Bloody Sunday referred to the way in which they had been able to turn the events of the day to their own advantage. So any suggestion that they might actually have borne any of the responsibility for some of the deaths would have had potentially catastrophic effects on the organisation's recruitment and levels of public support.

Yet over the years, despite the agreement developing, even in the British government, that the dead were innocent and the soldiers had fired recklessly, there were a couple of stories from reputable sources that went very much against the grain of the argument that the IRA had not fired that day.

227

Father Edward Daly was a priest in Derry on the day and rose to be Bishop of Derry. He was the priest who said the last rites over the body of the young Jack Duddy, shot down as he ran towards the Rossville Flats. He had also, in footage that became perhaps the most iconic from Bloody Sunday, waved his white handkerchief in his hand, bent over, as he escorted a group of men carrying Duddy's body past the soldiers. He had no doubt about the innocence of Duddy. Nor was his testimony doubted that no secret burials of IRA men could have taken place after the day. But this solid, most upstanding and reliable of witnesses had seen something else that day. He had testified about it at Widgery and had spoken about it to Saville.

Just before Father Daly led a group carrying Duddy past the army lines, he saw a figure moving along the gable wall of the last house at the end of Chamberlain Street. The priest saw a man in his thirties, wearing a brown coat, with a gun in his hand. He saw him fire 'two or three' shots around the corner at the soldiers. As Father Daly said, 'We screamed at the gunman to go away because we were frightened that the soldiers might think the fire was coming from where we were located.' Father Daly said that after firing the shots at the soldiers the man 'looked at us and then he drifted away across or into the mouth of Chamberlain Street'. Father Daly said he had never seen him before, did not recognise him but had shouted at him, with the others, because he was fearful that the gunman's presence might attract army gunfire in their direction. In the years that followed, and for the opening years of the Saville process, this mysterious figure became known as 'Father Daly's gunman'.

But in a city where the unprovoked nature of 1 Para's assault had become sacred writ there was at least one other shot that had become widely known about in the intervening years. This was the shot known to the army as 'the drainpipe shot'. This shot, which occurred very early in the firing, just before 16.00 and just before 1 Para went in, was observed by a large number of soldiers whose heads it went over. Major Loden recorded it in his diary, Soldier O recorded that it changed the whole nature of the operation, and it was the shot of which Colonel Wilford recorded, 'One of my senior officers who was standing with me at the time said, "That shot was aimed at us, sir."'

Many members of the army believed and recorded in testimony that the shot had come from the direction of the Rossville Flats. In fact it came from slightly nearer than that, from the top floor of the north-eastern end of Columbcille Court. It was fired by a civilian gunman, over the heads of the marchers at the tail end of the march.

This shot occurred very close to the time that the army fired the first shots of the day, wounding Damien Donaghey and John Johnston at the wasteground site where youths were throwing stones at the army. Over the years it had been suggested that the shot from Columbcille Court had been a retaliatory shot, but whichever order they came in they were so close in time that it was impossible that it was fired by anyone not already in a position to fire at soldiers.

Sean Keenan Junior, a member of the Provisional IRA, said he had been called over to remonstrate with the gunman by a woman who told him there were two or three young men with a rifle in a house.

In any case, it must have been widely known in Derry from soon after the events that though the people who had been shot were innocent, the soldiers had not gone into an unarmed area. Nevertheless the unwillingness of civilian witnesses to admit to having seen civilian gunmen became a very striking aspect of the civilian evidence. As, finally, were the number of people who eventually came forward and said that they had seen gunmen. It was not an easy position for a member of the community in Derry to admit to. The testimony of a number of witnesses to the Inquiry showed this. But as the evidence mounted it became impossible for the testimony of these people to be dismissed.

There was the evidence of another priest, Father O'Gara, who had testified to Widgery but died in 1982. On Bloody Sunday, after the shooting had finished, he went to Altnagelvin hospital, where, among other things, he broke the news to Barney McGuigan's wife of the death of her husband. But earlier that day he had seen something else. He recorded in 1972 how after firing had started he watched as 'a young man appeared from the Cathedral side of Kells Walk, unknown and unseen by soldiers, drew a pistol from his pocket, leaned over a wall at the end of Kells Walk and fired three shots quickly.'

Meanwhile, a young civilian woman called Monica Barr was inside her flat on the day. She said at the time, and testified to Saville, that after the shooting had started she looked out of her window and over to the Rossville Flats. There she saw, and had a clear recollection of it, 'a hand stick out of an open window on the eighth floor of Block 1 of the Rossville Flats... The window, as I recall it, was tilted inwards at the top and outwards at the bottom. The hand, which was holding a pistol, appeared from over the top of the window pane and pointed downwards. I remember one shot being fired from the pistol. The shot had a "pop" sound and was certainly different from the other shots I had heard earlier. Almost immediately I heard a "crack" and saw the wood at the top of the window frame splinter where I presume a bullet fired by a soldier below the flats had hit. At around the same time the hand disappeared. I think there may have been net curtains over the window as I am unable to describe the face or shape of the individual who fired the shot from the Rossville Flats.'

It was clear, however, that reminiscences of the day like this did not necessarily go down well with the local population. Another civilian who saw a gunman was Marian McMenamin. She was one of those who began to run down Rossville Street as the army Saracens came into the Bogside. Shooting had begun and, she said, 'as we were running away, I saw a civilian with a gun.' What is perhaps most interesting is what she said next:

> I hate myself for saying this; I have never told anybody about this before, not even my husband and we have been married for over twenty-five years. I feel disloyal to the innocent men who died on Bloody Sunday, but I did see him and I feel that the truth must now be told. The gunman was in an alleyway, near the pram ramp at the south gable end wall of Kells Walk.

She recorded that the gunman she saw was young, in his mid to late twenties, was on his own, and that he held his 'quite big, squarish, handgun in his right hand and had it held out in front of him, but not aiming it. He appeared from behind the wall, walked east towards Rossville Street, looked south towards the Rossville Flats' shops and then withdrew again.' She did not know where he had gone after that.

Perhaps most interesting is that line 'I hate myself for saying this.' Why would anybody hate themselves for telling the truth? Because, it soon became clear, anything that hinted that the army had any justification for opening fire went against the popular narrative of the day.

In February 2001 during evidence a man called William Harley told the Inquiry that he had seen a man fire five or six rounds at the army, possibly before any army firing. But in spite of repeated questioning he refused to name the man he believed he had recognised firing. Families of those killed on the day appealed to the citizens of Derry to 'break down the wall of silence' and announced that they were 'deeply saddened' by the refusal of some witnesses to co-operate in revealing what could well be 'unpalatable' facts.

Another civilian found himself in the same position. Charles McGill gave a statement to the Inquiry. And then a curious thing happened. Eversheds, the solicitors to the Inquiry who took down all the statements, revealed in a supplementary note to the statement that there was something McGill had told them that he said he was only telling them on the condition that it did not go into his statement. This was not procedure and the solicitors were forced to declare it. As a result McGill had, reluctantly, to give a second, supplementary statement. What McGill had not wanted to admit in his statement was that shortly after the main firing had stopped he had seen a man with a long coat and a rifle in Glenfada Park. McGill told him to 'fuck off '. He also saw a tray of nail-bombs being brought out. At 17.30 he saw three cars of Provos with guns come into the area. None of these things had been mentioned in his NICRA statement in 1972 and he had wanted to hold them back from this Tribunal. The reason, Eversheds recorded, was that 'he says he has to live around here and he only gave us the information after we assured him that his statement would only be signed when he had amended it as he wished.'

McGill had seen a number of people killed that day and he further said that he had not wanted to divulge the information about the civilian gunmen because he 'did not want people to use [it] as an excuse to detract from the enormity of what I had seen that day'. Questioned about his phrase that 'he has to live around here' he said in his oral evidence given in the Guildhall in Derry shortly afterwards that he now did not know what he had meant by that.

Meanwhile, Bernard Gillespie had admitted to seeing a man with a rifle at Columbcille Court. But he said that 'I didn't mention the civilian gunman at the time because I was very angry at what had happened that day and I was not going to give any help to the British army in saying that anyone had provoked what they did. I didn't want to give any credence to their argument that they had been fired on.' Slowly but surely similar tales started to come out. A journalist who testified said that he had spoken to a young woman who had seen a man fire a handgun in William Street but who had refused to make any reference to it in her statement.

Early in the shooting Michael Lynch saw a man in a parka jacket with the hood up come out of the north-east side of Glenfada Park North (the same part Soldiers E, F, G and H went in through) and fire two shots from a handgun at soldiers in Rossville Street.

As soon as he had fired the shots, he ran away in the same direction from which he had come from. I do not know what happened to the gunman after this. I was quite surprised to see the gunman as there had been a definite view beforehand that it was a civil rights march and that nothing should be done to give the soldiers an excuse to do anything. The whisperings on the street were that it would be a safe march. It almost seemed like he was acting out of frustration or was relieving his anger in some way.

Eventually, although there was certainly, if not a cloak of, then a tendency towards, silence in the city, dozens of civilians admitted in their testimony to Saville that they had seen civilians with guns on the day. Some saw them fire. Some saw them holding guns. Others– and this group was particularly large – saw a car or several cars of young men who, at various times from the period of shooting to around an hour afterwards, came into the Bogside laden with weapons. Certainly after the shooting it became clear that a large and relatively organised number of people turned up with arms to fire on the army. But one of the seldom commented-upon revelations was that if you add together all of the sightings of civilian gunmen by civilians that day it is clear that the Bogside was not simply dotted but covered with people armed and prepared to take on the army.

One other memory stands out from all of the testimony provided about civilian gunmen. It is from one William Breslin, a retired schoolteacher who, along with Ivan Cooper and others, had been involved in setting up the Derry Labour Party. In his statement he records a particularly telling exchange shortly after the shooting had died down. Breslin remembered that he had gone to the journalist Nell McCafferty's house where there were lots of people. They listened to the radio as the news came on saying that five people had been killed. While he was there a member of the Official IRA came into the house:

> While I was there, one of the Official Republicans came into Nell's house. I had always considered this man to be on the political wing of the Officials rather than in the Official IRA. He may have come to find out the Labour Party reaction to the events of the day. He did not talk about what he had been doing during the march. I said, 'There's five dead.' He said, 'I know, it may be the best thing that has ever happened.' I remember reacting angrily to this and I might well have thumped him but was restrained by Nell, or someone else. He quickly explained what he meant: 'This time the Brits have gone too far and they won't get away with it. They'll be condemned the world over.'

Breslin added another memory about this man. Years later he saw a photograph that the Saville Inquiry brought back to light. It was a photograph taken on the day, probably by an Italian photographer called Fulvio Grimaldi. It was of the man whom Father Daly saw with a gun at the end of Chamberlain Street. Breslin was particularly struck on seeing the photo because the man in it, the man who had fired up the street near where Jack Duddy was killed, was the man who had come into McCafferty's house. Breslin recognised him because he was wearing the same clothes in the photo as he had worn when he came into the house.

In the course of the Saville Inquiry the photo of this man and the man himself were finally to become public. And so, at last, were his comrades. After years of requests, searches and doubts, the IRA were going to have to account for what they had done.

When the Saville Inquiry was set up in 1998 it was hoped, and requested, that anyone with information about the events of Bloody Sunday should come forward. But from the moment that statements were gathered and even more so when civilians began to testify, it became clear that a gap existed in the evidence being given. The soldiers had said that they had faced gunmen, and many independent observers and civilians had seen civilian firing on the day.

In his opening statement, Edwin Glasgow QC for the majority of the soldiers pointed out the disservice that the silence of the IRA was doing not only to the case of his clients but to the Tribunal as a whole. Nobody from either wing of the IRA had come forward. So in the meantime, Glasgow submitted, the collecting of evidence and witnesses had been a 'wholly one-sided discovery' process.

In February 2001 a witness named a gunman he had spotted in the Bogside on the day. The man he named not only rejected the idea that he had ever been in the IRA, he also said he had not been on the march on the day. The following week William Harley was asked, but refused, to name the gunman that he and Father Daly had seen. Eventually he relented and had the name written on a piece of paper. But the name was not read out. Lord Saville expressed his frustration. The Inquiry was in what he described as a 'quandary' over the silence of witnesses about IRA activity on the day.

Finally Lord Saville warned that continued silence on the part of the IRA and silence about the IRA from citizens of the city would give the strong impression

– and would lead the Tribunal to have to conclude – that this had occurred because the IRA had something to hide.

Local author Eamonn McCann, who was close to the families, said during his evidence that it was the feeling of the families that 'for as long as IRA members do not come forward, then they are in effect polluting the truth about Bloody Sunday by not clearing up what they were doing.'

Eventually, after considerable pressure, five former members of the Official IRA at last approached the Inquiry, through a barrister, saying that they would be willing to give evidence on the condition that they were, like the soldiers, given anonymity. Over the course of the next two years they provided statements to the Inquiry and at the end of 2003 they constituted the last major block of witnesses to testify.

The first shots by the army on Bloody Sunday were those of Soldiers A and B, who fired at Damien Donaghey on the laundry waste- ground. The first known incoming round was either fired before, at almost exactly the same time or, most likely, almost immediately afterwards. This was the drainpipe shot that soldiers had thought had come from the direction of the Rossville Flats but which had in fact come from Columbcille Court. It was a single shot that dramatically changed the perception of the troops of 1 Para as they were about to enter the Bogside.

Considering the gravity of the act it was in some ways surprising that the gunman who fired that shot came forward at all. But he did and he was given the cipher OIRA 1. This man testified that along with an OIRA colleague given the cipher OIRA 2 he was on the Command Staff of the Derry OIRA at the time of Bloody Sunday. They said that they had come forward, like the other Officials, because of the requests made by the families. The evidence they gave turned out to answer, finally, some of the questions surrounding the last mysteries of the day. And they also provoked a final set of questions.

OIRA 1 and OIRA 2 claimed that they had gone to Columbcille Court the night before Bloody Sunday to retrieve a .303 rifle with a defective or missing sight but were afraid of undercover soldiers after a shooting incident earlier that day. They claimed, somewhat implausibly, that they had decided to return for the rifle the next day in broad daylight during the march while hundreds of troops were stationed around.

They claimed they heard that the army had shot Donaghey and Johnston and in retaliation fired a shot at a soldier by the Presbyterian church. Whether due to the defective sight or to bad shooting, the shot failed to hit the soldier OIRA 1 had aimed at. This, it seems, was the shot that instead hit and shattered the drainpipe on the side of the church.

A number of witnesses testified to the fact that at the bottom of the stairwell OIRA 1 and 2 were exiting from, they were immediately accosted by a group of people. There was some kind of altercation. A person who described himself simply as 'a Republican' and who was given the cipher RM 1 said that he wrestled the gun off the gunmen. A member of the Provisional IRA given the cipher PIRA 1 said in a statement to the Inquiry that he had raced up the stairs after hearing the shot and, using 'a few choice adjectives', asked the two what they thought they were doing, firing during a march. Others, including the Provo Sean Keenan Junior, got involved in the dispute as well.

Shortly afterwards Father Denis Bradley passed by and was told that a 'Stickie' (Official) gunman who had fired a shot had been chased away by 'the boys' (the Provos). He thought this was true because 'I had held a fear about the Official IRA's activities that day… There were some very irresponsible people in their organisation.'

What was perhaps most interesting about the Officials' line on this shot and other shootings that day was not just that they clearly failed, as they and the Provos had previously claimed, to remove all their guns from the Bogside but they had actually, at least in this case, positioned them in advance.

This contrasts strongly with what the Officials tried to claim to be the case after the event. For in media interviews immediately after Bloody Sunday they told very different stories. Journalists and others who had spoken to the Officials in 1972 were told by them that no Officials had fired any shots. Indeed, at a press conference on the night of Bloody Sunday, the Officials' spokesperson said that 'he could not speak for the Provisionals but to the best of his knowledge there was no shooting at all against the army in the William Street–Rossville Flats area.' The Official IRA wanted to ensure that there was no excuse whatsoever available to explain the army's firing in the Bogside when in fact they knew that they had fired a shot at the army at the very start of the shooting.

235

A few nights later, on 5 February 1972, OIRA 2, who had been with OIRA 1 when he fired the shot from Columbcille Court – either the first or the second shots of the day – addressed a rally in Kilburn, London. He told his audience that the IRA did not fire back at the army until the army had been firing for twenty minutes. In his Diary of Operations Major Loden recorded that the drainpipe shot occurred moments before the shooting of Donaghey and Johnston. If this is so then the Official IRA fired the first shot of the day. In any case OIRA 1 and OIRA 2 were involved in at least one round fired if not before the first then straight after the first army firing of the day.

The next Official who fired that day and came forward and admitted to firing was someone who was only known about over the years because a clergyman had admitted seeing him. The man who had been known for years as 'Father Daly's gunman' came forward to the Inquiry, was given a cipher and was from now on to become known as OIRA 4.

On Bloody Sunday OIRA 4 had been on the Command Staff of the Derry Official IRA. He claimed that none of the Officials on the march were on operational duty and that no attacks on the army had been planned for the day. He said that he did not know of any assurances being sought from the OIRA by NICRA that there would be no 'operations' on the march but said that he did not believe that 'such formal assurances' would in any case have been necessary 'as the Republican movement fully supported the purposes of the march and would not have risked injury to our families and friends who were attending the march'.

Notwithstanding this, OIRA 4 admitted that he attended the march with a loaded handgun in his coat pocket. He attended the march with the OC of the Officials and another member of the Command Staff of the OIRA.

He had gone on the march, he said, for peaceful reasons, and boasted that when he saw the rioting which was going on, since he was nearly thirty-four years old in 1972 and 'not one of the teenagers', he 'wasn't stupid enough to hang around'. Instead he did something that was far more dangerous and, in the kindest interpretation, 'stupid' than throwing stones at soldiers.

OIRA 4's version of events perhaps inevitably paints the picture of what he did in the most harmless possible light. The bare facts are these. As he and his colleagues headed down Chamberlain Street and into the area of the Rossville Flats car-park he heard a number of high-velocity shots from behind and the crowd began to run. If OIRA 4 is telling the truth on this matter, these would have been the shots fired by Soldier N.

OIRA 4 himself ended up at the location where Father Daly and others spotted him, at the gable wall at the end of Chamberlain Street in the Rossville Flats car-park area. It was while he was at that position, he said, that he saw that Jackie Duddy had been shot by the army. If this is true then his reaction was, like that of OIRA 1, swift enough to suggest that firing the weapon in his pocket had never been that distant a possibility during the march. The time between the shooting of Duddy, the first victim in the area, and the shooting of Michael Bridge, who was shot while shouting at soldiers for shooting Duddy, was very brief. But it was long enough for OIRA 4 to take his gun out of his pocket and fire. In his account, he 'lost his temper' on seeing that Duddy had been shot. 'The Brits were gunning down innocent civilians,' he said (by this point he had seen only one person hit). He took his 'short weapon', a .32 automatic pistol, out of his pocket and fired 'two, possibly three, shots' across the top of the car-park at the army Saracen vehicle at the corner of Block 1 of the Rossville Flats around which a number of soldiers were gathered. Then a soldier shot Michael Bridge.

These two or three shots were written off by OIRA 4 in his statement in an effort to paint himself out of the picture as completely as he could while admitting to firing a weapon in one of the most contentious areas of firing. He said, 'My memory is that none of the soldiers even appeared to realise they were being fired upon and none actually turned to return fire in my direction. I do not even recall seeing any of the soldiers reacting to the shots, which probably were not even heard over the sound of their own firing.'

> As I have said, my gun was a .32 calibre, a small and, looking back, pretty pathetic weapon, and I was probably well out of range to do any damage to the Paras or their Saracen. I didn't hear any pings or anything to suggest I hit the Saracen. Not only do I think I was out of range, I don't even know if I fired well enough to hit it, but I was just firing out of pure frustration.
>
> I never even thought about what was around the corner of the wall (northwards) because I was only concerned with firing at the Saracen and obviously not thinking straight. I wasn't holding my gun around the corner shooting blindly northwards as has been suggested. I was shooting in a westerly direction towards the Saracen in front of me, and the Paras near to the Saracen. I wasn't aiming at anyone in particular, I was just firing towards where I could see the shooting coming from.

Someone told me later that at the end of the wall, around the corner where I couldn't see, were a couple of Paras and I know now that I was very lucky not to be seen and to have got out of the whole situation alive. I don't think the soldiers even noticed me.

The minute I had fired I was confronted by people shouting at me to stop. They were yelling at me words to the effect of 'pack it in!' or possibly 'pack it in [OIRA 4]' if they knew me. I can't remember whether I knew any of the people who shouted to me, only that they wanted me to stop. Even Father Daly seemed to be shouting at me to stop from where he was attending to Jack Duddy. I was still mad as hell but these people brought me to my senses and I put my gun away in my coat pocket. It never left the pocket after that.

I know for a fact that Jack Duddy was already shot by the time I fired, and I'm sure when I think about it logically that my shooting made no difference whatsoever to what those Paras were doing.

The shots he had fired at the soldiers were, OIRA 4 insisted, 'incidental to the day'. If it looked as though this might have been a way to persuade himself, after the event, that his actions that day had no chance of having put civilian lives at risk, then at least one of his other pieces of evidence suggested that this was not his greatest concern even at the time. 'I think on the day I was wearing a dark blue or black duffel coat,' he said, but then added crucially: 'I was not wearing my glasses. I've had bad eyes all my life and I should have been wearing them that day, but I'm afraid vanity won through and I wasn't. I was not wearing them either when I fired my shots in temper.'

Like Martin McGuinness, OIRA 4 suffered from bad eyesight. But it seemed not to have occurred to him either in 1972 or 2003, when he signed his second statement to the Inquiry, that even someone with good, let alone bad, eyesight might have been unwise to fire a number of shots across an area dense with running civilians. Perhaps OIRA 4 was embarrassed about what he had done.

Perhaps he was unsure how he would face up to questioning over these matters. Perhaps the stress of speaking on oath simply got to him. But after thirty minutes of questioning in the Guildhall by Counsel for the Inquiry, OIRA 4 slumped forward in the witness box. Edwin Glasgow, representative of the soldiers, was nearest and leapt forward to give him first aid. The 66-year-old witness was rushed to hospital. The hearing was called to a halt and OIRA 4 did not return to the stand.

At the following day's hearing OIRA 4's legal representative made a short speech of thanks on behalf of those 'close to' his client. In particular, he said, 'they wish me to express their gratitude to my learned friend Mr Glasgow for his prompt and professional care of the witness and, in particular, they wanted me to thank him publicly for the kind and sensitive way in which he undertook that task.' It seemed in keeping with the confusing and strange nature of much of this Inquiry that towards its end a legal representative of the soldiers ended up saving the life of an IRA gunman.

There was one final strange tale of the Officials that should be added: about a man who refused to co-operate with Saville and who in the end cheated him, the families and the public of the truth. That was the story of a man known as 'Red' Mickey Doherty, a long-time Official IRA member.

Red Mickey had a number of claims to local fame. But one of them was that he was the only IRA member to have fired that day and been shot by a soldier in response. He was the only IRA gunman wounded on the day and his story is a curiously revealing one about the culture that existed and exists in his city.

On the day of Bloody Sunday, Red Mickey was involved in a firing incident just out of the main sector of the shooting. A number of soldiers reported a gunman with a rifle near the Bogside Inn, near Free Derry Corner. While 1 Para were in the Bogside, a civilian gunman fired a shot at a member of the Royal Anglian Regiment. The shot was recorded at around 16.15. Soldier AA was on Barrack Street.

> As I was advancing towards Charlotte Place I saw a man step around the corner of St Columba's Walk and Joyce St. He had a rifle at his shoulder aimed in my general direction. The man was about 5'8" tall and had very dark hair of medium length. He was wearing a quilted anorak and had a white scarf or handkerchief around his neck.
>
> I was carrying my 7.62 SLR rifle across my body. As soon as I saw the man I cocked the weapon and aimed it at the man. I fired one round from my rifle as I was still raising it from the hip. The man facing me fired at the same time as I did. I do not think I hit the man. I recocked my weapon but the man did not reappear. I heard the man's shot hit a wall somewhere above my head.
>
> I continued to advance to see if I could relocate the rifleman. As I came forward I came under fire from a gun port at the bottom of a bricked-up doorway of the derelict houses in Long Tower St. In all, three shots were fired at me in quick

239

succession as if a semi- automatic weapon were being used. I located the gunman's position by the muzzle flashes of this weapon. I could see the outline of a man behind the muzzle flashes.

My weapon was fitted with a special sight. I returned the fire at the gun port in the bottom of the doorway. I fired three shots, operating the bolt mechanism each time, and saw the body slump over the weapon that had been fired at me. I fired two more deliberate rounds at two other gun ports in the immediate vicinity of the one the gunman had been using.

I was then redeployed. I did not see what happened to the man I had shot. I did not fire again. I discovered that one of the rounds fired at me had hit another soldier of my unit. A round had gone through his flak jacket from side to side without injuring him. He had been some ten feet away from me at the time he was shot.

Although timings vary, it is generally agreed that these shots took place after the main body of firing in the Bogside. The Royal Anglian radio log gives the time of the exchange as 16.41, more than ten minutes after the Paras stopped firing.

In order to ensure that the casualty was not questioned by police, Red Mickey was not taken to hospital but to a house in the Bogside where he was given medical assistance for a gunshot wound. A number of journalists learned of the incident and on 31 January the Official IRA admitted in a press statement that one of their number had been wounded – but that he had been wounded after the main exchange of fire.

What was interesting was not just the silence of people in testimony about the matter of the wounded gunman but the fact that the OIRA who turned up to give evidence were unhelpful on the matter. The subject of the wounded gunman was of great importance. Yet over many years the Saville Inquiry failed to track down the gunman to give evidence. When asked about the case people refused to help, said they could not help, or otherwise obstructed the Tribunal. In fact the identity of the gunman was not only known to the RUC, he was very widely known in Derry. He was a local character. For years Lord Saville tried to get hold of testimony from Red Mickey Doherty about his role on the day. In fact, during the period when legal representatives of the soldiers and the Tribunal as a whole were desperately trying everything they could to get hold of him, he was there all the time. Throughout the Saville hearings Doherty had a stall just outside the hearings in the Guildhall Square, selling lighters. Many locals regarded it as amusing that this local 'legend' of the Official IRA was still succeeding in escaping the law.

One Republican called Liam O'Comain, during his oral evidence, even taunted the Tribunal about its inability to find Red Mickey. When asked a question about him by a representative for some of the soldiers O'Comain said, 'With respect,' and then recited a piece of doggerel: 'They sought him here, They sought him there, Saville sought him everywhere. Is he in Derry, Where does he dwell, That gentle giant, Red Mickey.' He went on to say, 'I loved that man, he was a gentle giant,' and agreed that it was funny that the Tribunal had not been able to put questions to his friend.

Red Mickey Doherty died in 2003 while the Tribunal was still trying to locate him to give evidence about his role in the day. He had been armed during the crucial period and was a well- known member of the Official IRA, but despite the pleas of the families and the continual attempts of the Saville Tribunal Red Mickey never made a statement about what he had been doing during the crucial minutes of firing. He never revealed whether he had a gun on him throughout the march, whether he had fired at other soldiers earlier that day or what he had done later when he was shot. One of the Inquiry's missing jigsaw-pieces went to his grave.

In January 2005 the 'Irish Republican Socialist Party' on behalf of his 'family, friends and comrades' unveiled a plaque to their comrade in the heart of the Bogside. It said: 'This plaque is dedicated to the memory of Revolutionary Republican Socialist "Red" Mickey Doherty, 1944–2003, founder member of the INLA and IRSP.' And then, proudly, it boasted: 'wounded on Bloody Sunday'.

And so Red Mickey was celebrated instead of questioned. He had been shot while he was firing a gun, had been covered up by an entire city and at the last, having evaded the truth, was memorialised not as a gunman but as a victim – and a hero.

While the Official IRA had only given a very sparse account of what they had done that day to the Saville Inquiry, they had succeeded in illuminating the situation around at least two of the controversies of the day. The little evidence the Provisionals gave was significantly less illuminating. Martin McGuinness had of course led the way and only after he had submitted his testimony did a number of other Provos follow with their evidence. Those who eventually did testify included the man (given the cipher PIRA 24) whom McGuinness had

241

replaced as OC of the Provos within two weeks of Bloody Sunday.

But he had not appeared willingly. PIRA 24 had been so reluctant to co-operate that in the end he was served with a subpoena forcing him to give evidence to the Tribunal. He told a representative of the Inquiry who had gone to see him that he had been threatened by the IRA and told that he was not to come forward. He said that the IRA had visited him to actively discourage him from giving evidence. When PIRA 24 eventually gave evidence on one of the very last days of witness hearings, in February 2004, he denied that the Provos had tried to stop him giving evidence. He said that his previous claims about intimidation had been 'banter'.

But this was not the only way in which PIRA 24 proved to be a contradictory witness. Martin McGuinness had said earlier, in his evidence, that he thought that the man who had been OC of the Provos on the day, and whom he had replaced, was alive. But McGuinness said that he did not know how he was or why he had not come forward. Yet during this time, and before McGuinness had given this evidence, PIRA 24 said that in fact he had had a number of conversations with McGuinness, including one six months earlier in which McGuinness had in fact asked him to give evidence. Which, if true, meant that McGuinness had seen him just a couple of months before telling the Inquiry in questioning that he had no knowledge of PIRA 24's current situation.

And though there were plenty of contradictions within the evidence given by the Provos who came forward, in essence – and in keeping with the suggestion that the organisation had determined who would give evidence – they all had the same story: that the Provisional IRA had taken their guns outside of the area of the march to arms dumps before the march started, that no member of the Provisional IRA had fired any shots during the period of the march and that none had carried any weapons on them during the march.

This story was clear. It was also suspicious. Indeed, in questioning McGuinness, Edwin Glasgow QC had asked him about the substantial number of press reports that suggested that the Provos had 'got their act together' as an organisation precisely to show a unanimity of opinion that supported the story provided by McGuinness. He was shown an article from the Irish News of 8 September 2003. Headlined 'Saville to hear from ex-Provos', it said that several members of the Provisional IRA had been given 'clearance' by the movement to co-operate.

Q: My question is this, and can I explain its importance, sir: we do not want to start another round of pursuing journalists to disclose their sources only to be told they are frankly confidential. Can you help this Tribunal to shorten that process by telling them who the sources within the Republican movement may have been, who were able to tell Roddy McGreggor on 8 September – no later than 8 September – that the movements were going on for these statements to be obtained?

A: I have no idea.

Q: You have no idea?

A: I have no idea, in fact, in relation to –

Q: We may have to ask him –

A: – the whole business of people who were former members of the Provisional IRA being given clearance, I did not seek clearance from anyone.

Q: I said I will not press it, I will not. Can we go to the next one, which is KM3.136, we will see if we have to go to Mr Mark Mullan as well, because closer to home in the Derry News, on Sunday 7th, this is the day before. His article starts: 'Senior Republicans in Derry have visited a number of former IRA members urging them to give evidence...' Without us having to pursue Mr Mullan, could you help this Inquiry as to who the senior Republicans in Derry who had been visiting people in this city were?

A: I have no idea, I do not even know if it is true.

Q: The last one is KM3.137, this was some four weeks later, on 30 September. You can see it all, I hope I am not editing out anything unfairly, it was really only the last paragraph: 'The legal sources said the evidence of the former members would support the testimony given by Mr McGuinness.' Again, to save us inviting the Tribunal to go to Mr Seamus McKinney and ask him who his sources were, could you tell us who the legal source was that told the Irish News on or before 30 September that testimony was being gathered to support you?

A: I have no idea.

Q: Again, in the light of those articles that we have been given, the same time as you, may I say, dating back to, as we saw, 7 September, can you help the Tribunal at all as to how it was that whereas the newspapers were being informed at the

243

beginning of September that this exercise was being performed, the statements all turned up simultaneously late the other evening, on Friday, 17 October, before Mr Ward gave evidence on the Monday; can you help the Tribunal at all about that?

Whatever the truth of the allegation, the Provos played it well. They were the last witnesses, said what they said when they wanted to say it, had the benefit of everybody else's testimony into which they could fit their own, and appeared to have some ability not only to decide who should come to give evidence but also who should not.

In this situation it was perhaps not surprising that the lawyers for the majority of the soldiers were reduced at points in their submissions to pointing out that the presence of so many members of the Provisional IRA on the march and at crucial points of the day was in itself sinister. There were certainly a large number of Provos around. Even the man who drove a lorry at the head of the march, Thomas McGlinchey, was a member of the Provisional IRA on the day.

And at the rubble barricade, the soldiers' representatives pointed out, in the location where a large number of the victims fell and where the soldiers said they had seen gunmen and nail-bombers, there were, caught on camera, a large number of Provos. Saville himself decided that there was nothing 'in itself surprising or sinister' about the number of identifiable Provos in key areas of the Bogside that day.

And they for their part stuck to their line. Despite what in the end became a considerable number of civilian sightings of gunmen in the crucial areas that day, the Rossville Flats, Glenfada Park and elsewhere, the Provos stuck to the line that the only shots they fired were later in the day, after the main shooting had happened, when the soon-to-be-replaced OC of the Provos (PIRA 24) along with the man about to supplant him (Martin McGuinness) apparently agreed that 'symbolic shots' should be fired at army observation posts on the city walls. About the first shots, about firing from the Rossville Flats, about whether or not a Provo had fired a Thompson submachine gun in the opening seconds of the firing during which the Provos' soon-to-be-OC was missing, there was only one stock response. It was the same response that the Paras had given. Denial.

While giving oral evidence Bernadette Devlin was characteristically clear in her dismissal of the very idea that there had been civilian gunmen firing at the army on Bloody Sunday. Everybody in the city would have known if members of the IRA had started shooting that day, she said. Indeed she claimed that any

IRA gunman would have been 'blamed and lynched', or at the very least ostracised and unable to live in the city any more.

The truth turned out to be very different. A number of men certainly did shoot on the day, and not only had they not been lynched, they had not even been blamed. It was clear, furthermore, that they were far from ostracised. Red Mickey was a jokey local hero. OIRA 1 and OIRA 4 were friends with people across the community. Evidence of the OIRA and others showed a city where people kept things from the Tribunal that the families and city had spent years trying to bring to light. It was not a city, as Devlin had claimed, where gunmen were unable to live. It was a place where gunmen could be excused, covered for and, eventually, memorialised.

CONCLUSION

On 15 June 2010 another march set off for the Guildhall in Derry. Relatives of each of the fourteen people killed all those years before carried photos of their loved ones. Beneath each photo was the single line: 'Set the truth free.' The silent procession was clapped as it moved through the scene of the killings in the Bogside. In front of the families a set of cameramen walked backwards, capturing the silent determination on their faces on this final stage of the journey. In the Bogside they were joined by Martin McGuinness for the walk to the Guildhall. At 2.30 another, larger, march that included Gerry Adams set off from the Bogside.

Again the sky was clear blue. And again the city was filled with press from around the world, including many who had been there that day. They had come to cover the end of the Bloody Sunday story.

And of course this time the march did end up at the square. The process of the release of Lord Saville's final report had been meticulously planned. At an approved time the families were let into the Guildhall to read Saville's findings in advance of their formal publication. Next of kin, widows, children and others went into the Guildhall through a square swiftly filling with people and expectations.

At an undisclosed location, another group of people were reading the report. At the same time as the families were allowed to see the report in Derry, the soldiers and their legal representatives were allowed to see it somewhere in London. It must certainly have been a grimmer process than its Derry counterpart.

It had taken twelve years, including five years to write and print. The finished work was 5,000 pages long in ten volumes. Easier to digest was a 60-page summary of the report's main findings, including attribution of blame. The families went over this inside the Guildhall.

The first sign that the findings of the report were pleasing to the families was when, shortly before the release-time, people gathered in the square began to cheer. Through the windows of the building some of the families of the dead were signalling to the crowd: they were giving the 'thumbs-up' sign. A few minutes later at 3.30 the huge screens placed in the Guildhall transmitted to the crowd of thousands the live proceedings from the House of Commons in Westminster. The Prime Minister rose.

> Mr Speaker, I am deeply patriotic. I never want to believe anything bad about our country. I never want to call into question the behaviour of our soldiers and our army who I believe to be the finest in the world. And I have seen for myself the very difficult and dangerous circumstances in which we ask our soldiers to serve. But the conclusions of this report are absolutely clear. There is no doubt. There is nothing equivocal. There are no ambiguities.

> What happened on Bloody Sunday was both unjustified and unjustifiable. It was wrong.

> Lord Saville concludes that the soldiers of Support Company who went into the Bogside 'did so as a result of an order ... which should have not been given' by their commander...

The crowd in the square in Derry booed at a little at the encomium to the British army. Otherwise the reception was entirely approving. They listened to a British Prime Minister in the British House of Commons report what Lord Saville had found.

That the first shot in the vicinity of the march had been fired by the British army. That 'none of the casualties shot by soldiers of Support Company was armed with a firearm.' That though there was 'some firing by republican paramilitaries', none of this 'provided any justification for the shooting of civilian casualties'. That Support Company lost their self-control and that either forgetting or ignoring their instructions and training there had been 'a serious and widespread loss of fire discipline'.

The Prime Minister also reported that Saville had found that 'despite the contrary evidence given by the soldiers ... none of them fired in response to attacks or threatened attacks by nail- or petrol- bombers' and that many of the soldiers 'knowingly put forward false accounts in order to seek to justify their firing'. He said to the House:

247

What happened should never, ever have happened. The families of those who died should not have had to live with the pain and hurt of that day – and a lifetime of loss. Some members of our armed forces acted wrongly. The government is ultimately responsible for the conduct of the armed forces. And for that, on behalf of the government – and indeed our country – I am deeply sorry.

It was a hugely significant moment for the population of Derry.

But those who were hoping for more were going to be disappointed. Saville did not find, the Prime Minister reiterated, that there was any conspiracy of senior politicians or senior members of the armed forces nor was there any evidence of an official cover-up. He highlighted the report's criticisms of Colonel Derek Wilford as well as the conclusions relating to another man, Martin McGuinness – who was standing listening in the Guildhall with his voter base. In relation to McGuinness the Prime Minister related that Saville's report 'specifically finds he was present and probably armed with a submachine gun' but concludes 'we are sure that he did not engage in any activity that provided any of the soldiers with any justification for opening fire.'

Then Prime Minister Cameron finished by paying tribute to the armed forces:

And let us also remember, Bloody Sunday is not the defining story of the service the British army gave in Northern Ireland from 1969–2007.

This was known as Operation Banner, the longest continuous operation in British military history, spanning thirty-eight years and in which over 250,000 people served.

Our armed forces displayed enormous courage and professionalism in upholding democracy and the rule of law in Northern Ireland. Acting in support of the police, they played a major part in setting the conditions that have made peaceful politics possible ... and over 1,000 members of the security forces lost their lives to that cause.

Without their work the peace process would not have happened.

He thanked the Tribunal for their work and acknowledged the grief as well as the perseverance of the families. But he hoped, he said, that 'the truth coming out can set people free.' He finished by quoting Lord Saville's conclusion.

What happened on Bloody Sunday strengthened the Provisional IRA, increased nationalist resentment and hostility   towards the Army and exacerbated the violent conflict of the years that followed. Bloody Sunday was a tragedy for the bereaved and the wounded, and a catastrophe for the people of Northern Ireland.

But, he stressed, 'we must move on.'

At 3.45 the families came out of the Guildhall in Derry into a cheering crowd. From a prepared platform a relative of each of the dead read out the conclusions of Saville on their relative and ended with the shout 'innocent'. It was a heady and moving moment, the final point of a search for justice that had taken nearly four decades and whose last stage had sometimes seemed just as unending.

Around 2,500 people had given evidence. Of them, nearly 1,000 had given oral witness testimony: 505 civilians, nine experts and forensic scientists, forty-nine journalists, 245 military, thirty-five paramilitaries and former paramilitaries, thirty-nine politicians and civil servants, seven priests and thirty-three Royal Ulster Constabulary officers.

In the Guildhall Square some of the most significant figures of the report milled around speaking to the crowds and giving instant-reaction interviews to the media. There was Father (now retired Bishop) Daly, delighted and beaming. There were some of the wounded as well as the widows, siblings and children. There too were some of the journalists who had been there on the day in 1972 and had in many cases given evidence to Lord Saville, returning for one last article on a story that had spanned their entire careers.

And there were the politicians too. John Hume was given a roaring cheer by the crowd when he emerged. And there, milling among the crowds and the families, were Gerry Adams and Martin McGuinness, looking beatific as they made their way among the crowds, shaking hands and hugging.

Gerry Adams was immediately calling for a Saville-style Inquiry to be set up into other atrocities allegedly carried out by British forces, including an Inquiry into the Parachute Regiment's shootings in Ballymurphy in 1971. There was no call from him for a fresh investigation to be opened into the La Mon Hotel massacre or Warrenpoint or Warrington or Enniskillen or Claudy or Birmingham, or into the disappeared like Jean McConville.

Nor was there any call for an investigation into another bloody day in 1972, the day that became known as Bloody Friday, when the IRA without warning set off twenty bombs across Belfast in the space of seventy-five minutes, killing nine and maiming and wounding 130.

In terms of political capital, the Saville process had always been a win-win for whichever government was in power when it came out. And of course it had only ever had one possible outcome. The Saville Inquiry would not have been ordered if there was any likelihood that a second British judge would come to the same findings as Lord Widgery. The point of the second Inquiry was to get a different answer. And, thankfully for the peace of Derry, it did.

Saville also finally found the right words to describe the actions of the soldiers who had done most of the killing that day. Of Lance Corporal F Saville concluded that he 'did not fire in a state of fear or panic. We are sure that he fired either in the belief that no one in the area into which he fired was posing a threat of causing death or serious injury, or not caring whether or not anyone there was posing such a threat.' Similar conclusions were reached in relation to the dead soldiers E and G, but also to Soldier H and others.

Nobody knows where any of the soldiers – apart from Colonel Wilford – criticised in the Saville Report now are. Fearing his former comrades, the soldier who started it all, Soldier 027, is probably now living abroad – certainly with a new identity. Part whistleblower, part fantasist, he was somebody whose evidence, Saville finally concluded, could not be trusted unless there were other sources to back it up. Perhaps this was his own fault. Perhaps it was not – the result, instead, like Soldier L, of being haunted by what he had been part of. In any case, believing yourself on the run from your former enemies and your former comrades cannot be an easy life.

The future of others of the soldiers may yet be even more uncertain. The Director of Public Prosecutions will have to decide over the months and years ahead whether to prosecute those soldiers who can be proved to have killed that day. Even if he decides not to, there is at the very least the prospect that a number of soldiers could – as they were warned when they testified – now be tried for perjury in deliberately misleading the Tribunal. The prospect of civil actions mounted by the families also hangs over those soldiers who fired and killed that day. Some of the relatives believe that no good can come from prosecuting soldiers so long after the event. Others have expressed a desire to pursue just such a course of action. Perhaps Soldiers F and H have decided it is sensible to spend the rest of their retirement outside the jurisdiction of the courts of the country they spent their lives serving and disgraced so badly. In any case, the shooting soldiers may not yet have spoken in public for the final time.

Among the higher command, General Ford managed to escape serious censure of any kind from Lord Saville. It was in some ways a surprising conclusion. It had been Ford's decision to use 1 Para for the arrest operation. Saville himself described 1 Para as a force with 'a reputation for using excessive physical violence, which thus ran the risk of exacerbating the tensions between the army and nationalists in Londonderry'. He concluded, however, that General Ford 'did not have reason to believe that there was significant risk soldiers would open fire unjustifiably'.

As their history has shown, there are some tasks for which the Parachute Regiment are remarkably effective. Acting as a scoop-up force in the middle of a civil rights march, albeit one that had in part descended into rioting, was certainly not one of them.

Colonel Wilford, painting in Belgium, would doubtless agree with some of this. Perhaps his silence since the release of Saville suggests that he has learned from his earlier appearances in the media. Or maybe he is planning to respond at some later point, when he has had time to absorb the enormity of what Saville has achieved. At any rate, if he studies the whole report he can never again claim that no one has shown him the evidence of what his troops did that day. And if Colonel Wilford in the latter part of his retirement still feels blind devotion to his men, he might reflect on what might have been if the men under his command had held the same standards of loyalty towards him as he had so desperately held towards them.

If the soldiers and certain commanders remain concerned that the law will at some point come for them, there are of course others who believed themselves soldiers and commanders that day who have no such fear.

Under the terms of the Good Friday Agreement every IRA killer is currently free. Much of the leadership of Sinn Fein consists of people who without that agreement would currently remain in prison. It is highly unlikely that McGuinness, Adams or any of the other former leaders of the IRA will ever now face trial for the hundreds of murders they and their organisation committed.

Yet in the final report there was a small surprise from Lord Saville. On the issue of the agent Infliction he was cautious. Agreeing that there was no reason for thinking that Infliction would have been motivated to mislead his handlers, in the end he decided, 'We consider that [Infliction's] account by itself does no more than raise the possibility that, notwithstanding his denial, Martin McGuinness did fire a Thompson submachine gun on "single" shot from the Rossville Flats on Bloody Sunday.'

The report concluded that 'someone probably did fire a number of shots at the soldiers from the south-west end of the lower balcony of Block 3 of the Rossville Flats ... probably at a stage after soldiers had opened fire in that sector.' Perhaps McGuinness fired those shots, but he was probably mistaken if he ever had it on his conscience – and told anyone – that he had actually fired the first shot.

And what of the person who, against considerable competition, was the most elusive figure of the whole process?

In the final report Saville wrote at length on Infliction. He also published an intriguing new exchange with the Security Service that had employed the agent. In 2003 solicitors for the majority of the families had written a letter to the Inquiry outlining four questions they wished the Security Service to answer. Among them was whether the Service had deliberately put the identity of Infliction at risk by making him potentially identifiable to McGuinness. And they also asked whether the information put forward had in fact been knowingly false.

The Security Service replied in a letter dated 22 October 2003. The Service said that McGuinness 'might well have told others the same information as he told Infliction' and that 'Infliction did not have a uniquely close relationship with Martin McGuinness.'

> The Service considered and considers that it is unlikely that, if Infliction's report is true, Infliction would have been the only person to whom Martin McGuinness spoke about this matter in the years following Bloody Sunday. Further, if it is true, it is likely that others who were present on the day of Bloody Sunday itself would also be aware of Martin McGuinness' role. For these reasons the Service assesses that, if the report is true, a number of people are likely to know this information, and that with the passage of time Martin McGuinness may not remember exactly who he has told or who he believes might be aware of what he did.

The Service rejected the suggestion that they had knowingly put Infliction's identity at risk by releasing the material, saying that they continued to have 'an obligation to ensure that Infliction's right to life is protected, and would not knowingly have released material publicly that it assessed would place Infliction's life at risk'.

Other conclusions tucked away deep inside the final publication also showed that the picture was not in all respects simpler after a twelve-year search for the truth.

As well as the firing from the Rossville Flats the report found the 'likelihood' of much other civilian gunfire on the day. Even just in the area of the earliest shooting, where Donaghey and Johnston were shot and OIRA 1 fired, Saville concluded that there was more firing than any civilian had admitted to. He cited the case of Teresa Bradley, a woman who saw a man with a handgun firing to the north from the first floor of Kells Walk, and concluded:

> We have no doubt that OIRA 1 fired the shot that hit the drainpipe on the side of the Presbyterian church; and we equally have no doubt that there was other paramilitary gunfire in this sector before soldiers of 1 PARA went into the Bogside. The evidence suggests to us that this was probably firing by members of the Official IRA.

As far as the Provisional IRA went, the report concluded:

> There is no evidence that suggests to us that any member of the Provisional IRA used or intended to use the march itself for the purpose of engaging the security forces with guns or bombs. Nevertheless, we consider it likely that Martin McGuinness was armed with a Thompson submachine gun on Bloody Sunday and we cannot eliminate the possibility that he fired this weapon after the soldiers had come into the Bogside. Furthermore, we are unable, notwithstanding their evidence, to exclude the possibility that other members of the Provisional IRA may also have carried arms.

Over the years since 1972 many millions of words have been written about Bloody Sunday. Yet even the Saville process – thorough, exhausting and incomparable as it is – has not answered and cannot answer all the questions of the day. Only the surviving shooters – the soldiers and civilian gunmen – can know what it was that made so many soldiers fire at unarmed civilians that day.

Today the peace process in Northern Ireland is holding, as it largely has since 1998. Breakaway splinter-faction Republican groups on an almost daily basis

253

continue to attempt to murder, intimidate and harm. But so far Republicans have succeeded in preventing any substantial movement of people back to the cause of 'armed struggle'. People say that the province is tired of violence.

But the IRA's appeal has diminished before and resurfaced. Its ability to continue is reliant on myths – some based in truth, some wholly on lies. Foremost among the myths of the IRA has been the notion that political violence is the noble reaction of the oppressed. Countess Markievicz was not oppressed when she murdered, nor was violence the only available outlet for her politics – but she is commemorated in statues in Dublin. Sean Russell of Sinn Fein died on a German U-boat during World War II, helping the Nazis, yet is commemorated by a statue in Dublin. Irish society has a strange relationship with violence, and at its core on all sides is the problem that it remembers murderers as heroes while forgetting not only their victims but all those who eschewed violence from the start, even while suffering the same problems, holding many of the same opinions and in many cases working for the same ends as those who chose to kill.

In the years since Bloody Sunday and especially since the publication of the Saville Report, an idea has been encouraged that in the wake of the murderous behaviour of soldiers of the Parachute Regiment it was not the IRA's fault that it grew and behaved as it did. It suggests that after Bloody Sunday Catholic youth in the north of Ireland could not help joining the IRA, that no serious IRA violence had gone on before and that people only joined because they had to join in the wake of this outrage.

This makes the IRA the legitimate, respectable and understandable voice of outrage and suggests that after Bloody Sunday who could not torture and maim civilians, plant bombs in shopping centres and 'execute' any suspected opponents for thirty years?

The IRA existed and was murdering innocent civilians, police and soldiers long before Bloody Sunday. And they continued to do so afterwards. But if Bloody Sunday becomes rewritten not as a terrible and undeniably incendiary event but rather as the ignition and cause of the conflict, then not only are the actions of all those who killed before that day forgotten, but all the atrocities after that day risk being excused.

Many people did choose the path of violence. Many others said with

Bernadette Devlin that they would not condemn those who travelled that path. But many others realised that they had a moral choice and remained moral beings even after the Parachute Regiment had made their fatal visit to the city.

Hugh Barbour was sixteen years old at the time of Bloody Sunday – the day he saw Barney McGuigan shot through the head with a single bullet from Soldier F's rifle. The years since had not, he admitted, been easy. 'After Bloody Sunday I tried to block all my memories of what I had seen. I have found it very difficult coming to terms with what I experienced.' But with hindsight he thought what he had seen at such an early age was actually 'a positive experience for me' because 'it made me see the reality of the troubles. I had witnessed what one person could do to another when I saw Barney McGuigan and I knew I could never justify doing this to another human being. I saw reality that day. If I had been a hundred yards up Rossville Street and had not seen Barney McGuigan shot I would have joined the IRA.'

Another man who was young on the day, Leo Friel, felt the exact same reason to move away from violence. 'For months after Bloody Sunday', he said, 'I struggled and I wanted to get back at the British army in any way possible. I was even thinking about joining the IRA. Then I thought back to what had happened to Barney McGuigan and I just couldn't do it. I wasn't the type of person that could do that sort of thing to anybody.'

Others had immediately felt impelled to join the IRA but had been dragged off that course and realised there were other ways to channel their justifiable rage. One who had seen the events of the day, Alfie McAleer, related that he was thinking of joining the IRA the day after Bloody Sunday. In fact, he said, he would 'have probably joined that night if I had known where to go. However, the place where I worked had a club at the top of Beech Wood which was used as a rallying point. The next day this was opened and I joined other local people making phone calls, asking local business- men to close their shops as a mark of respect. I put my energy into that – if it had not been for this I would have joined the Provos.'

Barney McGuigan's son, Charles, meanwhile would have been better justified than most in deciding that he should avenge the army, the security forces or the government that stood behind them. But nor did he choose to do so in the years after his father's death. To Lord Saville he recounted how, 'at the time of my father's death, my mother cleared a space in our kitchen and made me kneel under the Sacred Heart picture and swear to her that I would never do anything about my father's death that would bring shame on the name of the family. Having lost her husband, I believe that my mother was determined that she would not lose any other member of her family as a result of what had happened.' He finished, 'I have honoured that promise to this day.'

All of these people, and many others, realised that they had a choice. And, like many others who have no memorials and are rarely recognised, they made the most important decision of all. They decided that in response to murder they did not have to become murderers themselves. If the peace in Northern Ireland is ever secured fully it will be when the exaltation of the men of violence is consigned to the past and people exalt instead men and women of peace like those who set out one cold, bright afternoon, marching for justice, and managed for the course of a lifetime never to lose sight of their goal.

SOURCES

There can now be few minutes in history more documented than those surrounding Bloody Sunday. Thanks to the Bloody Sunday Inquiry website (www.bloody-sunday-inquiry.org), all of this evidence is now freely available to the public. It comprises the most valuable and exhaustive source of information about the day.

The initial evidence of the Inquiry was collected into 160 volumes. These bundles alone contain between 20 and 30 million words. In addition, there are thirteen volumes of photographs, 121 audiotapes and 110 videotapes.

As well as sitting in on hearings, over the course of almost a decade I read all witness statements, testimony and much else. Though it was something of a labour, I did not want to translate this into a laborious book.

In an effort to make this book as accessible as possible I have avoided the practice of footnoting specific pages and paragraphs in excerpted material, choosing instead to point the reader to the relevant statement and/or day of testimony. If anyone wishes to follow up a quote they can do so by way of the notes to each chapter (see page 317).

The material for this book breaks down into three main types.

Witness statements: the Saville Inquiry requested anybody with information about the day to come forward. As a result some 2,500 statements were taken by Eversheds, the solicitors acting for the Inquiry. Not all these people were called to give evidence.

Each statement given to the Saville Inquiry has a reference number. For instance, Colonel Wilford's statement is coded 1110. Others begin with a letter. Some statements, particularly those of controversial figures involved in the day, run to hundreds of pages. In each case I thought it better to point readers to the statement and its primary identification number since any phrase can be looked up within the body of that statement.

As well as the actual statement each individual's statement includes all relevant documents relating to the person; for instance, any Widgery evidence, photographs, maps and any additional comments over the years (for instance, transcripts of media interviews).

Tribunal sittings: Almost 1,000 of those who submitted witness statements to the Inquiry were questioned on their statements over the course of a five-year period (2000–05). There were also a series of preliminary hearings (1998–2000) that constitute vital background. For reasons of length as well as flow I have generally favoured the more tightly written source of witness statements, where the questioning and the statement material are similar. But where questioning brought new information to light I have cited these transcripts. In each case the full TS of the day referred to is available on the Bloody Sunday Inquiry website.

Final Report: Lord Saville's final report was published on 15 June 2010. It is ten volumes long, comprising, in total, over 5,000 pages. It is also available in full online. Obviously the full report remains the most substantial investigation of the events of the day. I take its findings to be conclusive with only a couple of exceptions. Where those exceptions are taken I have indicated in the text where and why.

NOTES

Chapter 1 – A Victim

Geraldine McBride (née Richmond) statement, AM45 Geraldine McBride testimony, Day 145, 146

Thomas Eamon Melaugh statement, AM397 Soldier 227 testimony, Day 371

Also re Soldier F, see Soldier 040, Soldier 134, Soldier 025 Sean McDaid statement, AM174

William Patrick McDonagh statement, AM192 Hugh Barbour statement, AB10

Paul James McLaughlin statement, AM350 Tony Morrison statement, AM439

Brian Ward statement, AW6 Andrew Barr statement, AB12

Brian Joseph McCay statement, AM100 Charles McGuigan statement, AM269 Róisín Stewart statement, AS34

Kevin Vincent McGonagle statement, AM254 Soldier F statement, 167

Soldier F testimony, Day 375, 376

Dr R. T. Shepherd and Kevin O'Callaghan, Report on the pathology and ballistic evidence following the Bloody Sunday shootings, E2, esp. E2.0046 – E2.0048, E2.0056 – E2.0057, E2.0078, E2.0081

Eileen Collins statement, AC72

Seamus Carlin statement, AC39

John Patrick Friel statement, AF32

Noel Millar statement, AM477

James Patrick McCafferty statement, AM60

Eamonn Baker statement, AB2

Chapter 2 – The Scene: Derry

David McKittrick, Seamus Kelters, Brian Feeney and Chris Thornton, *Lost Lives: the stories of the men, women and children who died as a result of the Northern Ireland troubles,* Mainstream Publishing, 1999, passim

Kevin Myers, *Watching the Door: Cheating Death in 1970s Belfast*, Atlantic Books, 2006, p. 118

Patrick Doherty statement, AD96

Peter Taylor, Brits: *The War Against the IRA*, Bloomsbury, 2001, p. 94
Glasgow submission, Day 51

Sandra Doherty statement, AD101

Chapter 3 – What Happened?

INQ 2030 statement, C2030

Soldier O statement, 575

General Sir Robert Ford statement, 1208

Father Daly statement, H5

Final Report, Vol. I, Ch. 3

Final Report, Vol. VIII, Ch. 165

Final Report, Vol. II, Ch. 12

Final Report, Vol. IV, Ch. 55

Chapter 4 – The First Inquiry

Sir Edward Heath statement, KH4

Sir Edward Heath testimony, Days 282, 283, 285, 286, 287, 289, 290, 291

Hansard, 1 February 1972

Sir John Peck, *Dublin from Downing Street*, Gill & Macmillan, 1978, pp. 3–4

Joseph Doherty statement, AD76

Geraldine McBride statement, AM45

Soldier 027 statement, 1565

The Report of the Tribunal appointed to inquire into the events on Sunday, 30 January 1972, which led to loss of life in connection with the procession in Londonderry on that day by The Rt. Hon. Lord Widgery, O.B.E., T.D.

Hansard, 29 January 1998

Chapter 5 – The Conspiracies

Martin Hegarty statement, AH62

James Toye statement, AT13

Opening statement by Lord Saville, Friday 3 April 1998

'Ford memorandum', attached to General Ford statement, B1123 Tony Geraghty, *The Irish War: The Military History of a Domestic Conflict*, HarperCollins, 1998, p. 44

Minute of meeting between Edward Heath and Lord Widgery, 1 February 1972, attached to Sir Edward Heath statement, KH4

Channel 4 documentary, see Lena Ferguson statement, M25, and Alexander Thomson statement, M84

Edward Dillon statement, AD45

Hugh V. Kelly statement, AK10

Ivan Cooper statement, KC12

Ivan Cooper testimony, Day 419

Paul James McLaughlin statement, AM350

Thomas Mullarkey statement, AM452

William Lindsay statement, AL15

Pauline Anne McDermott statement, AM186

Final Report, Vol. VIII, Ch. 167.52

MoD email cited in Paul Bew, 'The Bloody Sunday Inquiry: was it worth it?', *Daily Telegraph*, 14 June 2010

'His Lordship blew his top' and related, see Philip Jacobson, 'Riddle of the Derry guns', *Sunday Times*, 14 August 2005

Final Report, Vol. X, Appendix 1

Fern Lane, 'Bloody Sunday rifles – new revelations', *An Phoblacht*, 18 August 2005

Alan Harkens statement, AH8

Lieutenant 026 statement, 1544

Captain Conder statement, CC1

Final Report, Vol. VII, Ch. 137.3

Soldier 1766 statement, C1766

Eileen Collins statement, AC72

Eileen Collins testimony, Day 161

Noel Moore statement, AM416

Map of 'missing casualties' provided by Mr Glasgow, 0S7.34

List of 'missing casualties' provided by Mr Glasgow, 0S7.35-38

Edwin Glasgow, Day 51

Father Edward Daly testimony, Day 75

Professor Terence O'Keeffe statement, H21

Final Report, Vol. IV, Ch. 58 + 60

Chapter 6 – The Firebrand: Bernadette Devlin

Hansard, 31 January 1972

'Daughters of Ireland', *Independent on Sunday*, 9 March 1997

Bernadette Devlin, *The Price of My Soul*, Pan Books, 1969

Eamonn McCann, *War and an Irish Town*, Pluto Press, 1993 edn.

The Battle of the Bogside, documentary, Vinny Cunningham (director), 2004

BBC News, 26 June 1970

Bobby Heatley statement, AH110

Michael Havord statement, AH46

Margot Collins statement, AC148

Leo Friel statement, AF35

Eamonn Deane statement, AD15

John McGowan statement, AM258

Bernadette McAliskey (Devlin) statement, KD4

Bernadette McAliskey (Devlin) testimony, Day 112

Hansard, 1 February 1972

Tim Pat Coogan, *The Troubles: Ireland's Ordeal 1966–1996 and the Search for Peace*, Palgrave Macmillan, 2002 edn., p. 126

Dictionary of Irish Biography, entry on Bernadette Devlin

Bernadette Devlin McAliskey, 'Bloody Sunday: put Britain in the dock', *Guardian*, 15 June 2010

Chapter 7 – The Shooters

Captain Mike Jackson statement, CJ1

Captain Mike Jackson testimony, Day 318

Soldier 112 testimony, Day 320

Soldier A statement, 20

Soldier A testimony, Day 297

Soldier L statement, 342

Soldier L testimony, Day 381

Soldier S testimony, Day 332

Details of 'Colonel Callan' in Chris Dempster and Dave Tomkins, *Fire Power*, Corgi, 1978

Soldier 202 statement, 2111

Noel Kelly statement, AK17

Noel Kelly testimony, Day 62

Joe Friel interview with Jimmy McGovern attached to Joe Friel statement at AF34.107-AF34.108

Widgery Report

Soldier H statement, 262

Soldier H testimony, Day 377, 378

Chapter 8 – The Colonel: Wilford

Colonel Wilford statement, 1110

Colonel Wilford testimony, Day 312, 313, 314, 315, 316, 317, 320, 321

Tim Pat Coogan, *The Troubles: Ireland's Ordeal 1966–1996 and the Search for Peace*, Arrow Books, 1996, p. 158

BBC, *Remember Bloody Sunday*, 1992, at Inquiry audio tape 3, also TS attached to Colonel Wilford statement, 1110

Peter Taylor, *Provos: The IRA and Sinn Fein*, Bloomsbury, 1997, pp. 125–6

Channel 4 News, 1997, at Inquiry video 6

Today programme, 6 July 1999, TS at X3.6.1, attached to Colonel Wilford statement, 1110

'Row after Colonel calls victims' relatives "republican fronts"', *Independent*, 7 July 1999

'Enjoying retirement in Belgium', *Irish Mail on Sunday*, 20 June 2010

'Bloody Sunday officer sued for libel', *Daily Telegraph*, 12 November 2000

Final Report, Vol. VIII, Ch. 171

Major General Peter Welsh testimony, Day 282

Chapter 9 – The Whistleblower?: 027

Soldier 027 statement, 1565

Soldier 027 testimony, Day 246, 247, 248, 249

Tom McGurk statement, M56

Tom McGurk, 'The testimony of Soldier A', *Sunday Business Post*, 16 March 1997

027 letter to Belfast paper at 027 statement, Appendix 6, 1565.008

Agreement between the Northern Ireland Office and Soldier 027, 6 July 2000

Final Report, Vol. X, Appendix 1

Material relating to Soldier 036, 1631

Final Report, Vol. VIII, Ch. 166

Joseph Mahon statement, AM18

Anonymity Hearings, 26–27 April 1999, TSS AH001, AH002 Lord Saville Ruling: Names in Public Domain, 24 May 2001

Testimony of Soldier F, Day 376

Final Report, Vol. IX, Ch. 179

Tom McGurk, 'The good Soldier', *Sunday Business Post*, 13 June 2010

Tom McGurk, 'The bloody truth has finally set them free', *Sunday Business Post*, 20 June 2010

Chapter 10 – Agents and Handlers: Infliction

Opening statement to Inquiry by Christopher Clarke QC, Day 8 Attached to Martin McGuinness statement, KM3

'McGuinness fired the first shot on Bloody Sunday', *Independent*, 7 April 2000

Discussion on submissions relating to Infliction, Day 214

Ruling on public interest immunity, time-delay procedure, anonymity, screening and venue applications, 19 December 2002

Ruling on Applications for anonymity, screening and redactions of documents and other material made on behalf of the government and government agencies, 14 April 2003

'Julian' statement, KJ4

'Julian' testimony, Day 325, 326

'David' statement, KD2

'David' testimony, Day 330

'James' statement, KJ2

Observer B statement, KO2

INQ 2241 statement, C2241

'Widow walks out over Bloody Sunday "farce"', *Irish Independent*, 14 May 2003

Martin Ingram statement, KI2

Martin Ingram testimony, Day 329

David Shayler statement, KS2

David Shayler testimony, Day 327

Annie Machon statement, KM12

Annie Machon testimony, Day 327

Officer N statement, KN1

Officer A statement, KA2

Officer A testimony, Day 326, 327

'Court orders eviction of MI5 whistleblower David Shayler', *Times*, 12 August 2009

Officer B statement, KB3

Officer B testimony, Day 327

Chapter 11 – The Prime Minister: Edward Heath

Sir Edward Heath statement, KH4

Sir Edward Heath testimony, Days 282, 283, 285, 286, 287, 289, 290, 291
Lord Carver statement, KC8

Widgery Report

Chapter 12 – The Terrorist: Martin McGuinness

Submissions relating to Martin McGuinness, Day 61

McKittrick et al., *Lost Lives*, pp. 1466–7

Ann Harkin statement, AH10

Ann Harkin testimony, Day 59

Mitchel McLaughlin statement, AM340

Mitchel McLaughlin testimony, Day 80

Joe McColgan statement, AM123

Joe McColgan testimony, Day 104

Eugene Lafferty statement, AL1

Eugene Lafferty testimony, Day 64

James Ferry testimony, Day 179

Noel Breslin statement, AB116

Eamonn Deane statement, AD15

Eamonn Deane testimony, Day 106

Bernadette McAliskey (Devlin) statement, KD4

Nell McCafferty statement, M54

Liam Clarke and Kathryn Johnston, *Martin McGuinness: from guns to government*, Mainstream, 2001

INQ 2245 statement, C2245

'McGuinness in new spy claims', Liam Clarke, *Sunday Times*, 4 June 2006

'This is what McGuinness won't tell you', Liam Clarke, *Sunday Times*, 6 May 2001

INQ 21, General Sir Michael Rose, statement, C21

INQ 21, General Sir Michael Rose, testimony, Day 284

Martin McGuinness statement, KM3

Martin McGuinness testimony, Days 390, 391

John Barry testimony, Day 194

Liam Clarke testimony, Day 387

Soldier 227 statement, 2204

Eamonn McCann (ed.), *The Bloody Sunday Inquiry: the families speak out*, Pluto Press, 2006

Chapter 13 – The Soldier: 'F'

Soldier F statement, 167

Soldier F testimony, Day 375, 376

Department of Industrial and Forensic Science report, 29 February 1972, D0047, also testimony of Colonel Overbury, Day 243

Soldier 027 statement, 1565

Soldier 027 testimony, Day 246, 247, 248, 249

Professor Terence O'Keeffe statement, H21

Donna Harkin testimony, Day 171

Joseph Doherty statement, AD76

Chapter 14 – The IRA

Father Daly statement, H5

Colonel Wilford statement, 1110

Father O'Gara statement, H19

Monica Barr statement, AB16

Marian McMenamin statement, AM363

William Harley statement, AH36

William Harley testimony, Days 76, 77, 78

Charles McGill statement, AM230

Charles McGill testimony, Day 69

Bernard Gillespie statement, AG32

Chris Myant statement, M91

Michael Lynch statement, AL38

William Breslin statement, AB112

Glasgow, Day 51

Eamonn McCann testimony, Day 87

OIRA 1 statement, AOIRA1

OIRA 1 testimony, Day 395, 396

OIRA 2 statement, AOIRA2

OIRA 2 testimony, Day 392

PIRA 1 statement, AM508

PIRA 1 testimony, Day 409

RM 1 statement, ARM1

RM 1 testimony, Day 424

Denis Bradley statement, H1

OIRA 4 statement, AOIRA4

OIRA 4 testimony, Day 394

Soldier AA statement, 908

Liam O'Comain testimony, Day 417

PIRA 24 statement, APIRA24

PIRA 24 testimony, Day 426, 427

Martin McGuinness statement, KM3

Martin McGuinness testimony, Day 390, 391

Final Report, Vol. VIII, Ch. 146–53

Conclusion

Hansard, 15 June 2010

Saville Report, passim

Hugh Barbour statement, AB10

Leo Friel statement, AF35

Alfie McAleer statement, AM37

Charles McGuigan statement, AM269

ABOUT THE AUTHOR

Douglas Murray is a bestselling author and journalist based in Britain. Author of a number of specialist reports and books, including: '*Bosie: A Biography of Lord Alfred Douglas*' Lambda award for gay biography (2000); '*Neoconservatism: Why we need it*' 2005; '*Victims of Intimidation: free speech within Europe's Muslim communities*' (2008); '*Bloody Sunday: Truths, lies and the Saville inquiry*' Christopher Ewart-Biggs Memorial Prize for promoting peace and understanding (2011); '*Islamophilia: A Very Metropolitan Malady*' (2013); '*The Strange Death of Europe: Immigration, Identity and Islam*' *The Sunday Times* No. 1 best seller in non-fiction (2017), published in more than 20 languages worldwide; 'The Madness of Crowds: Gender, Race and Identity' *The Sunday Times* best seller, *The Times* and The *Sunday Times* book of the year. Contributor to *The Spectator* since 2000 and Associate Editor at the magazine since 2012. He has also written regularly for numerous other outlets including *The Wall Street Journal, The Times, The Sunday Times, The Sun, The Evening Standard* and *The New Criterion*.

INDEX

INDEX

All members of the armed forces given anonymity are referenced as 'Soldier', regardless of rank.

282

Made in the USA
Las Vegas, NV
14 November 2024